Created and Directed by Hans Höfer

INSIGHT GUIDES

POLAND

Edited by Alfred Horn and Bożena Pietras
Introduced by Lech Wałęsa
Translated by Susan Bollans, Thomas Fife and
Ginger Künzel

HOUGHTON MIFFLIN COMPANY

APA PUBLICATIONS

POLAND

Second Edition
© 1995 APA PUBLICATIONS (HK) LTD
All Rights Reserved
Printed in Singapore by Höfer Press Pte Ltd

Distributed in the United States by:	Distributed in Canada by:	Distributed in the UK & Ireland by:	Worldwide distribution enquiries:
Houghton Mifflin Company	**Thomas Allen & Son**	**GeoCenter International UK Ltd**	**Höfer Communications Pte Ltd**
222 Berkeley Street	390 Steelcase Road East	The Viables Center, Harrow Way	38 Joo Koon Road
Boston, Massachusetts 02116-3764	Markham, Ontario L3R 1G2	Basingstoke, Hampshire RG22 4BJ	Singapore 2262
ISBN: 0-395-66439-X	ISBN: 0-395-66439-X	ISBN: 9-62421-152-3	ISBN: 9-62421-152-3

ABOUT THIS BOOK

With cultural traditions stretching back 1,000 years, with beautiful landscapes and friendly people, Poland has long been a travel destination of great interest. But today it is more than that. The country in which the Warsaw Pact was founded produced a powerful grassroots movement which comprehensively cast aside the old order. The victory of the Solidarity trade union transformed life in Poland and provided an inspiration for the other peoples of eastern Europe. This dramatic opening-up of a closed society was bound to attract the attention of Apa Publications, whose formula of pairing insightful text with the best photojournalism has created more than 180 Insight Guides.

What makes this book's approach unique is its daring departure from the customary guidebook practice of sending writers into a country or city to observe, explore and report their findings. Instead, Apa sought out expert writers within Poland, pairing their valuable insights with its own proven expertise in producing an internationally renowned series of guidebooks. What is on offer, therefore, is not Poland as filtered through the sensibilities of foreign observers, but Poland as seen through the eyes of indigenous writers. It is the next best thing to staying with a family in the country, sharing their joys and frustrations about the place they know and love.

The Authors

Project editor **Alfred Horn** was given the task of assembling an expert team of writers and photographers. In his days in the European Parliament, Horn had committed himself to establishing greater cultural and environmental cooperation with Eastern Europe. On the 50th anniversary of the German invasion of Poland, he organised an international culture project in Gdansk in co-operation with Solidarity. As a result, he persuaded **Lech Walesa**, the trade union leader who rose to be president of the new Poland, to write the book's introduction as well as a very personal article on "Gdansk – The Cradle of Solidarity".

The whole book was the result of such amicable co-operation. Horn contributed a piece on Treblinka and, as a German himself, went over the history section and the essays with the Polish authors to ensure that they were free of palliative references towards the Germans. It was Horn's intention that, as far as possible, Polish authors should be entrusted with the task of presenting an account of their country to an international readership.

Bozena Pietras, from Crakow, took over the role of ensuring constant communication between Polish authors and Apa's editors. Her prime area of study at Crakow University was modern Polish history, much of which she herself helped to create working as a journalist and activist in the Opposition. A fellow student at Crakow, **Waldemar Paclawski**, took on the difficult task of writing the history of the country and contributed the article on Catholicism.

The young team of authors was reinforced by **Professor Jachowitz**, long-time dean at Crakow University. As chairman of the respected Ecology Club of Poland (PKE), he was a representative of the opposition at the "round table" discussions when the old order came to an end. After World War I, Jachowitz was put in charge of the rebuilding of Gdansk and he contributed his experiences to that

Pietras   *Horn*   *Strauss*

chapter. He also provided material and ideas for the article on the environment. The threads of this article were sewn together by **Tomasz Parteka** from Gdansk, chairman of the foundation Ökobaltika and spokesman for the European Society for Ecology and Culture. Having ended his studies with a thesis on the cultural dimensions of regional planning, he was well suited to produce an informative – and amusing – article on "Rural Poland".

Jacek Ziarno and **Mariusz Urbanek**, two specialist journalists and authors of scientific work in this field, were responsible for the articles on the Jews and the ethnic minorities in Poland.

Originally from Warsaw but living in Frankfurt, **Ewa Malicka-Kingston** wrote about Polish literature. Her movement between two cultures also inspired her to produce a second article on "The Art of Survival" in which she hilariously exposes the cunning and notorious mischief that her countrymen are wont to employ when it comes to making ends meet.

A further much-travelled European involved in the project is art critic **Dr Thomas Strauss**, author of numerous publications on the east European world of art. Here he gives us a glimpse "behind the mirror" of the extremely varied Polish art scene.

Dr Andreas Remin is professionally involved in "Business in Poland". The Cologne lawyer was born in Crakow and reports from his daily involvement in helping to set up joint ventures with Polish business partners – providing an interesting glance at another reality of Poland today.

Having been for several years Warsaw correspondent of the south German newspaper *Süddeutsche Zeitung*, the journalist **Thomas Urban** was well placed to offer his contribution on the most recent history of the country. In exposing some of the old wounds inflicted by the Germans, he pleads for them to be given a real chance to heal.

Local Talent

The descriptions of the cities and regions of the country are solely the work of Polish specialists, all recognised authors.

Maria and **Przemyslaw Pilicki** concentrate on the capital Warsaw and its surroundings, while the royal city of Crakow and the region of Malopolska are described by **Stanislaw Klos**. **Lidia Dlugolecka** and **Maciej Pinkwart** examine the mountain regions from the point of view of the nature-loving rambler and **Lech Szaraniec** describes his homeland of Silesia with a real feeling for the cultural variety of the region.

Wlobziemierz Lekki, from Poznan, knows this west Polish metropolis, the surrounding country of Wielkopolska and the coastal strip of West Pomerania like the back of his hand, while Gdansk and East Pomerania are extensively covered by **Janusz Uminski**. The region of Masuria is described by another local, **Jan Baldowski**.

Barbara Kryszkiewiecz assembled all the vital pieces of practical information in the "Travel Tips" section, which have been updated for this edition by **Clare Griffiths**.

The English-language edition was produced in Apa's London office, under the supervision of editorial director **Brian Bell**. The exotically-accented text was checked for accuracy by **James Lewis**, guided through a variety of Macintosh computers by **Jill Anderson**, and proof-read and indexed by **Gillian Delaforce**.

Malicka-Kingston   *Remin*   *Parteka*   *Drinkhut*

History

Features

Maps

TRAVEL TIPS

**For detailed information
see page 293**

WELCOME TO POLAND

An introduction by Lech Wałęsa

For more than a millennium, Poland has played a vital role in European history. The country's situation in the heart of Europe has always made it a bridge between two great cultural spheres. The resultant diversity of influences has helped to shape the mentality of its people: tolerance towards differing opinions and ways of life, an evident open-mindedness for new ideas and hospitality towards strangers.

Neither oppression nor the centuries of brutal violence perpetrated by neighbouring countries have succeeded in stifling Poland's liberal spirit. Even during times of great upheaval, when Poland was obliterated from the map of Europe, the safeguarding of national culture, the recollection of a glorious past, Christian-humanistic tradition and simple human solidarity continued unabated. These values still abound in present-day Poland, and in such a cultural climate there was never room for any one "truth" or a power monopoly of any one doctrine; never room for a regimentation of man or a curtailment of his liberty.

Countless wars have been waged in our country. Huge armies constantly swept across our land – they wanted to rule the whole of Europe and in their attempts to do so they incessantly inflicted deep wounds on Poland. Innumerable testimonies of a glorious history and priceless treasures of a highly developed culture were thus lost. Nevertheless, Poland has retained its beauty – the splendour of its rebuilt cities, the enchanting quaintness of its villages and the peaceful expanses of countryside in which they lie.

You are cordially invited to acquaint yourself with Poland – its kind-hearted people and its diverse culture. Soon you will come to appreciate just how inseparably this country is linked with Europe. Recent events have also made it plain that these links are of mutual advantage. Poland will most certainly be able to add its wealth of historic experience to a new form of cooperation within Europe.

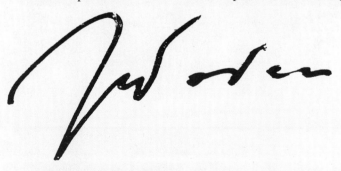

Preceding pages: Aneta Kreglicka, Miss Poland and Miss World, 1989; intensive cultivation in the Beskidy Mountains; the town hall in Wrocław; a brass band from Silesia; advertising for Solidarity. <u>Left</u>, Lech Wałęsa.

375: The invasion of the Huns triggers the great migration of nations, during the course of which Slav tribes settle in the territory that is present-day Poland.

966: Polish court adopts Christianity. Count Mieszko I has himself and his followers baptised. He succeeds in unifying *Polanie* and neighbouring tribes under his rule.

1000: In Gniezno the first Polish church province is established. The German Emperor Otto III visits the city and is accorded a friendly welcome.

1024: Bolesław I Chobry receives the Pope's blessing and is crowned King of Poland.

1226: Duke Konrad Mazowiecki summons the German Order of Knighthood to Poland to support him in his struggle against the Prussians.

1241: A Polish army under Henryk Pobozny stops the Mongol advance at Legnica. Cracow is burned down.

1309: The Order of Knighthood has consolidated its power and rules over a large territory along the Eastern Baltic Sea, including the Hanseatic city of Gdańsk.

1325: Polish-Lithuanian alliance is formed against the Teutonic knights.

1364: Foundation of Cracow University.

1386: Poland and Lithuania are fused into a larger realm by the marriage of the heiress to the throne Jadwiga with Grand Duke Jagiełło. Poland gains access to the Baltic ports.

1410: The victory over the German Order of Knighthood at the battle of Grunwald/Tannenberg establishes the preconditions for a greater expansion of power in the unified realm.

1466: In the second peace of Toruń, the German Order of Knighthood recognises the sovereignty of the Polish kings and cedes territory at the mouth of the river Vistula, including the city of Gdańsk, to Poland. The Jagiełłones now rule from the Baltic Sea to the Black Sea.

1505: At the Imperial Diet of Radom the king grants unprecedented and extensive rights to the nobility. Thereby "rule of the nobility" is established as a spècific Polish form of government.

1525: Under Duke Albrecht of Hohenzollern, the "Order State" that had been secularised in the wake of the reformation, becomes Polish feudal tenure.

1543: Copernicus publishes his book on planetary motion.

1552: A decision of the Imperial Diet establishes the right of religious tolerance. The cultural and denominational tolerance thus afforded makes Poland a centre of tranquillity in the turmoil of the religious wars that raged throughout Europe.

1564: Bishop Hosium of Ermland calls the Jesuits into the country. That is the start of the counter-reformation.

1569: With the union of Lublin, Poland and Lithuania are now officially united to form an "inseparable whole".

1600: War with Sweden.

1618–48: Thirty Years' War.

1621: East Prussia falls to the Elector Georg Wilhelm of Brandenburg. The fates of this region are henceforth determined in Berlin.

1655–60: War with Sweden.

1683: King John III of Poland (John Sobieski) credited with expelling the Turks from Vienna.

1772: With the first partition of Poland begins the subjugation of the country by its neighbouring states.

1791: The Polish reform movement, headed by King Stanisław August Poniatowski, proclaims a liberal constitution.

1795: With the third partition of Poland, Austria, Prussia and Russia occupy the country, despite fierce resistance. The uprisings during the next century do not result in liberation.

1800s: Numerous uprisings are staged against foreign rule.

1892: Foundation of the Polish Socialist Party.

1918: After the military defeat of the occupation forces, an independent Polish state is proclaimed on 7 October.

1920: Under President Piłsudski, Poland stops the advance of the Red Army at the Vistula and occupies part of the Ukraine and Lithuania. Gdańsk becomes a "free city".

1921: After heavy fighting between Poles and Germans, Upper Silesia is divided at a conference of ambassadors.

1926: Piłsudski stages a coup to regain power; rulership becomes ever-more authoritarian.

1939: On 1 September World War II starts with the German assault on the Polish garrison on the *Westerplatte* in front of Gdańsk. On 1 November the Eastern territories of Poland are annexed by the Soviet Union; German rule is enforced throughout the rest of the country.

1944: The Warsaw rebellion is the culmination point of an embittered and protracted resistance by partisans and the Polish *Armia Krajowa*.

1945: The "Lublin Committee" proclaims itself the provisional government. All opposition forces are made to resign by the communists, supported by the Soviet army. At the Yalta and Potsdam conferences Poland's territory is extended in the west. In the east large territories fall to the Soviet Union and their republics. In the west the *Oder/Neisse line* is established as the border to Germany.

1952: Poland becomes a "people's democracy" lead by the "United Workers Party".

1955: Founding of the "Warsaw Pact" and "Treaty of friendship, cooperation and mutual assistance" with the Soviet Union and other Eastern bloc states.

1956: After strikes and unrest in Poznań, the National Communist Gomulka takes over the leadership of the country.

1970: In the wake of the "new *Ostpolitik*", Willy Brandt, the Chancellor of West Germany, signs the "treaty concerning the basis of normalisation of mutual relations between Poland and the Federal Republic of Germany".

1976: Widespread civil unrest after price increases.

1980: Strikes in Gdańsk spread throughout the country. Formation of an independent union "Solidarność", Solidarity.

1981: Party and head of state Jaruzelski proclaims martial law on 13 December and thus pre-empts a planned invasion by troops of the Warsaw Pact. The opposition is declared illegal and joins the underground.

1989: The communist leadership declares its willingness to share power with the opposition headed by Lech Wałęsa. After an unexpectedly clear election victory, the Solidarity candidate, the Roman Catholic intellectual Tadeusz Mazowiecki, becomes the leader of the government.

1990: After unification, Germany formally recognises the Western border of Poland at the Oder/Neisse line. In the November presidential elections, political allies, Lech Wałęsa and Tadeusz Mazowiecki, are rival candidates. Lech Wałęsa wins by a small majority.

1993: The remains of exiled war-time leader General Sikorski are flown home. Poland's first woman prime minister, Hanna Suchocka, resigns. The last of the 60,000 Soviet troops based in Poland leave.

1994: Poland applies for membership of the European Union.

A GLORIOUS PAST

Poland is too often viewed as a tragic country whose fate is ever to be conquered and partitioned. This is a top-heavy view of history, for these tragedies apply only to about a quarter of Poland's story, which for the rest was significant, heroic and glorious.

Poland saved Europe from the Tartars at the beginning of the Middle Ages and from Islam at the end of the 17th century, when King Jan Sobieski lifted the Turkish siege of Vienna with an expeditionary force of Polish cavalry (1683). Indeed, to a large extent, "Christian Europe" owes its survival to Polish feats of arms. Even in 1921 Lenin had to revise his strategy for world revolution after Polish cavalry defeated the advancing Red Army on the Vistula river.

After the union with Lithuania in the 15th century, Poland became a mighty kingdom and commonwealth stretching from the Baltic to the Black Sea and including large areas of Belorussia and the Ukraine. Odessa was once a Polish port. It is these episodes which give Poles the pride and power to overcome their very real – but nonetheless subordinate – sufferings.

Early days: A Roman chronicler writing in about the 4th century AD described "a land beyond the Carpathian Mountains inhabited by a strange people who played the flute beautifully, but who do not know the use of the sword". The Romans knew these people because their land lay in the so-called Amber Route to the Baltic coast which produced then, as it does still, some of the purest amber in the world.

Poles, however, were not destined to enjoy such peace for very long. Their lands were coveted by Germanic tribes in the west and by the *hordes* from the East. Historically the original Slav settlers pre-dated even the Teutons or Deutsche in modern Germany. Berlin and Leipzig are Slav names.

In the second half of the 10th century, on territories inhabited by Slavic tribes closely related to each other by language, creeds and customs, the Polish State was founded, and its boundaries by about the year 1000 were

Preceding pages: A glimpse of Warsaw's bustling past. Left, Canaletto's view of the city.

approximately the same as they are today.

The unification of those tribes was carried out by the dukes of the Polians (from *pole* = "field"), a tribe living in the basin of the River Warta. The first Polish ruler recorded in history was Mieszko (about 963). From the mid-11th century, the centre of the country gradually moved from territories situated on the River Warta (Gniezno, Poznan, Kruszwice) to those on the upper River Vistula (Cracow, Sandomierz). Other important settlements included Wolin, Gdańsk, Szczecin, Opole and Wrocław, fortified towns surrounded by merchant suburbs.

In 966, Mieszko introduced Christianity. Because Poland adopted Christianity after

the Roman rite, its cultural development proceeded mostly in conjunction with other countries of Central and Western Europe. There was also at this time some contact between Poland and the Scandinavian countries, which were undergoing a similar cultural development. However, Poland as the easternmost country within the orbit of Latin culture was in constant contact with the civilisation of Eastern Europe, and the influence of Byzantine culture. Poland even had temporary contacts with the expansive Asiatic civilisations.

The adoption of Christianity suited the international policy of a young state. Poland

had been subjected to the pressure of the bordering German March and tried to establish direct relations with the Empire as well as with Bohemia, which was already Christian and in a similar situation. The entire early period of Poland's history was a series of attempts by Polish rulers to make themselves independent from Germany.

The invasion of the Mongols in the 13th century put paid to the flourishing development of the Polish cities – but only briefly. It was during this time that Wrocław, Cracow and Poznan decided to adopt the Magdeburg Municipal Law, which afforded good conditions for economic development.

Nevertheless, the old dynasty managed to uphold the idea of a Polish state during two centuries of feudal dismemberment. By the end of the 13th century, the kingdom managed to consolidate itself again – initially within the framework of the Union of Bohemia. Not until Władysław I Łokietek came to power was this difficult task successfully concluded. He was crowned in 1320 in Cracow. The restored *Corona Regni Poloniae* received a modern constitution and a stable currency during the reign of his son, Kazimierz Wielki (died 1370). It was said of this king that he found a Poland built of wood, and left it built of stone. The "polonisation" of Małopolska also came about during this time.

The most important development, however, was that a Polish identity, the prospect of becoming a Western civilised nation, managed to gain a foothold. Thus, for example, the church that was attempting to regain cultural autonomy and political sovereignty, protested vehemently – and ultimately successfully – in Rome against the appointment of Germans in high office in Polish dioceses. The last Piast king was less successful from a military point of view. He had a dense network of fortified castles built throughout the country, but the expansion to the eastern territories and the continuing annexation of Lwów and the Pripet marshes left other areas of the kingdom vulnerable and resulted in the loss of all Silesia.

The Jagiellons: After the death of the last Piast ruler, the Polish throne fell to the Hungarian line of the royal family of d'Anjou. Soon after, however, the kingdom was united with the Grand Duchy of Lithuania. The new ruler, the Grand Duke of Lithuania,

Władysław Jagiełło and his subjects converted to Christianity and Jagiełło married the Polish queen Jadwiga d'Anjou. The immediate reason for this union was the continuing threat posed by the German Order of Teutonic Knights.

The claims of Germany over Polish territory have been a running issue since time immemorial. The causes of World War II can even be dated back, almost precisely, to 1410. That was the year of the battle of Grunwald, when a combined Polish, Lithuanian and Tartar force defeated the Grand Order of Teutonic Knights in one of the largest medieval set-piece battles. The knights, having spread false propaganda that

Knights had only been invited into Poland for the limited purpose of putting down an unruly tribe who were rebelling against the Polish king.

Having ruthlessly and successfully accomplished their task, the knights, unemployed since the Crusades, looked enviously and aggressively at the rest of Poland. Although defeated at Grunwald, the issue of East Prussia, the area they had colonised, was to remain a Polish-German issue right up to the time of Hitler. Then it became perhaps the greatest *causus belli* of all time.

Commonwealth and Kingdom: The new king, Kazimierz Jagiellończyk (1447–92) became known as the "father of Europe". Of his nine

Poland was a heathen country, had enlisted the help of English archers. But on this occasion, five years before Agincourt, the archers did not stand their ground and fled before the onslaught of Polish cavalry.

During the period of the Grand Order's greatest power, Malbork Castle was the residence of the Grand Masters (1308–1457). After 1457 it became the residence of Polish kings. In its heyday it was one of the greatest strongholds in medieval Europe. But the

Left, trade flourished in the Middle Ages. **Above**, the Grand Master of the Teutonic Knights swears the oath of allegiance.

children, one son became a cardinal, four became kings, one was canonised and the three daughters were eventually married off to become the mothers of the heirs of the greatest dynasties in Western Europe.

Nevertheless Jagiellończyk and his successors did not manage to convert this exceedingly favourable family constellation into real political power. This was primarily due to the very strong economic position of the nobility, which, as a reward for its participation in the wars, was granted numerous and far-reaching privileges. The result was that the peasants, who had virtually lived the lives of serfs since 1496, as well as the townsfolk, were forced to the brink of economic destitution.

During the reign of the last Jagiełłons – Zygmunt Stary (1506–48) and Zygmunt August (1548–72) – the country once more enjoyed a cultural and political boom. The Polish language became the *lingua franca* of the Eastern European nobility. The Polish, Ruthenian and Lithuanian nobility, which was quite used to the co-habitation of people of different denominations, readily accepted the revolutionary teachings of Luther and Calvin. At the time of the Reformation, the state of the German Order of Knighthood was also secularised, i.e. subjugated to the secular administration of the Hohenzollern

life had been characterised by the growing power enjoyed by the Lithuanian and Ruthenian aristocratic families. Their huge estates in the east afforded them economic independence and enabled them to rise to the highest official posts. There they pursued solely their own interests, without any consideration of matters of state. At the same time powerful and aggressive forces developed within the adjoining European states: in the west the Habsburgs, in the southeast Turkey with its ambitions to conquer the continent, Moscow under Ivan the Terrible in the east, and Sweden in the north.

When the Jagiełłon dynasty came to an end, the Sejm, the Polish parliament, intro-

emperors and thus closely aligned with the Prussian house of Brandenburg.

Despite the fact that religious wars were raging in the west, the traditional and reformed religious denominations in the territory ruled by the Polish crown continued to live quite amicably side by side. Religious tolerance was a central element of the "golden period of liberty", as the Polish state ideology was known at the time. In 1569 the union of the Polish crown with Lithuania was renewed and a "Republic of the two Nations" was proclaimed.

Elective monarchy and hamstrung policy: In the mid-14th century, political and economic

duced an elective monarchy. However, Henri de Valois, the first king to be elected (in 1573), decided to return to France immediately after his coronation to rule there as King Henry III.

The next king, Stefan Batory (1576–86), Duke of Transylvania, was a superb military strategist but constantly had to struggle to find sufficient funds to wage war: the powerful nobility evaded all state taxes and the war treasury was bankrupt. Despite the fact that the defence of the state could no longer be guaranteed, Stefan Batory managed to consolidate Poland's position in the east of Europe by conquering Livland and establishing fortifications on the eastern border.

In 1587 the Swedish royal family of Wasa took over the monarchy. Zygmunt III Wasa and his successor Władysław IV and Jan Kazimierz ruled Poland until 1668, but economically the country continued to decline. All too readily during that century, the new rulers allowed themselves to become embroiled in the tumults of war.

During the time of the Reformation, domestic peace and quiet was ensured. The Counter-Reformation, in turn, which had been organised by the Jesuits active in the country since 1564, helped intensify internal political conflicts. The aristocratic families which ruled like little kings in their prov-

form of foreign trade. Until the end of the 16th century, constant wars were waged in the border regions of Poland. Despite being heavily outnumbered, the commanders of the Polish army were excellent tacticians. But even their numerous victories in the battles against the Swedes, Muscovites and Cossacks in the Ukraine could not prevent the country from getting ever weaker. The brutal, five-year Swedish occupation of Poland (1655–60) resulted in the death of a third of the population.

In 1657 East Prussia shook off the yoke of Polish rule. The last great victory of the Polish army and, simultaneously, the last act of the "Republic of the two Nations" in

inces and hardly wasted a thought on the well-being of the state, were most enamoured of this fundamentalist model of Roman-Catholicism; after all, it justified their own bigotry and their baroque style of life.

While the wealthy families continued to live a reckless life of pleasure, the country itself declined. Agricultural production was maintained at a relatively high level, but the cities lost much of their importance. Only the Hanse city of Gdańsk was involved in any

Left, King Batory of Pskow. **Above**, an ambassador from Vienna begs Polish help against the Turks.

European policy, was the victory over the Turkish army in the battle before Vienna in 1683. The glorious victor, King Jan III Sobieski, sent the standards wrested from the Muslim enemies to Rome and was subsequently hailed as the "Liberator of Europe".

However the "Saviour of the Occident" could not uphold the sovereignty of his own country. Poland had long since become a veritable toy in the hands of the neighbouring powers, which were only waiting for a favourable moment for a final show-down.

The internal disintegration of the feudal republic contributed to paving the way for subsequent conquests.

DEPENDENCY AND DIVISION

Like the Sword of Damocles, a threatening coalition of the neighbouring states against Poland had been hanging over the country ever since the mid-17th century. The desperate internal instability of Poland itself had made a decisive contribution to this danger: while throughout the rest of Europe the nobility was subordinate to the absolute power of the monarch, in the Polish Sejm, the parliament of the aristocracy, any individual delegate could, by means of the "liberum veto", stop any and every debate without even being compelled to make a sensible counter-proposal.

Under these prevailing conditions, an effective governing of the state was neither possible for the king nor indeed for any other legislative body. Politically, the state was thus to all intents and purposes hamstrung; economically, because of the rapid disintegration of the domestic market and the lack of organised foreign trade relations, it was heading straight for bankruptcy. The mighty neighbours – Prussia, Austria and Russia – took this opportunity of persuading, or cajoling, Poland's leading families to support their claims. In 1717 the Sejm had passed a law putting the privileges of the Polish nobility under the protection of Russia, thus allowing the czar to intervene practically at will in all domestic matters. After 1732 the other neighbouring countries were permitted to intervene in all matters pertaining to state rule in Poland.

Up until 1763, the rulers of Poland were mainly princes from Saxony. But for them a sojourn in Warsaw was supremely uninteresting – at least in comparison to the courtly refinement and entertainment afforded in their splendid home city of Dresden. Consequently they just collected their allowances and left the country to look after itself.

Reform and betrayal: In 1764 Stanisław August, from the Poniatowski family, was elected king. As the young monarch had been brought up in the spirit of the French enlightenment, he did his level best to revi-

Left, Poland's "neighbours", Josef II, Catherine the Great and Frederick the Great, divide the country between them in 1772.

talise the state. His endeavours at reform and in inspiring a cultural movement that had a decidedly national character received a great deal of support from the intellectuals and the aristocratic youth. First successes were soon apparent: some form of discipline returned to the Sejm and the tax system was reformed. But the new customs offices, which were to provide the treasury with additional income, were prevented from functioning efficiently because of intervention from Berlin. A patriotic confederation, which had formed in 1768 in Bar with the slogan "faith and liberty", was disbanded by the Russian army. Soon the whole country was seething in turmoil and Czarina Catherine II therefore decided to accept the Prussian suggestion of a partition of Poland – a proposal that she had previously rejected. In 1772 huge areas of the country were annexed by Prussia, Austria and Russia.

In view of the danger to the very existence of the state, comprehensive reforms were imperative. A strong government was set up, which, among other things, institutionalised the first Ministry of Culture in the world. In the four-year legislative period of the Sejm, from 1788 to 1792, the whole political system was restructured and an army of 100,000 soldiers was recruited. The citizens were granted full civic rights and on 3 May 1791 the first modern constitution in all Europe was proclaimed. This new constitution granted political power to the citizens, allowed the cities self-determination and afforded legal protection to the peasants.

For Catherine II this manifestation of Poland's sovereignty was a serious blow. She now demanded the absolute loyalty of the members of the power elite who received their funds from Russia. In 1792 this elite formed a confederation in Targowica which proceeded to declare the constitution null and void and requested military aid from St Petersburg. The battles between the supporters of the constitution and Catherine's army were waged for several months. At the last session of the Sejm, the king, who was under extreme pressure from Russia, was finally forced to agree to the annulment of the constitution and a second partition of Poland. One of the consequences of this was that Gdańsk and Toruń became an integral part of Prussia.

Then in March 1794 General Tadeusz Kosciuszko proclaimed a national uprising in Cracow. After a spectacular victory in the Battle of Racławice and bloody unrest in Warsaw, the uprising was put down by the Russian and Prussian armies.

In 1795 Poland was partitioned for the third time, and this time disappeared from the map of Europe altogether. The last Polish monarch, Stanisław Poniatowski, died in 1798 in detention in St Petersburg, a lonely and embittered man.

Emigrants and Emperors: Now either in exile or dispersed throughout Europe, the Polish liberation front tried to drum up support for their cause. They saw their greatest hope in France: the Polish legions that had been formed in 1797 in the south of Italy fought on the side of Napoleon Bonaparte. Later, when he became Emperor Napoleon I and negotiated the peace treaty with Czar Alexander I, he managed to enforce the re-establishment of a small "Duchy of Warsaw".

In 1809, after the defeat of Austria, the Duchy was expanded. But the overthrow of the Emperor, who was revered in Poland and at whose disposal the Poles had placed thousands of soldiers and officers as well as food for his Russian campaign, resulted in a new partition of the country. Wielkopolska and Pomerania remained part of Prussia, Cracow and its environs became a non-aligned mini-republic; Galicia was ceded to Austria and the rest was fused into what became known as "Congress Poland", a constitutional monarchy under direct union with Russia. Such rights and liberties as were afforded to them by the Vienna Congress in 1815, the Poles used to help carry out a variety of tasks that had been specified in the constitution annulled on 3 May 1791.

In 1816 a university was founded in Warsaw, which soon became a decisive factor in the promotion of scientific and cultural contacts with other centres of Europe. The idea of a national revival was also evident in the establishment of independent domestic industry and modern state administration structures.

Patriotic associations and conspiratorial groups were secretly formed, inspired by the Polish romantic poets. Above all there were repeated conflicts with Russia's stifling bureaucracy. The November rebellion of 1830 gathered momentum and developed into a full-scale war with the Russian empire. The republic managed to survive for ten months, before it was defeated after a series of dramatic battles. One of the positive effects of the resultant new wave of emigrants was unbounded admiration throughout western Europe for the freedom fight in Poland. The exiled political leadership concentrated on making the preparations for an armed uprising. In the European revolution year 1848, the Poles also sought to re-establish their national sovereignty, but were as unsuccessful as all other rebellious peoples farther to the west. A further uprising in 1863 was crushed by the Czarist army.

The nation in God's hand: "Boze coś Polskę"/ "Almighty God, grant us Poles a free home-

equation of "Polishness" and "Roman Catholicism" gained a firm hold in the minds of the people – all the more so as the church was the sole remaining supra-regional institution of any importance. It was therefore no coincidence that the national movement came to be based in the sphere of influence of the paternalistic-Catholic imperial Austrian realm; in Galicia and, above all, in Cracow.

Together with the Roman Catholic church, these groups prepared the renaissance of the Polish state – despite the resistance of the intolerant clerical policy of orthodox Russia and protestant Prussia.

The First World War: Between 1914–1918, the front between the German-Austrian and

land" – thus the hymn of the Polish resistance movement. Despite the singularly unsuccessful outcome, despite the number of casualties, the idea of a common, united Polish nation continued. It was primarily the Roman Catholic church, whose clergy had become increasingly outspoken in favour of national resistance, that was now the guarantor of Polish continuity.

At a time when national culture, language and custom could only continue in constant conflict with the occupation forces, the

Above, Wrocław is occupied by hostile forces (1741).

Russian armies ran right through Poland. Clad in the uniforms of inimical armies, Poles had to fight against Poles.

All warring factions tried to lure the support of Poland by making promises. The collapse of the old order in Europe and the attitude of the future super powers, the USA and the Soviet Union, was a decisive factor in giving Poland a new, historical chance.

In 1917 President Wilson declared that "there should be a united, independent and autonomous Poland". The fledgling Bolshevik regime declared the partition and occupation of Poland to be contrary to international law.

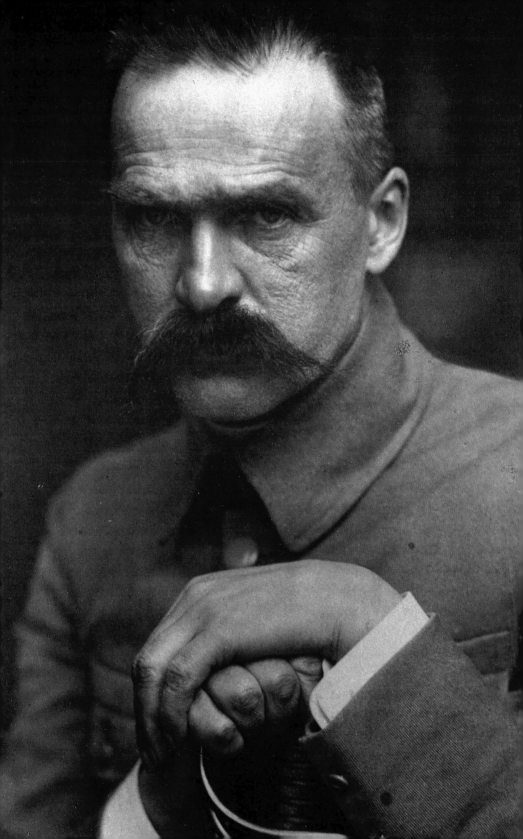

In 1918 the banners of rebellion fluttered over the debris of the dynastic empires throughout Europe. Liberty was writ large – larger than it had ever been after 1848 and before 1989.

Now regionally organised, in October 1918 the Poles disarmed the Germans and Austrians whose leadership had been overthrown and who were too exhausted even to consider a continuation of hostilities. In Poznań weapons for a Polish rebellion were collected. A national government, free from all Bolshevik ambition, was established in Lublin and in Lwów fervently patriotic high school pupils fought street battles with the Ukrainians, who had also started an uprising. In Warszaw, Józef Piłsudski took charge of all military and civil tasks and on 11 November 1918 the Republic of Poland was proclaimed. Because of the uprisings against the Germans in Silesia and Greater Poland, and also as a result of of the war against the Red Army and the skirmishes with the Lithuanians and Czechs, the actual borders of the Second Republic were not officially drawn until 1919–21.

Thus a state evolved that was, to all intents and purposes, in the Polish political tradition, although it now had to carry the hereditary burden of the partition and was hence faced with the integration of three different institutional, legal and economic systems. On Polish territory, the sixth largest in Europe at the time, ethnic minorities constituted a third of the total of 27 million inhabitants: Ukrainians, Belorussians, Jews, Germans, Ruthenians, Lithuanians and Czechs. In 1921 a general, political consensus resulted in the acceptance of a democratic constitution, based on the French model. After the election victory of the National Democrats in 1922, Gabriel Narutowicz became the first president of the new republic. Piłsudski was compelled to tender his resignation. Narutowicz did not last for long: he was assassinated that same year.

Although the parliamentary constitution protected the fledgling democracy from

monopolistic claims of the central executive, its barely proven control mechanisms were insufficient to afford total freedom to political forces. The coalition governments of the 1920s worked in an atmosphere of mutual distrust and disunity.

The attempt to turn the high-flying modernisation plans into reality did not really get off the ground – not surprising, considering the vast number of problems the country faced. The currency reform ultimately proved advantageous, but it entailed an unpopular limitation of social rights. As was the case in other European states at the time, this in turn encouraged radical political groupings to question the legitimacy and leadership mandate of parliament.

Only within the army did a strong, supraregional link to the new, united state emerge. In May 1926 the long-awaited boom in the economy began to materialise. Piłsudski, who had long been the *eminence grise*, immediately seized this opportunity to lead his loyal military units into Warsaw. After several days of street battles the coup succeeded and Piłsudski again managed to gain total control. A new political strategy of restructuring was introduced.

The patriot of federation: Piłsudski was a patriot through and through – but neither in the Polish nor the Lithuanian tradition. His lodestar was the Jagiełłonian idea of creating a strong political and military structure. In view of the conditions prevailing at the time, in his opinion only a federation could guarantee the security and development of the peoples wedged in the corridor between Germans and Russians, between the Baltic Sea and the Black Sea.

A first political step to turn this idea into reality came about in 1919 with the establishment of a Polish-Ukrainian Confederation. For centuries the vast expanses of the Ukraine, originally populated by nomads from the east, had been the grain store for Poland, later for the ever more powerful Russian empire. Piłsudski supported the Ukrainian nationalists and it was the marshal himself who rode at the head of his resplendent cavalry into the capital city of Kiev. However, this move was destined to be only

Left, Josef Piłsudski led the Second Republic to independence.

a brief episode in the Russian-Polish war, which lasted from April to October 1920. The Ukraine soon became a Soviet Republic, and the local supporters of a federation with Poland, if they did not manage to save their skins by fleeing, were arrested and executed.

The Red Army, meanwhile, went about turning Trotsky's command into reality: "Over the corpse of bourgeois Poland" they were to march into Berlin – firmly in socialist hands at the time – to add impetus to the continuation of the world revolution. The Polish army – with the assistance of the French general Maxime Weygand – managed to thwart the Soviet advance near

Piłsudski the sole remnant of his earlier, highly ambitious plans.

On the stage: Piłsudski started his career as a revolutionary. But as far as his political inclination was concerned, he was a thorough pragmatist. Throughout the last 10 years of his life – he died in 1935 – he had a formative influence on the power structure of the state. In theory the structure of the democratic order remained untouched. In practice, however, all the key positions in the army and the administration were held by fervent Piłsudski supporters. A loyal elite was forged from the group of erstwhile soldiers who had fought for independence under his command. Moreover, a substantial

Warsaw. This "miracle at the Vistula" forced the Bolsheviks to slow down the advance of the revolution.

The marshal bade farewell to the idea of a federation, but gave orders to occupy Vilnius. Vilnius was as vital for the Poles as it was for the Lithuanians, who had only just achieved their own sovereignty. Although the occupation by Polish troops directly contravened the regulations of the League of Nations, the new eastern border was soon recognised by the adjoining states in the west. Nothing remained of the grand idea of a central European federation, except the 1921 military alliances with Romania and France – for

portion of the intelligentsia found employment in the state administration. Also the influence of the aristocracy, who, for centuries, had owned the landed estates, increased year by year. The socialists in turn, – initially supporters of Piłsudski – soon lost any illusions they may have had and joined the opposition.

The undoubted charisma of the marshal was cleverly marketed and his political premises were successfully popularised. The equality of all religious denominations – specified in the constitution – was retained, not least due to his political dexterity, and despite the pre-eminent position of Roman

Catholicism. His *savoir-vivre*, his adherence to the traditions of the Polish multi-national state, his preference for horses, sabres and swords; all this fused in the eyes of his countrymen to make him the embodiment of a popular hero.

This paternalistic leadership ideal was underscored by a cult of strict bureaucracy as well as the propagation of the obedient and loyal citizen. The encouragement of such characteristics was not only designed to guarantee survival for a nation wedged between "traditional enemies", but also to enable Poland in the long run to play a mediatory role between the "wild east" and the "civilised west".

the Piłsudski clan came from the National Democracy camp. Particularly in rural areas this movement was inseparably linked with the Roman Catholic hierarchy. It propagated the concept that people had a natural right to their land, their language and their traditions. Roman Dmowski, the chief ideologist and strategist of this movement at that time, deemed the ultimate solution of the nationality conflicts the most important task of any political agenda. The various peoples were to be settled on their own respective territories and a system of peaceful co-existence was to be established. The movement also called for racial purity.

The Jews, who made up more than 8 per-

Parliament was left with only a very few legislative functions. Using an impending coup as a pretext, legal proceedings were instigated against the socialist deputies. The judiciary managed to save face by remaining independent and passing purely symbolic sentences, but nevertheless the young democracy lost much of its credibility. Piłsudski not only sanctioned this development, he even consented to the new, restrictive constitution on his deathbed.

The only significant opposition against

Left, Lwów – melting pot of cultures. Above, the gateway to world trade: Gdynia.

cent of the population, were the prime target of attack. But also loyal, often non-denominational citizens, whose families may have been "polonised" for hundreds of years, became the victims of these persecutions. The main pretext for these attacks were the socialist ideas of Utopia propagated by the Jewish intellectual scene.

When in the late 1930s the feeling of external threat increased, it soon became clear that Poland lacked anyone of the calibre of Piłsudski; the kind of figure it required to maintain the integrity of the state. The influence of Nationalism grew apace and the government camp became ever-more aligned with the national democracy movement. On the extreme right wing of the national democracy groups, fascist tendencies became evident. Violence against minorities was no longer an isolated occurrence.

Economy: In the period between the two world wars, Poland had become a relatively homogeneous economic unit. Beforehand, however, the preconditions to achieve that had had to be established; provinces that had been characterised by totally diverse influences for centuries had to be economically integrated. After all at the time there existed a combination of radically different elements within Polish society: the efficient "Prussian-style" industrial machine, an easy-go-

ing "Austrian" Bohemian way of life and "Russian" dynamism, which all had to be brought under one roof.

The process of assimilation – particularly with regard to legislation and infrastructure – took a long time. A modern port was built in Gdynia and linked to the highly industrialised Silesia by a rail. Nevertheless, even during the fat years of prosperous economic growth there was a dearth of funds for an independent Polish investment policy. Heavy industry, for example, remained wholly under the control of France and Germany. The annual capital transfer to foreign banks was five times higher than any domestic invest-

ments. The primitive banking system levied the highest interest rates in the whole of Europe; the prime lending rate was three times higher than in the United Kingdom or in Switzerland. Even in 1939 it was still not possible to regain the level of industrial production that had prevailed in the time before World War I.

Almost 65 percent of the population lived tied to the land in rural areas. With the exception of Greater Poland and Pomerania, the agricultural structure remained backward. Seven-tenths of the rural population was only marginally involved in the circulation of goods and currency.

The catastrophically high birth rate as well as the sluggish pace of industrialisation caused a drastic decline in the overall standard of living and triggered a fresh wave of emigration. During the time leading up to the Great Depression (1926–30) approximately 200,000 people left Poland annually. In subsequent years, the over-population led to further sub-division of the rural estates and thus to lower revenues. The rural population, which was largely illiterate and highly indebted to provincial usurers, remained in a suffering, seemingly divinely ordained, state of lethargy.

The power of the idea and the idea of power: Traditionally the age of maturity for a Pole is 21. Only then is he or she granted full rights of Polish citizenship. The Second Republic of Poland never quite managed to celebrate that anniversary. With the implementation of Polish sovereignty in 1918, the dream of national independence had been achieved. But despite this totally new situation, the disputes concerning the proper form of government continued to erupt. And soon it became only too evident that the question of sovereignty would continue to be the main problem.

In 1921 the idea of a state was a very modern concept for the Poles. The aim was to create a homogeneous, democratic political system. This system withstood the continuing efforts of the Roman Catholic church to raise Catholicism to a state religion. A renewed sense of independence, including the feeling of being liberated from patriotic obligations, was endemic in intellectual and

Left, bowing before Polonia. Right, the Church of St Michael in Vilnius.

LWÓW AND VILNIUS

The reunification of Germany has entailed an unequivocal and final renunciation of the former German Eastern territories. At the same time Poland has gained a secure western border and millions of new Polish citizens in Wrocław, Malbork and Szczecin are guaranteed a right to their homeland. Many of these people had had to leave their homeland once before – when they were expelled from the former Polish Eastern Territories, now part of Lithuania, Russia and the Ukraine. Luckily, nobody in Poland has any intention of reclaiming these territories and thus triggering yet another tragic migration of the region's peoples.

Instead it is becoming ever more apparent that it is only through inter-cultural exchange and the overcoming of national isolation tactics that there will be common access to cities and regions that are characterised by a shared cultural history.

This point is clearly demonstrated by the former Polish cities Vilnius/Wilno and Lwiw/Lwów, with their marvellously rich, multi-cultural traditions.

Marshal Józef Piłsudski, the Polish leader during the inter-war years, once compared Poland to a pretzel: the most worthwhile part was on the edge, he claimed, in the

middle there was only a void. That is understandable because Piłsudski himself hailed from the border region near Vilnius. Despite their peripheral location, Lwów and Vilnius did not take second place to the capital city.

In free Poland during the inter-war years both cities developed into centres of intellectual life. Regaining them had been a considerable task for the young Poland. Vilnius, although largely inhabited by Poles, was regarded by the Lithuanian republic as their actual capital and Lwów, also with a Polish majority, had to be defended against claims from the Ukraine.

In the years of Polish partition, Lwów had become an important city – even richer and bigger than Cracow. It was located on the junction of the major trade routes and its population was made up of a variety of cultures and nationalities. As early

as 1894 an electric tram was in operation in Lwów. In this autonomous capital of Galicia science and literature were allowed to develop and flourish in comparative freedom. The university – renamed in 1919 after King Jan Kazimierz – brought forth superb humanists.

The mathematical department of Lwów, which was founded by Stefan Banach and Hugo Steinhaus, was once the leading such institute in the world. It was in Lwów that Rudolf Weigl developed the vaccine against typhoid. The Lwów theatre was deemed one of the best in the country and two legendary Polish actors, Leon Schiller and Wilam Horzyca, were members of the ensemble. In the local radio station there evolved the satirical programme *Funny radio waves from Lwów*, once popular throughout the country.

Until the renewed demise of Poland, Lwów was never relegated to the status of a provincial city.

Only after protracted disputes was Vilnius, the former capital of the Grand Duchy of Lithuania, returned to Poland in 1922. The interaction between two national cultures over many centuries had determined the stature of this city.

Marshal Piłsudski was a descendant of Lithuanian dukes. Adam Mickiewicz, the Polish national poet, began his famous epic poem *Pan Tadeusz* with the exclamation: "Lithuania, my fatherland!"

The literary tradition that was inaugurated in Vilnius by Mickiewicz and Slowacki, was further developed by the Nobel prizewinner, Czeslaw Milosz. Antoni Golubiew and Pawl Jasienica were also active in Vilnius during the inter-war years. Both authors have a place of honour in Polish literary history. Stanisław Cat Mackiewicz, in the post World War I period prime minister of the government in exile, began his political career in the city.

Both Lwow and Vilnius still retain abundant evidence of this multi-cultural diversity. In Vilnius the Gorny Zamek Giedymina, the baroque Church of St Casimir and the Gothic Church of St Ann characterise the harmonious city landscape. In Lwów you will find cathedrals of the Armenian, Greek-Orthodox and Roman Catholic church, and the city remains the only one which is simultaneously the seat of three archbishops.

academic circles. Creativity now knew no bounds and flourished – so much so that there appeared to be a veritable explosion of a cultural renaissance. Through contact with the west, the belief that Poland was, once again, well and truly a member of the European family was strengthened.

The cinema became the main attraction in the cities. The big screen was dominated by down-to-earth romances, in which a country bumpkin Cinderella found fulfilment of her love in a dramatic, but ultimately victorious, climb to a higher social strata. The small theatres in Warsaw flourished, the night life in the large cities was fully on a par with any recherché refinements that may have been offered in Paris.

In Europe: In the 1930s Poland's foreign policy situation deteriorated rapidly. Stuck in the doldrums of the world economic crisis of 1929, the plans for domestic modernisation and social improvements collapsed. After 1935, the government, which was having to rely even more strongly than before on the traditional forces of the army and the landed gentry, passed a new, far more authoritarian, constitution.

In Warsaw the slogan of a "superpower Poland" found popular favour. Despite all endeavours to achieve a rapid, national consensus, in this tense situation there was far too little freedom of movement for such a conflict to be solved. As far as the propagandists were concerned, the Polish "superpower" should, with the assistance of its culture, influence the whole of central and eastern Europe and, at the same time, form a military protection wall to the East. An alliance with Berlin or Moscow was out of the question, but when Hitler occupied Bohemia and Moravia after the Munich agreement, Marshal Edward Smigly-Rydz, in turn, gave orders to annex a slice of Bohemia, which Poland had claimed since 1918.

In this atmosphere, a young generation waited for the solution to the mystery of independence. On 11 November 1939, it intended to celebrate its 21st birthday, together with the republic. But as it happened matters were to turn out very differently. Another power sought to find its *Lebensraum* in the east.

Right, Warsaw in the 1930s – one of the world's elegant cities.

44

In autumn 1938, the German Reich under Adolf Hitler summarily confronted Poland with a number of political demands, including the return of the "Free City" of Gdańsk and access to East Prussia across the so-called Polish corridor.

Neither Great Britain nor France made any attempt to halt the growing expansion of the Third Reich to the east. The only obstruction to Hitler's plans was the uncertainty of how the Soviet Union would react to these claims. In fact, after Hitler's troops invaded Czechoslovakia in March 1939, the Soviet Union agreed to collaborate with the "Greater German Reich".

In response, Great Britain and France concluded a friendship treaty with Poland, assuring each other of mutual military assistance in case of a German attack on any one of the countries. It entailed a huge risk of world war.

On 23 August 1939 Germany and the Soviet Union concluded a "non-aggression pact". In an additional, secret protocol both countries specified their territorial claims against Poland: Eastern Poland was assigned to the Soviet Union, while the remainder – the whole of the western and central territories – was to come under Hitler's control.

In the late evening of the 31 August 1939 the Soviet parliament ratified the Hitler-Stalin pact; only a few hours later the German Wehrmacht marched into Poland, without any prior declaration of war. Poland was the first country to offer military resistance to Nazi aggression. A popular myth has grown up that Polish cavalry charged German tanks. What really happened was that detachments of mounted infantry and cavalry met German panzer divisions. The cavalry, whose duty it was to charge the infantry following behind the tanks, naturally had to gallop towards oncoming armour in order to attempt this objective.

Two weeks after the German invasion of 1 September 1939, the Russians invaded from the East. There were cases of Polish soldiers caught in the middle of this crushing on-

slaught who fought the Germans in the morning and Soviet forces in the afternoon of the same day. The Government fled over the border to Romania, but the citizens of Warsaw put up a final heroic defence of the city. Nonetheless Poland was overwhelmed and by the beginning of October it was all over. Winston Churchill commented...

"Following the defeat, large regular Polish forces formed abroad and strong underground forces at home (largest among occupied countries). Poland was left longest under the devastating regime of Nazi occupation, suffered the greatest losses in human life (over 6 million) and the greatest material losses (38 percent of national property, estimated at 16.6 thousand million dollars according to the 1939 state). Poland was the only occupied country which never collaborated with the Nazis in any form and no Polish units fought alongside the German army.

To the Nazi terror Poland replied with a mass resistance movement, one of the strongest in Europe. Patriots in their hundreds of thousands in a variety of organisations flocked to the resistance movement. Poles fought in France, Norway, Africa and Italy; took part in the Battle of Britain and in countless naval engagements, including the Battle of the Atlantic."

Chaotic flight: Both numerically and technically, the German army was far superior to the ill-prepared Polish forces. The Polish soldiers, who had been mobilised within only a few hours, tried, in vain, to resist a German army that had attacked their country from the north, west and south along a front of 995 miles (1,600 km). An additional factor limiting the operational capabilities of the Polish forces was the chaotic flight of thousands of civilians, primarily Jews, desperately seeking to escape from persecution by fleeing to the east.

Although Great Britain and France declared war on Germany on 3 September 1939 and Poland thus had legitimate hopes for military support from the allied forces, no help was forthcoming; not a single shot was fired in the West and Hitler completed his "Blitzkrieg" of Poland quite unhindered.

During the last week of September, a friend-

Left, the free city of Gdańsk – a calamitous bone of contention between Germany and Poland.

ship treaty was concluded between the Soviet Union and the German Reich and there were fraternisations between German and Soviet soldiers on Polish soil. In the subsequent months, the German Wehrmacht occupied Denmark and Norway and conquered France. The Soviet Union occupied the Baltic states and eventually large areas of Finland and Romania too.

Resistance and underground: Once the Polish campaign had ended, West Prussia, Greater Poland and Upper Silesia were swallowed up by the German Reich. After various unsuccessful attempts to establish a puppet state, Germany declared the rest of occupied Poland a general *gouvernement* with its ad-

of hopelessness. Corruption and human rights abuses abounded.

In 1939, as political compensation for their failure to provide any effective military answer to Hitler's aggression, Great Britain and France undertook to sponsor the rebuilding of the Polish army abroad. At the same time support was granted to the government in exile. This government was headed by General Sikorski and represented a political spectrum that ranged from moderate nationalists to socialists. Polish soldiers, primarily refugees from occupied Poland, joined the British army. On their uniforms they wore a stripe with the inscription "Poland" and as a further symbol of recognition, a white Polish

ministrative seat located in Cracow.

The Soviet Union set about the annexation of occupied East Poland and began with the "russification" of its newly-won territory. This was personally undertaken by the head of the Communist Party in the Ukraine at the time, Nikita Khrushchev, who later, on Stalin's death, became the first Secretary of the Soviet Communist Party.

The military and political downfall of Poland was a severe shock for the Polish people and it forced them into a painful reappraisal of the situation. Terror, torture, death and starvation, and the suppression of any liberal traits, further intensified the general feeling

eagle with crown. They fought at the front in Norway, France, North Africa and later in Holland and Germany.

By mid-1943 Poland had succeeded, with the help of the allied forces (which by then included Russia), in establishing an underground army of approximately 500,000 troops, which regarded itself as the army of the government in exile in London. In addition there were thousands of partisans as well as communist party brigades, who received their arms and their orders from Moscow.

Between 1942 and 1944 the resistance forces provided a continuous threat to the German occupation forces: bridges were blown up, supply lines and centres of armaments production were sabotaged.

In the civilian sphere, too, there was a great deal of activity in occupied Poland. The education system was clandestinely organised so that thousands of young Poles could sit their high-school diplomas and even go on to further education. An underground administration and press network managed to continue functioning; there was even a police force and law courts.

Where the massive resistance movement encountered retaliation from the occupation forces, these institutions helped the threatened population as best they could. Thus, even during the period of occupation in Poland, a

destruction of the Polish people, its expulsion or "germanisation", the extermination of Jews and Gypsies as well as the settlement of Germans in the newly "liberated" areas.

This aim was to be achieved in accordance with a "legal punishment system". Craftsmen and labourers were deported to do forced labour in the Reich. Artists, scientists and priests were taken into "protective custody", often a synonym for deportation to a concentration camp. Anyone who attempted to resist had to reckon with brutal retaliation. Mass executions were the order of the day.

Since 1940 the Germans had established a number of camps on Polish territory, which, in January 1942, were semi-offically re-

feeling of national cohesion and moral strength prevailed.

Hitler's reign of terror: With the help of a chauvinistic propaganda, the party apparatus and its organisations – above all the *Waffen SS* and the *Gestapo* – Hitler applied his brutal theories concerning racial purity. In accordance with the guidelines of the propaganda ministry, Poles were regarded as *Untermenschen* – a sub-human species. The final aim of National Socialist policy was the

Left, much of Warsaw was destroyed during World War II. **Above**, the Polish resistance involved both the military and civilians.

fashioned and enlarged to function as extermination camps. People deported to these camps were officially described as "vermin". Before they were killed, they were abused as slave workers and used for medical experiments.

From 1942 onwards the prisoners of these camps were killed by poison gas and the corpses incinerated. Of the more than 5 million Polish concentration camp inmates, more than 3.5 million were killed – 3 million of those as a consequence of the *Endlösung* (final solution) as had also been planned for the Jews.

In conjunction with the executions in the

camps there was also the *Action Reinhand* which simply meant that those who had been condemned to death were robbed first of any valuables they may have had. In the fiscal year 1943–44 this brought the Deutsche Reichsbank a net profit which totalled no less than 100,047,983,91 Reichsmarks.

Soviet-occupied Poland: In Moscow, Stalin propagated the occupation of Poland as an "act of liberation from the capitalist system by a fraternal nation". A precise census was carried out, and subsequently the Soviet administration foisted Soviet passports on every Polish citizen.

One Stalin method that was especially successful was the expulsion of whole sec-

tions of the Polish population from their traditional homelands. Stalin was of the opinion that it was possible to expel anyone or anything: the nation from its identity and its land, the family from home and hearth. His aim was that ultimately, people would lose their self-esteem and sense of identity.

Stalin's reign of terror was based on rather different premises to Hitler's. He believed that his victims would ultimately surrender to a system in which they were forced to do slave labour and were pressurised day and night by functionaries or police.

In February 1940 the deportation of Polish citizens to Kasachstan, to the Russian Arctic

and to Siberia commenced. State officials, judges, foresters and small farmers were the first to be deported. Eventually whole families, merchants, members of the self-employed classes, university professors and teachers followed. In one year almost 2 million Polish citizens were deported in cattle wagons. A large percentage was taken to concentration camps for "re-education". By 1942 more than half of the people deported were no longer alive.

The battle for political supremacy: When Hitler attacked the Soviet Union in June 1941, the leader of Poland's government in exile, General Sikorski, convened with Stalin and was granted the concession that a number of Poles deported to Soviet camps should be released in order to set up a Polish army. Stalin was even prepared to annul the pact with Hitler concerning the partition of Poland, but peremptorily rejected the Polish demand to be allowed to re-establish the pre-World War I border of Poland. This new Polish army was transported via Iran into the Middle East and later played an important role in the allied landings in Italy.

This was a complete U-turn by Stalin. When a Red Cross commission inspected Katyń in Russia, occupied by the German Wehrmacht in 1943, they found a mass grave of thousands of Polish officers who had been executed three years previously by the Soviet NKWD. As a result of this crime, the Polish government in exile in London severed all contacts with the Soviet Union. At the time Stalin was totally convinced of his victory over Germany and he believed that the Soviet expansion to the west would obliterate any memory of Katyń. He even had the temerity to invite Polish communists to Moscow. Just a few years previously many of them had barely escaped the execution that Stalin had ordered for all members of the Polish Communist Party. (In 1938 the Polish Communist Party, at the time illegal, had been disbanded because of a "betrayal of the world revolution"; the party had collaborated with the Socialist Party and the Peasant Party in Poland. Some 5,000 comrades invited to the Soviet Union at the time were murdered on Stalin's orders).

For the Polish communists at the time

Left, members of the Polish resistance. Right, stone memorials to indescribable suffering.

TREBLINKA

Everybody knows the horrific photographs taken in the concentration camps. Anyone who is not blind, or does not deliberately close his eyes, will never be able to forget them: starved children with silent despair in their eyes, clinically clean gas chambers, perfect killing machines. And inscribed even above the entrances to the gas chambers is the omnipresent and deeply sarcastic motto of the master race: ARBEIT MACHT FREI ("work makes you free") – mockery of Treblinka's victims even unto their death.

As modern technology brings world events ever closer, so the list of human atrocities gets longer and longer; napalm attacks on Vietnam, genocide in Biafra, man hunts in Chile, the murder of children in Romania. But there is still no event in history which bears any comparison with the barbarous deeds perpetrated by the Nazis in the concentration camps of Poland. Here, a whole people was to be systematically exterminated – in complete orderliness, according to predetermined plans, in well-planned stages.

They were not only Jews and Gypsies, not only those in opposition to the Nazis, but also simple folk who merely wanted to continue living as Poles in Poland, who made their way to the gas chambers in Treblinka, Auschwitz, Birkenau, Majdanek and the many other camps.

This was the ultimate fate that befell all those who, in the opinion of the occupiers, were no longer useful as "work slaves".

The concentration camp at Treblinka provides one of the most chilling reminders of the Nazi atrocities: the site was strategically well-chosen; about 60 miles (100 km) to the northeast of Warsaw, with its own rail terminal linked with the international railway network to Russia. At the junction there was a large supply depot for the German advance to the east. Some convicts were occasionally allowed to work there a few days longer – for the "final victory".

It is practically a historical certainty that the two extermination camps, Treblinka I and II, were built directly along the demarcation line that the German Reich and the Soviet Union had drawn straight through Poland when they divided the country between them. The intention of the Germans was probably to be able to lay the blame at the Russians' door. In 1943, when the mass graves of Katyń, where Stalin had had 4,000 Polish officers interred, were discovered, German propaganda hypocritically made use of the massacre for their own purposes. By then, the military situation had changed of course.

In November 1943 the Nazis closed the Treblinka camps and obliterated their bloody traces. Before that they had committed 2,400 murders per day. Documents were rapidly burnt, all possible eye witnesses were liquidated; the SS literally tried to let grass grow over the site of the horrors they had committed.

But their hasty attempts at a total cover-up failed – a few dozen eyewitnesses escaped from their captors and conveyed the cruel truths about the camps to the rest of the world. In 1964 a commemorative site was at last inaugurated that tried to do justice to the unequalled human tragedy that this place represents.

The architect Adam Haupt and the sculptor Franciszek Duszenko – both professors at the Art Academy in Gdańsk – commemorated the 800,000 victims with simple stone tablets. Concrete sleepers mark the path to the cobblestone death ramp, the final stop for the countless cattle wagons in which the prisoners were transported to the Treblinka camp.

For the former crematorium the artists created a "visionary picture of hell": the site of that indescribable horror is now covered with basalt rocks that were melted and fused with each other at a temperature of 2,000°C. A central monument of massive ashlar granite piled up to a high altar commemorates the uprising of the prisoners on 2 August 1943.

The Treblinka memorial is just one example of the dignified earnestness with which the Poles view their tragic history. They allow the wounds to heal slowly.

We in the west – particularly in Germany – would do well to make quite sure that the old scars never break open again.

there were two tasks: on the one hand they wanted to strengthen the Soviet Power, on the other they wanted to overthrow the Polish military. In autumn 1941 the newly organised Polish divisions fought side by side with the Soviet army at the Eastern front. As a sign of their identity, these soldiers wore the Piast eagle – without crown – on their helmets.

In January 1945 the Soviet army had reached the pre-war border of Poland. After a compromise suggestion by Great Britain, the future Polish-Soviet border was to run along the Bug, ergo a little farther to the west than before the war. Stalin refused to accept this. In order to pre-empt the "sovietisation" of Poland, the Polish government in exile in

side, most of them just youths. After the capitulation of the rebels, Hitler ordered the total destruction of the city. Eighty percent of the buildings were blown up and the remainder went up in flames. Despite the destruction, about 2 million people were living among the rubble when the Red Army crossed the Vistula in January 1945.

At the conference in Yalta in February 1945 Roosevelt, Churchill and Stalin, the three leaders of the Superpowers, agreed that after the termination of hostilities in Poland, free democratic elections should be held in the country. The allies made no objection to Stalin's desire to establish governments amicably inclined to Moscow in Eastern

London sent their own troops to liberate the Polish cities – but in vain.

A last chance both to break the resistance of the Germans in Warsaw and to secure the country's independence from the Soviet Union was to be a military action on the left bank of the Weichsel in Warsaw. The Warsaw Uprising of 1 August 1944 ultimately turned out to be unsuccessful because Poland received no support from Great Britain and the Soviet Union did not allow the allies to send aid to the Polish areas that were occupied by the Soviet army.

The uprising continued for 63 days and claimed 200,000 casualties on the Polish

Europe. In their eagerness not to offend Stalin, the British government even banned Polish forces from the Victory Parade held in London.

In April 1945 the fraternisation of American and Soviet troops at the river Elbe settled the future border between the Western and the Eastern sphere of influence on the continent which heralded the end of the war in Europe. On 2 May the Soviet army marched into Berlin and Soviet and Polish flags flew on the Brandenburg Gate.

Above, the fate of Poland was decided by **Churchill, Roosevelt and Stalin in Yalta.**

One party state and planned economy: In summer 1944, a Polish administration was introduced in liberated Poland, controlled by communists. That same year a "manifesto of progress" was published, settling a new social and economic order. The transformation of society began with slogans of justice and democracy, a reform of agriculture and the nationalisation of industry.

This revolution from above started without any support from the people, and was accompanied by terror and fear. As Stalin did not trust the Polish communists, he ordered the Soviet secret service to start up operations immediately behind the front lines. He took charge of the network of agents that had previously worked for the Gestapo and checked the allegiance of the Polish population to the communist party. Poles who stood by their conviction were either executed and buried in the forests, or, if they were lucky, forced into exile. Those willing to compromise were offered employment and living quarters and promised a party career.

The military and civil administration of the Polish underground, which had previously worked in close cooperation with the exiled government in London, was systematically disbanded. Stalin had no intention of adhering to the guarantee for a democratic Poland planned by the three Superpowers.

Only after mid-1945 did the terror abate somewhat; but fears continued in Poland. Soviet advisers urged Polish communists to make promises to the people and at least give the appearance that democratisation was taking place. Again and again the communists declared themselves willing to cooperate with non-communists and again and again the slogans of the Progress Manifesto were repeated. Poverty and fear, the rage against the old regime and the vacillating attitude of the church in these revolutionary times, made many Poles susceptible to promises of this kind.

When vast numbers of refugees, including the prewar and war time politicians and the exiled government in London returned to Poland, the communists and their police and military administration had already done their worst. Politicians who had been active – legally and in the underground – had been isolated, had had to stop work and leave the country. Many were killed.

The Polish communists who determined the development of the new state and who had initially been prepared to cooperate with all democratic forces in the country soon had to bow to pressure from Moscow and intensify their attitude to non-communist groups. Political blackmail became widespread. Power was retained by the functionaries of the security police. Their motto was: "Communism from Vladivostok to Gibraltar".

In June 1948 the head of the Polish communists, Władyslaw Gomulka, was accused of "right-wing national tendencies" and imprisoned. Some months later the Socialist Party was forcibly integrated with the National Unity Party, the PZPR. With the agreement of Stalin, power was transferred to his faithful, but totally incapable, communist henchman Bolesław Bierut.

The reconstruction of the economy: In 1945 the Poles found themselves with a new state with geographically favourable and historically acceptable borders. However, since 1939 more than 6 million Poles had been killed. One-third of the national property had been lost and two-thirds of the industrial potential had been destroyed. A tangible hope for an economic upswing was in the areas from which up to 1947, 3.5 million Germans had been expelled. But there, too, the war had left its mark; after the war the Soviets had removed all the region's surviving industrial plant and shipped it to the Soviet Union.

Agricultural reform did not bring about the desperately needed economic results. In 1946 industries, both large and small, were nationalised. As compensation for the loss of Polish property abroad, more than US$200 million were repaid to the country, but under pressure from Moscow, the Poles had to forgo help from the Marshall Plan. The communists foisted a centralised planned economy on to the country; the private trade and service sector was abolished in 1947. As the new economic bureaucracy was incapable of replacing the liquidated private sector, the black market flourished. Paradoxically, this state of affairs was laid squarely at capitalism's door.

Thanks to the endeavours of the people, from 1947 onwards Poland managed to keep to a three-year plan of industrial and agricultural growth. Soon the average per capita income was back at the level it had been before the war.

THE COMMUNIST STATE

In 1948 Europe entered the long dark tunnel in its history known as the Cold War. With the blockade of Berlin the era of Stalinism also began for Poland.

In March 1948 the prime minister, Józef Cyrankiewicz, received instructions from Moscow to establish a governing unity party. This was to include the remnants of the Polish Socialist Party (PPS) and the Polish Workers Party (PPR). The pre-communist Peasant Faction, the United Peoples Party (ZSL) and the Democratic Faction (SD) were allowed to remain independent but under the auspices of the communists.

Stalinism takes hold: In the December of 1948 the founding congress of the PZPR/Polish United Workers' Party took place. Bolesław Bierut, a former member of the Comintern and at the time president of the republic, was appointed first secretary. With the embodiment of the pre-eminent role of the PZPR in the new constitution on 22 July 1952, the last chance to establish a democratic society in Poland passed.

Adoption of Marxism-Leninism as an infallible ideology, the amassing of armed forces on a huge scale, centralised economic planning and concentration on heavy industry as well as the power monopoly of the PZPR and its front organisations were the characteristic traits of Stalinism in Poland. This model was transferred directly from the Soviet Union to all countries of the Eastern bloc and was retained, virtually unchanged, until the end of the 1980s.

Officially the constitution was quite democratic: it guaranteed civil rights and a democratic government elected by parliament with a president and a states council. The parliament itself, the Sejm, was voted by general election. In reality, however, it was little more than a farce. The "working people in the city and in rural areas", according to the letter of the constitution nothing less than the true rulers of the country, were only helpless victims of the state. The party alone, the politburo, the first secretary and the privileged elite of the nomenclature were the ones who really wielded all the power. In effect, it was a dictatorship of the party over the people.

The conviction of Stalin and his minions that the Soviet bloc was constantly threatened by an invasion from the "powers of American imperialism" led to the recruitment of an enormous Polish army (400,000 troops). The officers were trained in a Political Military Academy (WAP, founded in 1951). In 1955 Poland became a member of the Warsaw Pact, which was intended to be the reply to the founding of NATO. Moreover Poland became a full member of the COMECON, the Union of Mutual Economic Aid, founded in 1949.

Top priority was accorded to building up the steel, coal, iron and armaments industries. In order to accommodate the flood of migrant workers from rural areas who were now required to take their places on the production lines, whole new cities and suburbs were built virtually overnight. On the outskirts of Warsaw and in Nowa Huta near Cracow these municipal, architectural monstrosities can still be seen in all their ghastliness. The supply of foodstuffs was largely handed over to the newly established PGR (national property – the Polish version of the Russian collective farms), whose gross inefficiency resulted in disastrous consequences for both productivity and quality.

The Roman Catholic church was generally regarded as a reactionary relic of the old system and totally inimical to the communist regime. Priests and laymen alike were openly attacked and constantly threatened with arrest. In 1950 the financial assets of the church were confiscated and in 1952, Cardinal Stefan Wyszynski, the primate of Poland, was exiled to a monastery.

The intention of the system was to fashion new, socialist man: in effect that meant the abolition of humanitarian ideals. Political terror and repression reached its climax between 1951 and 1952.

Everyday life became a nightmare. All contacts with the outside world were immediately denounced; in bogus trials innocent people were arbitrarily accused of being

Left, in "Manifest" (here a picture by Wojciech Weiss) the Communists outlined their vision of a new Poland.

spies and sentenced to internment or death. There were also executions without trial (in 1990 mass graves were found dating from this time). Many people were deported to the Soviet Union and simply vanished without trace. A dense network of informers infiltrated factories and offices, the schools and the universities.

The propoganda, of course, told a different story. The news was full of stories about the construction of gigantic collective combines, factories and other buildings and tales of rising work quotas. The ever-increasing number of success stories perpetuated the course that Stalinism had planned. Monumental sculptures and paintings in the style of socialist realism provided additional visible proof of the superiority of the new system and its ideology.

And yet the omnipotence of Stalinism in Poland never quite reached the level that it did in the other states of the Eastern bloc. The political trials never developed into a series of propaganda trials. It proved impossible to eradicate the bourgeois and intellectual milieu, and the Roman Catholic church also survived the times. The collectivisation of agriculture met with strong resistance from the farmers and could only be carried out slowly and incompletely. Nevertheless, the memory of the brutalism of the Stalinist years was for ever engraved upon the mind of the nation.

Stalin died in March 1953. Within two years the liberalising effect of his death was being felt in Poland. In December 1954 the despised Ministry of Public Security (Ministerstwo Bezpieczenstwa Publicznego) was disbanded and the laws of censorship were relaxed. Wladysław Gomulka was released from prison. There was no further talk of collectivisation.

In June 1956 the worker protests in Poznań, which started with the slogan "bread and liberty", showed that the country needed a new party leader whom the people could trust and who would handle the national problems pragmatically. This man turned out to be Władysław Gomulka. After Khrushchev had personally assured himself of his loyalty, everything seemed plain sailing. The era of Stalinism in Poland had come to an end.

1956–80 national communism: In October 1956 Gomulka managed to free Poland from total control of the Soviet Union. This fact determined the political life of Poland for the next 25 years. Gomulka was of the opinion that there were "various ways to Socialism" and he managed to prove that Polish communists could look after the affairs of their country on their own account, without having to take constant instructions from Moscow (Imre Nagy in Hungary was not so lucky). Gomulka managed to achieve three vital concessions: an independent church, free agriculture and an open political forum. These concessions were only designed to be of a transitional nature, until the party had found a firm footing, but matters turned out differently.

The church was stronger than ever before. Within the framework of its self-administration, the church continued to run its priest seminars, its own social and intellectual societies and its own university (KUL – the Catholic University of Lubin). It thus became the only really independent church in the whole of the Eastern bloc.

Sociologists who adhered to the party doctrine had prophesied that the extensive industrialisation and urbanisation would ultimately change the cultural patterns of traditional society and would sever the close ties between the people and the church. They couldn't have been more wrong. The Polish church did not lose her adherents – on the contrary the church turned out to be a place of refuge and the driving force behind the Polish opposition.

The same kind of fate befell the collectivisation plans of the agricultural programme. Gomulka had no intention of committing the same errors that had led to the death by starvation of millions of people in the Ukraine 20 years previously. More than 80 percent of the arable land thus remained in private hands, while collective farming was only retained in the areas where it had already been introduced (e.g. on the huge, former German estates in the west of Poland). The experts did not regard that as a problem. In time, the small, private farms would disappear of their own accord, as the state had other means of making it plain to the farmers that private industry was not worthwhile. In practice that meant granting privileges to the

Right, "High Noon" looms in Poland – a gunfight or a peaceful exchange of power?

Solidarność

WYBORY

Jaruzelski gorszy od Hitlera
Bo WIARĘ odbiera!

WŁADZE NIE D...

DNIE
'89

collective sector and neglecting the private sector, measures which ultimately ended in unmitigated disaster.

Within 40 years the government managed to lead the country to the very brink of starvation. Poland, traditionally an agricultural country, was ruined, despite its fertile soil. The population was plagued with food rationing and queuing in front of grocers' shops. Nevertheless private agriculture managed to survive.

The demands for pluralism in political life were accommodated by the leadership through the licensing of several political organisations. However, the fact that these were all united under the one roof of the

alties. By this time there could no longer be any doubt that the government had lost the confidence of the Polish people.

The establishment of an organised opposition came about in stages. The protests of March 1968 not only mobilised the students, but also the whole intelligentsia. For the first time the names of several dissidents became well-known, e.g. Adam Michnik, Jacek Kuron and Karol Modzelewski.

The unrests in December 1970 in Gdańsk and Szczecin succeeded in moulding a generation of intransigent yet embittered workers. Between 1975 and 1976 the changes in the constitution, which resulted in an even greater dependency on the Soviet Union,

National Union Front – under the patronage of the party – meant that any ideas of pluralism were pure illusion. Soon it became clear that neither Gomulka nor his successor, Edward Gierek, backed up as they were by a total lack of any constitutionality, were prepared to adhere to the promised concessions. The sphere of civil liberties was considerably curtailed. Again and again (1968, 1970, 1976 and 1980) dissent broke out. The slogan of the protestors was "Bread and liberty". The protests were either organised by labourers or students and intellectuals. They had to be forcibly put down by the government and there were frequent casu-

contributed to the organisation of a national dissident group within the KPN (Committee of Independent Poland).

In June 1976 when the workers in the tractor plant in Ursus and the armaments factory in Radom were punished for their participation in a protest action, intellectuals founded the KOR (Committee to defend the workers). For the first time intellectuals and workers were unanimous in pursuing a common goal and from this moment on one could talk of an organised, supranational opposition. The committee worked quite openly (although not legally) as information and coordination centre for the whole country.

With the investiture of the cardinal of Cracow, Karol Wojtyła, as Pope in 1978 and his visit to Poland in 1979, the psychological barrier of fear was also destroyed.

August 1980–December 1981, Solidarity: In summer 1980 government attempts to implement drastic price increases for foodstuffs and consumer goods caused a wave of public strikes. The epicentre of the protest was in Gdańsk, in the Lenin shipyard, whose tradition of resistance went back to December 1970, when workers had been killed in front of the gates when they denounced price increases. The KOR members were involved right from the start of the political agitation. Included on the list of the 21 demands posed

committee from all the provinces of the country formed the national coordination committee of the independent, self-administered trade union "Solidarność", known in the West as Solidarity. The 37-year-old Lech Wałęsa was elected chairman. Just a few months later the "Farmers' Solidarity" ("Solidarność Wiejska") was permitted as an official organisation.

In the 15 months of its activity Solidarity proved to be a peaceful reform movement which, with its 10 million members, represented the whole nation. It could only defend itself with its own ideals. On 13 December 1981, the head of the party, General Jaruzelski, proclaimed martial law. Solidar-

by the strike committee were the right to strike, the right to form independent trade unions and the permission to erect a monument for colleagues who had died in the 1970 uprising. In return the workers declared themselves willing to accept the leading role of the party.

The agreement between the workers and the government was eventually signed on 31 August 1980. As an immediate consequence of this event, representatives of the strike

Left, the people support Solidarity. **Above**, with Tadeusz Mazowiecki at his side, Lech Wałęsa holds a first press conference in October 1980.

ity was officially disbanded and its most prominent members were imprisoned. A wave of repression started; all remnants of constitutionality disappeared.

1981–89, Martial Law: The next eight years in Poland were characterised by an ever more acute economic crisis. The opposition centred around the church. During the state of martial law and for some time afterwards the church was the only truly independent institution that could afford to offer its protection to anyone requiring it. The church was, at the same time, a forum for political discussion, meetings, lectures, theatre performances, tuition and the dissemination of illegal literature, publicity and magazines.

Life was divided into two spheres – the official, legal, everyday routine and the unofficial, illegal, underground work. The government proved incapable of coping with the economic and political crisis. Also, under the leadership of Mikhail Gorbachev, the Soviet Union for the first time no longer showed any imperialistic tendencies. An invasion, such as had already been planned in December 1981, was therefore no longer a realistic possibility by the latter half of the decade. In autumn 1988 the party agreed to share political power. In the "round table" talks in spring 1989, the conditions between the party and representatives from Solidarity were specified. The path towards democracy had finally been levelled.

After the change of power: For the elections, Solidarity founded citizen committees to represent the opposition. Even during the "round table" talks, the communist party had reserved the right to form the government. But in the election of June 1989 the communists were so soundly thrashed that any attempt of doing so failed. Ultimately Tadeusz Mazowiecki was entrusted with the task of forming a government. A journalist by profession, he had already acquired authority as the editor-in-chief of the *Tygodnik Solidarność* in 1980–81, and later, during his imprisonment, he enjoyed a high popular esteem.

The new government, the first freely elected non-communist leadership in a Warsaw Pact state, took office on 12 September 1989. It had to concentrate on two primary problems: the political reorganisation of the state, a revival of democracy and political and social pluralism; and the avoidance of an impending economic collapse.

The minister of finance, Balcerowicz, began implementing a drastic economic reform programme which broadly followed the recommendations of the World Bank and the International Monetary Fund. After massive price increases and drastic reductions in the state budget, the inflation rate fell below 10 percent. The zloty became the first freely convertible currency within the COMECON. Poland began talking confidently of joining the European Community well before the end of the century.

But the country rapidly confronted the problem faced by all post-communist governments in Eastern Europe: it was difficult to implement radical economic reform without mature democratic institutions in place. As shops found a ready market for expensive Swiss watches and American jeans, further sacrifices today in return for better living standards tomorrow was not a proposition that appealed to the third of families who were already living below the poverty line. As one jaded Solidarity deputy described the joys of governing: "It's like repairing a rusty threshing machine in a dark barn."

No-one discovered this truth more bitterly than Lech Wałęsa: it seemed to many nothing short of a fairy-tale when the former labour leader became president, yet within a couple of years much of his popular support had drained away and he was being unfavourably compared with Napoleon. Prudently, he ordered bullet-proof glass for the Namiestnikowski Palace when renovating it as his Warsaw residence.

Wałęsa fell out with Hanna Suchocka, a 45-year-old lawyer who became prime minister in 1992. Unable to hold together a seven-party coalition *and* keep the president happy, she lasted less than a year. In the ensuing elections in September 1993, Solidarity, which had splintered politically in 1991, was humiliated and a communist-dominated coalition led by Alexander Kwasniewski, a dapper 38-year-old sophisticate who presented himself as a social democrat, came to power. His promises of more jobs, better education and health care, and higher pensions had more appeal than the prospect of further austerity offered by most rival parties – even though he was notably vague about how he was going to achieve his promises.

But at least Poland faced its problems as a free nation. In 1993, the last of the 60,000 Soviet troops which had been based in Poland for 48 years departed, and the remains of Poland's wartime hero General Wladislaw Sikorski, which had rested in a British war cemetery for 50 years, came home to Cracow. Pessimists, however, were perturbed by the social unrest to the west following Germany's reunification and by the political instability to the east as Russia, beset by economic problems even worse than Poland's, threatened to veer to the right.

Right, a memorial in Poznań recalls the victims of the first strike.

THE OPPOSITION SPECTRUM

The political opposition in Poland crystallised out of the student revolt in March 1968. The protests succeeded in unifying the intellectuals against the regime, and indeed most of the present-day members of parliament in Poland belong to this generation.

The workers rebellions in December 1970 and the formation of the "committee to defend the workers" (KOR) consolidated the Polish opposition. Political dissidents, scientists, writers and artists were all members of the KOR. Together with industrial workers, they opposed the totalitarian state that was ruled by a party "nomenclature", prepared the establishment of independent trade unions and, despite an official ban, published newspapers and books.

The founding of Solidarity in 1980 was thus the result of a long process and came about through the efforts of a whole people.

A brief biography of three leading figures may be taken as *pars pro toto* for the changing fortunes on the way to opposition.

Mieczysław Gil: Born in Gace Slupieckie, a village near Kielce, Gil started as a worker in 1963 at the Lenin steelworks (now Sendzimir steelworks), the biggest industrial enterprise in Poland and prize exhibit of the communists. Like others of his generation he joined the Communist Party and played an active role in the political youth movement. At the age of 19 he was a fervent believer in their ideals for a glorious future.

In 1968 he began to experience his first doubts. He was fully in favour of the striking students. He refused to do service in the Workers' Militia – notorious for its hard-nosed delight in beating up students – and was consequently suspended from work.

The period between 1970 and 1980 – a time of deceptive stability under Edward Gierek – was relatively tranquil for him. He started to get involved in journalistic work. His first reports appeared in the student magazine *ITD* and he also wrote for the *Cracow Daily*. After 13 years, he was employed by *The Voice of Nowa Huta*. During the strikes in 1980 he became the spokesman for the protesting steel workers, founded a committee for metal workers in the "NSZZ Solidarity" and was appointed chairman.

In January 1981 he was elected chairman of Solidarity for the region of Małopolska. He resigned his party membership and became one of the best-known opposition leaders of Cracow.

After 13 December 1981 he organised the workers' strike at the Lenin steelworks in Cracow and, after the proclamation of martial law, joined the underground opposition movement. In January 1982 he was arrested and sentenced to four years imprisonment. In 1984 he was released, but not re-employed by the management of the steelworks. He moved back to his home village and from there organised the work of the, meanwhile prohibited, Solidarity in that region. In 1986

he founded a public workers committee in Nowa Huta and headed the strike of the collective in 1988. Eventually he became a close ally of Lech Wałęsa at the "round table" negotiations.

In 1989 he was a list member of the "Solidarity Committee" and a candidate for a seat in the Sejm. He won his ticket with more than 90 percent of the votes – more than anyone else in Poland. After the resignation of Geremek, he became leader of the faction and is currently also head of Solidarity in Nowa Huta.

Krzysztof Kozłowski – the fervent Catholic: Kozłowski was a scion of a landed family with a long social and political tradition. His grandfather had already been deeply involved in agricultural and education matters. His father served as a soldier in the army of Marshal Jozef Piłsudski and was a deputy in the Sejm, the Polish parliament, from 1930 to 1939. His uncle, Leon Kozlowski, was prime minister of Poland from 1934 to 1935.

In the 1950s Krzysztof Kozłowski studied at the Catholic University in Lublin, where he sat his PhD in philosophy.

In December 1956 he became editor-in-chief of the *Tygodnik Powszechny*, a weekly magazine, whose publication was repeatedly banned for political reasons. He also joined the "Club of Catholic Intellectuals".

This included Tadeusz Mazowiecki, later to become Polish prime minister, as well as senators Andrzej Wielowieyski and Andrezej Stelmachowiski.

In the 1970s, Krzysztof Kozłowski became closely associated with the gradually evolving political opposition and was one of the founders of the "Society for scientific courses", an independent, autodidactically orientated organisation.

In 1980 he unequivocally supported the striking workers. Together with Helena Bortnowska he worked as a consultant for

Left, Jaruzelski. **Above**, Lech Wałęsa.

the metal workers of Nowa Huta and, during the time of martial law, he supported the underground work of Solidarity.

In December 1988 he was a member of the committee and took part in the "round table" discussions for political reforms and mass media. On 4 June 1989 he was elected to the senate on the ticket of the "Solidarity Committee". As chairman of the senate committee for social communication he was involved in the democratisation of the media. At the request of the prime minister he joined the Ministry of the Interior and became chairman of the Office for State Security.

Seweryn Blumsztejn – the 1968 generation: Blumsztejn is a member of the post-war generation, a generation that grew up in the totalitarian, communist state. In the politically tumultuous 1960s, which also ushered in a new era in Poland, he enrolled at the university to study history. With his circle of friends which included Adam Michnik and Jacek Kuron, he started his opposition role at the University of Warsaw. They founded the "Club of Objectors" and organised numerous discussion meetings with intellectuals throughout the country.

He was repeatedly arrested during those years. His lodgings were frequently searched and disciplinary actions were instigated against him at the university. All this had a profound effect on his political thinking.

Later Blumsztejn wrote passionately about those years of student upheavals. "What remains is the memory of an ocean of sewage that slushed across public life and the disgusting, hate-filled party apparatus. I think before the time of Solidarity there was something like a generation of March 1968. March was their moment of political initiation, their embryo was the democratic opposition of the 1970s."

In the 1970s he became fully involved with the KOR and was publisher of the first uncensored magazine in Poland. In 1980 he edited the daily news service of the agency Solidarity/AS. When martial law was proclaimed, he happened to be in Paris. He immediately founded a Solidarity subsidiary there and sent medicines, printing presses and independent publications to Poland. In 1984 he tried to return to Poland but was stopped at the border and sent back to Paris.

He returned again in 1989 and became the editor-in-chief of the *Gazeta Wyborcza*.

"*Nie damy sie* – we will not give in!" Like a leitmotif this sentence has been repeated in all the great speeches made by the leaders and heroes of the country for the last two centuries, from the first division of Poland to the 1980s. Even Tadeusz Kościuszko, who fought against the English as a general of George Washington and later led the uprising of his people against the Russians, employed these words. Later on they turn up in the speeches of Józef Piłsudski, who commanded the forces of the young country at the "Miracle of the Vistula", when the Red Army was defeated and forced to abandon its attempt to advance into Central Europe. And finally, they are inseparably linked with the figure of Lech Wałęsa, the workers' leader from Gdańsk who played a crucial part in the defeat of the communist system.

"We will not give in!" The Poles always had plenty of reason to express their defiance with this rousing declaration. It has lost none of its significance today, nor is it likely to do so in the future.

There is a profound feeling amongst the Poles that they are repeatedly going to be subjected to national misfortune, against which they will fight, but with no chances of succeeding. In the history of the Polish people, chapters in which they are the heroes alternate with chapters in which they are the victims, and the transition is only too often very abrupt.

There is not, however, very much they can do about their main problem, their geographical position: in the west they have the Germans, in the east the Russians. In their relationship to both countries military conflict has historically played a much more prominent part than peaceful coexistence. And the three countries have accordingly not got a good word to say for one another. The Russians find their neighbours unreliable and much too happy-go-lucky for their liking. In German "Polish economy" is an expression denoting a shambles.

To the Prussians in particular, with their authoritarian state, their dynamism and their moral code which frowned on every kind of

instinctive behaviour, Poland was not merely a mystery, but a positive horror. In the year 1814 a Prussian field marshal wrote to Baron von Stein: "Disorder and a life of chaos is the Pole's element. No – these people deserve to be trodden underfoot!" And Bismarck's opinion a few decades later was much the same: "The Pole has to be beaten until he loses heart."

Some decades after this the Nazis gave another demonstration of how the Poles should be taught by the Germans to mend their ways. When they occupied the country, they established a reign of brutality and cruelty: it will be a long time before the name of Auschwitz ceases to haunt all attempts at rapprochement, to say nothing of reconciliation between the Germans and the Poles. Nor can the older generation erase the memory of the suppression of the two Warsaw uprisings in 1943 and 1944.

Friendships: The general disparagement of their neighbour on the part of Germany and Russia, which paved the way for the crimes of World War II, was occasionally interrupted by waves of enthusiasm for Poland, for example when the Poles rebelled against the scourge of the czar and the discipline of the Prussians in the revolution years of 1830 and 1848, even though both uprisings were unsuccessful. The first lines of a very popular song of the time in support of Poland ran as follows:

*"Forward little Poland
And as in David's day,
A sling your only weapon,
The great Goliath slay!"*

Something vaguely reminiscent of these waves of sympathy emerged after the imposition of military rule at the end of 1981, when the West Germans sent millions of aid packages to the crippled country.

The postwar years were a time of bitterness for the Poles. The initial euphoria of the reconstruction gave way to the feeling that once again they had no control over their fate. When the pressure of the Stalinist regime let up with the death of the Soviet dictator, the Poles rebelled several times, in

1956, 1968, 1970, 1976 and 1980 – without success. Each time the system (in Polish eyes a foreign power that had imposed itself on the country) fought back. On a day-to-day basis they were thus forced to come to terms with their fate whether they liked it or not.

They also drew some comfort from their highly developed ability to make fun of every kind of authority, with jokes ranging from the harmless to the bitingly sarcastic. The victims of political humour, who in Polish literature up until then were primarily the Germans and Austrians, were now most commonly the Soviets.

Ridicule, fine irony in the old-established Polish style and subtle sarcasm experienced a strong revival. Polish satire has a long and glorious tradition, kept alive to this day by the priceless cabarets that are still part of regular entertainment in the towns. Amongst its neighbours, Poland acquired the reputation of being the "jolliest barrack in the socialist camp".

The jokes however often fell into the category of black humour, as the following two, of which there are any number of different variations, illustrate quite clearly. They are based on the fact that a lot of Poland's industrial and agricultural products were siphoned off to the east, while the country got little back in return. The first of these short jokes went as follows: "We have been given a million pairs of shoes from the glorious Soviet Union – to sole." And the second: "We give the Russians coal and they take meat from us in return."

Victory: In that historic year, 1989, the Poles finally reaped the benefits of their resistance when, after more than four decades, they finally succeeded in shaking off the totalitarian system that masqueraded as socialism. When the communist party was voted out of office and later disintegrated, fury over the half-ruined country that it had left behind was mixed with pride on the part of the Poles that they had been the first to triumph over the system.

The breakdown of the socialist system all over Eastern Europe is linked in the vast majority of Polish minds with two names: Pope John Paul II and Lech Wałęsa. The former Cracow cardinal visited his home country in 1979, one year after his election as Pope, and was received by an entire nation with an enthusiasm that knew no bounds.

The barrier of fear that had been created by a government based on force had finally been broken down. More than 10 million people, which is almost a third of the population, saw the Pope with their own eyes. No-one could fail to be aware that this was a nation in the process of rediscovering its identity.

The next step was a general protest only a few months later under the leadership of the free trade union Solidarity, which manifested itself in a wave of strikes precipitated by a rise in the price of sausage and meat. The young, dynamic electrician Lech Wałęsa emerged as the leader of the workers; he and his advisers in Solidarity were the first to find a peaceful but eventually successful way of putting up constant resistance to the totalitarian system.

Even when military rule was imposed the Poles did not give in, one of their main strengths being the alliance between the workers and intellectuals that continued to hold firm. In true Polish tradition, the best-known artists in the country lent their support to everyone who they felt was fighting for the independence of Poland. Included amongst them were the film directors Krzysztof Kieslowski, Andrzej Wajda, Krzysztof Zanussi, and even the expatriate Roman Polanski, the composer Krzysztof Penderecki and the writers Stanisław Lem and Andrzej Szczypiorski.

The exiled Czeslaw Milosz, who was awarded the Nobel prize for literature just when the "Summer of Solidarity" was in full swing, filled the whole nation with pride; the movement in support of intellectual and political independence acquired fresh impetus. The artists and writers used their international reputation to help the other Poland – the real Poland, as it proved to be – assert itself; they also helped to show the world what was really going on.

Disillusionment: After the political change and the liberation from the confines of the system, divisions in Polish society that had existed before the war reasserted themselves, and it was as if the German occupation and the 45 years of communist rule had never been. Once again the old argument was resumed about whether Poland belonged to the East or the West. What the Poles have in common with the East, the Russians, the Belorussians and Ukrainians is that they are also a Slavic people. What bound them throughout their history to the West and still keeps them firmly linked to this half of Europe is Western culture, the Renaissance and the Enlightenment, and their religious faith, which they share with a number of Western European countries.

When the debris of the communist system had been cleared away, however, the old hostilities between the Poles and their neighbours were shown to be still very much alive. It was not only the relationship between the Poles and the Germans that was troubled once again by the emotions of the past: Lithuania, Belorussia, the Ukraine and Czechoslovakia also brought up old grudges

they had against the country.

Some of the issues involved are not that old. At last it was possible to talk not only about the German past of Silesia, Pomerania, West and East Prussia but also the expulsion of the Germans from Poland after the war and the fate of the German minority.

The Lithuanians demanded a guarantee that their capital Vilnius would not be annexed again as it had been in 1920 under Marshal Piłsudski, who had pushed the border of Poland further east to absorb consider-

Father Jerzy Popiełuszko, a popular figure in the Church, died a martyr for his political beliefs.

able chunks of Belorussian and Ukrainian territory. And the Ukrainians asked what justification Piłsudski, a figure who is incidentally greatly admired by the workers' leader Lech Wałęsa, had had when he led a Polish army of invasion into their capital, Kiev, in 1920. In Czechoslovakia the people had not forgotten that after the Munich Dictate that gave Hitler Sudetenland, the Poles took advantage of the situation to get a share of the land themselves and invaded a part of Bohemia.

The Poles were confronted with the fact that they still had to come to terms with much of their past, and were eventually forced to acknowledge that in their conflicts with their neighbours, even those which had taken place this century, they had not always been the victims. Amongst the aspects of their past that did not necessarily show the Poles in a good light, was the relationship of the majority of the population to Jewish citizens. For too long certain dark chapters in Polish history had been suppressed, and it had been taboo even to mention them.

These included the pogroms during the first two years after the war, which culminated in the murder of 46 survivors of the concentration camps by an hysterical mob in Kielce, a town in central Poland, and the anti-Semitic campaign of 1968, as a consequence of which thousands of Jewish intellectuals left the country: an irreplaceable loss for Polish science and art.

Looking west: However, like people of their age everywhere else in the world, Poland's younger generation is not interested in carrying on the conflicts and arguments of yesterday. For years the West has been the main attraction.

The majority of young Poles found it hard to understand the revival of the West's interest in the Soviet Union, Russia and *perestroika*, when they themselves had been tormented for years with Russian language instruction and pre-military training. When they were allowed to choose between several different subjects at school after the removal from power of the communist party, Russian fell by the wayside and over 90 percent took English as their first foreign language. Even German was noticeably more popular than the language of Poland's eastern neighbour. The motto of the younger generation is quite simply: return to Europe.

The heart of Warsaw's city centre on Saturday afternoons is a sight guaranteed to take the unprepared visitor by surprise: in front of the city's three largest department stores, Wars, Sawa and Junior, once the pride of the Gierek era and the symbol of the more western-oriented consumerism of the 1970s, the streets are crammed with hundreds of Poles.

Nothing is left of that western atmosphere. In the midst of the monotony of everyday life in Warsaw and the ruins of the socialist economic system, the Poles are once again practising the difficult art of survival. The atmosphere of this weekly occasion closely resembles that of an Oriental bazaar. The goods for sale are spread out on cloths, on the pavement itself or the bonnets of the ubiquitous Polski-Fiats. Here would-be buyers will find virtually anything and everything they could want, from bananas to ladies' underwear – the booty of weekend trips to Berlin or visits to Turkey – excursions that are vital to survival in Poland.

The initial stages of a market economy are difficult. Many Polish families have found themselves beset by financial problems due to the sharp rise in prices with which wages have not kept pace, or to the main breadwinner suddenly finding himself out of work. Work has never been the Poles' favourite way of solving their problems, and they accordingly started looking for other ways out of their economic crisis.

Risk of fines: The buying and selling of goods is generally seen as the most lucrative and direct means of supplementing income and the market at the Maszalkowska and Aleje Jerozolimskie crossroads, in the heart of Warsaw, is the final destination of many a carefully planned trading expedition. Whether they come from an easterly, westerly or southerly direction, the individuals embarking on such trips always incur a certain amount of risk in the form of customs inspections and fines imposed by the police. To circumvent these impediments requires

cunning, imagination and a true Polish talent for survival.

Goods dumped: The phenomenon of the "Polish market" in West Berlin is a particularly notable example of such Polish cunning. Taking advantage of the allies' agreement to allow the citizens of the Eastern bloc free access to West Berlin, the Poles flooded in at the beginning of 1989, loaded down with goods of all kinds that they had accumulated on their journey through Poland and the former German Democratic Republic. The goods were dumped at low prices, but the people selling them still made themselves a considerable profit.

Once the word got round that on the site of the old Potsdam Station cigarettes, vodka and champagne were being offered at half what they normally cost, the "Polish market" was soon swamped with buyers. All attempts by the West Berlin authorities to put a stop to the illegal trading merely served as yet another challenge to the ingenuity for which the Poles had in the meantime become notorious. When rumours started circulating of stricter controls being implemented at the border crossings between East and West Berlin, the Poles soon thought of an alternative route where they would not be subject to customs examinations: the underground from east to west.

It is not only Berlin, however, that is affected: equal numbers of Polish smugglers and black-market dealers pour into Vienna, which is having similar difficulties coping with them. In the meantime complaints about the Poles have been coming from everywhere imaginable, even from regions as remote and unlikely as Nepal.

The profits from these trips are usually reinvested on the spot in high-tech equipment or other categories of article hard to come by in Poland, which will then be sold at a profit back home. The money made, however, is always in excess of the costs of the trip, and as long as there are no signs of any kind of fundamental change in Poland's economic situation, these trading expeditions are likely to continue.

Not all Poles, of course, have resorted to the "trade tourism" described above. Many

Preceding pages: Czech President Vaclav Havel visits Poland in 1990; German Chancellor Helmut Kohl adds his weight to reconciliation talks. Left, many Poles are optimistic about the future.

have sought and found opportunities of earning money without it being necessary for them to go abroad, and are simply making capital out of the current situation and the fact that, with the country in a state of transition to a market economy, there is an absence of legal regulations in many areas of economic life. The commission business is flourishing, and dubious "agencies" spring up overnight, but none of these activities contributes to the prosperity of the country.

Most of such behaviour is attributed to the fact that Poles are very independent in their thinking, and see laws and regulations more as "suggestions" as to how something might be done than as rules which stipulate how

something must be done. The question of where this independent Polish thinking came from and whether or not it can be explained by the tragic past of the Polish nation, has never been satisfactorily resolved.

Centuries of foreign rule, when it was a patriotic duty to show resistance to the state, have left their mark and resulted in the sharp distinction between nation and state that is typical of Poland today. Even in postwar Poland under the communists the Poles identified with the concept of nation much more strongly than they did with the state, i.e. with the people's government or the peoples' party in power, which was in any case seen

primarily as a puppet of Moscow. The Poles always conspicuously say "us" when referring to themselves, the Polish people, but "them" when talking about the state and its institutions to which they are subject. It will be interesting to see if and how their attitudes change, now that Poland has become a democratic republic again.

There is no doubt that this individualism and their unshakable faith in the tenacity of the Polish spirit also helped the Poles to survive the worst periods under the communists. In particularly critical phases, such for example as that which followed the introduction of martial law in December 1981, the Poles demonstrated for all the world to see that they do not give in that easily.

Although under martial law the independent trade union Solidarity had been dissolved and the mere mention of it was punished with a spell in prison, the Poles continued to show where their sympathies lay by taking small resistance elements out of their transistor radios and pinning them on to the lapels of their jackets, in place of their banned Solidarity badges. Alongside these they frequently sported buttons which said: "Down with the military junta" – and underneath this in tiny letters: "...in El Salvador". To an outsider such demonstrations of resistance may seem childish, but they did much to keep the Polish spirit alive and make it clear whose side the people were really on.

This was not the only form of protest that became popular when the country was under martial law. Every evening at half-past seven, the time when the most important news programme of the day was broadcast on television, people ostentatiously poured out of their homes and whole families could be seen on the street talking to friends and neighbours. Many also reinforced their demonstration of contempt for state propaganda by standing their television sets in the window when they left home.

To fight or to submit: Throughout their history the Poles were continually being confronted with the dilemma of whether to succumb to the state or fight and being forced to decide for one or other alternative. They always chose to fight. This inborn heroism in the Polish character has repeatedly driven generations of Poles to rebel even in the most hopeless situations, even when they knew for certain that they were going to be defeated and that the severest of punishments awaited them. Polish history is characterised by one uprising after another, and at first glance every single one of these uprisings seems only to have resulted in greater misfortune and more deaths. Where else other than in Poland could an uprising have occurred like that which took place in Warsaw in 1944? With the Red Army already poised on the opposite bank of the Vistula awaiting its chance to "liberate" the city, the Poles took up arms in a last desperate attempt to liberate themselves. For 63 days large parts of the city were free and in Polish hands – but at what a price. To an outsider this bloody episode may seem senseless, a useless waste

the Polish people, and as long as there is hope there will be Poles who are prepared to sacrifice everything to fight for freedom, Polishness and a better future. It was hope that gave this people the strength to triumph over history so that today, against all odds, Polish is still spoken in the heart of Europe.

In the meantime the trials and tribulations of everyday life still have to be coped with and the people continue to think up all kinds of clever ways of surviving on a day-to-day basis. At present emigration is a favoured solution, and the queues at the German and other western consulates indicate that the Poles have swiftly calculated the advantages that are possibly to be obtained from future

of human lives, but it is typical of the Poles' uncompromising will to survive as a free nation, whatever the cost may be.

Even after the war Poland was the only country in the Eastern bloc where there was resistance to communist rule in the form of repeated strikes, unrest and demonstrations, which often resulted in shootings and deaths; resistance that was maintained with a persistence and determination that was one day inevitably going to bring about a change. Hope has always been a life-giving force for

Left, who will buy? **Above**, the ubiquitous "Polish Market" – a bracelet is scrutinised in Cracow.

developments in Germany as a result of reunification.

This would seem to contradict what we have said about the Poles' love of their home country, but it is only an apparent contradiction. In the first place, every Pole who emigrates takes his Polishness intact with him to the foreign country of his choice – their disastrous history has made the Poles true experts in the art of living as emigrants. And in the second place, those applying for visas in the present wave of emigration are almost certainly doing so with the unspoken thought that they will return as soon as life in Poland is really worth living again.

The airline stewardess announces: "We have just flown over the Polish border," and all heads turn and look out of the window. Far below the landscape is gradually turning into a colourful mosaic and the first impression is one of a country totally different in appearance from its Western neighbours.

The fantastic brightly-coloured carpet of small fields and meadows is what the new visitor to Poland notices first. If a weaver had taken all the colours available and put them together at random to make a rug the effect would not be very different: there is the yellow of rape, the ochre-coloured fields of wheat and rye and green squares of bushy-topped potatoes. Narrow strips of land are separated from one another, and hardly any of the farmers have more than one diminutive field to till. A further surprise is the number of trees lining the roads. Such avenues are all too rare elsewhere in Europe, where "efficient agriculture" has had them felled; here they have been preserved, providing a bright green border along the way.

The reasons for this system of land ownership do not lie very far back in history. When the communists came to power in 1945 the large estate farms that existed were divided up and parcelled out to the landless rural population. The communists hoped that by introducing such radical land reform they would quell misgivings among the rural poor and win their support against the capitalists and large landowners.

This was unique in the Eastern bloc. In the same period the governments in Czechoslovakia and Hungary took all the land away from its private owners and formed giant collective farms. This special Polish situation meant that, contrary to the intentions of those who had engineered the policy, it was decades before communism really took a real hold in rural areas. Today over 75 percent of the land belongs to 2.7 million private farmers; only a quarter of land is state and cooperative property.

The picture changes as the plane crosses

Preceding pages: northern Poland's farmland and lakes are still remarkably unspoilt. **Left,** a Harvest Festival procession.

West Pomerania. Here, too, there are brightly-coloured strips, but here they are much longer and wider. In this region an enormous area is taken up by the agricultural cooperatives with their state monoculture.

The villages, too, are different here. In the rest of Poland they are apparently scattered at random, some just as they have developed over the centuries, the embodiment of harmony between man and nature with the church right at their centre. The villages that have been built since the introduction of the centrally planned economy, however, are not the same at all.

They are laid out geometrically, and consist of large blocks of houses surrounded by

munist government, which was finally replaced by Solidarity. Full of colour and variety in the areas with a private economy, grey and monotonous in the areas fully under the control of the state.

Taking to the roads: There are still no motorways in Poland; the roads usually go through the villages. There is no sense of isolation on a drive through the country; there is always a possibility of turning off, stopping and getting out, and soon being in the midst of village life. It is as well not to drive too fast, in order not to miss a host of interesting details. The road seems too narrow for modern needs and is lined by huge old trees, limes, maples and poplars, occa-

small allotments. This is where the agricultural cooperative workers live – under similar, although slightly worse conditions than in the towns. The cooperatives are organised along the same lines as industrial production. The towns are surrounded by another type of village: badly-planned settlements that have been built for the so-called "working peasants". These people are no longer peasants, but neither are they workers. They work in the factories in the towns in the daytime and on their own little piece of land in the evenings, keeping a pig or a cow for their own needs.

This then is Poland after 40 years of com-

sionally interspersed with apple and cherry trees. Much of the traffic consists of carts, pulled by one or two horses and rolling along at an unhurried pace. They are almost certainly returning from the market in the nearest small town where the driver has sold a pig he has fattened himself. He is master of his own affairs in a centuries-old tradition that communism was unable to change. In the evenings caution is advised: such carts are not always lit.

Every village has its wooden crosses, which are always decorated with flowers and lovingly looked after. As mentioned, the centre of the village is dominated by the church, where on Sundays the whole village gathers for mass.

The architecture of the old houses will tell the visitor what region he is in. In Pomerania they are wide but low, seeming to crouch under the wind. In Masuria they are smaller, and sometimes thatched. In the mountains they are built of wood with stone foundations and a pointed roof. Old cottages in a dilapidated state are replaced by new, square ones with flat roofs, built of "Ytong" blocks. The reason for the preponderance of this ugly style is a regulation, in force for many years, which only permitted this type of construction. Some anonymous official in Warsaw evidently thought it would be cheaper. Other

gering across the village street on his way home after a few drinks at a neighbour's or the village festival.

With a good map to hand, the asphalt road can be left for a dirt track with no problem. It is down such tracks, lined by old trees, that one comes across some of the most interesting relics of Polish history, such as an old farm, a silent witness of the revolution. Most of these farms were destroyed after 1945; their owners, members of families who had lived in them for centuries, summarily evicted. Destroyed, plundered, demolished – they are frightening ruins. Some, however, were saved and have been faithfully restored by their new owners: often well-known

types of building are now allowed, and in 10 years' time the country will probably look completely different.

The villages are lively and colourful. The houses are surrounded by a mass of trees and shrubs, and children play in the road. It is necessary to keep a sharp eye out for all the vehicles that are constantly joining or leaving the road: motorbikes, bicycles, tractors, agricultural vehicles. On Saturdays and Sundays particular care is advised on the roads. There will be many a local inhabitant staggering

Left, the ploughman at work. Above, a well-earned rest.

writers, artists, musicians and composers.

On foot: Visitors are well advised to take their time and leave the car or bus to take a little walk or even a long hike. Breathing in the smells of real village life, peeping into the cowshed or the paddock, you will be welcomed by the farmer and meet both rich and poor. The priest is the best person to begin with, since the Polish village exists "in the shadow of the church". Traditionally three people mattered in village life: the estate owner, the taverner and the priest. War and the communists drove out the first two but the priest steadfastly remained. He is still the highest moral authority and even the resident communists had to reckon with him.

Polish village life successfully survived the social revolution. The Catholic traditions and strong family ties remained intact and the church was present at every important occasion in life: village existence revolved around christenings, weddings and funerals. Even party secretaries, who otherwise claimed to be atheists, had their children christened – secretly and in the next village.

To dismiss the Catholicism of the Polish village as antiquated and old-fashioned is to make a grave mistake. For 40 years the church was a rock in the sea of communist domination. The government distributed tractors, seeds and fertilisers and decided

The mixture of private and state ownership became a breeding ground for corruption and theft; local cliques and peasant mafias flourished. Amidst the grey monotony of the planned economy a few model farms stood out. People who were particularly loyal to the government were able to obtain certain advantages, and in this way large private farms developed, financed by credit and boasting new, modern machinery, equipment and furniture.

The church, the shop, the pub, the local administrative office and the buying centre for cereal and livestock – these are the focal points of village life. This is where information is swapped and money and goods change

what taxes were to be paid. But the souls of the people were and still are ruled by the local priest.

The villages were not helped by the conviction that communist rule was only a temporary episode. The farms developed sluggishly if at all, and they were run merely to feed the family. The future was uncertain, agricultural policy was constantly being changed. There was criticism of the situation: "As long as the land is in private hands, this is not proper communism".

But it was, after all, the communists who had divided up the land themselves. The farmers felt their land did not belong to them.

hands. Time in the village is measured either by the natural rhythm of work in the fields or the opening times of the offices and suppliers. The local bureaucracy battled against the natural order for a long time; now all this is set to change with the restoration of self-administration in the villages. At last the rural population will be making their own decisions about themselves on their own soil.

What are the country people like? This depends on the region, but villagers are usually interested in foreigners, open and helpful and eager to talk to strangers – and sometimes not above playing tricks on them as well. Someone from the mountains in the south of Poland, asked whether it is far to a particular place will say, "not far, just round that little hill over there." And it will take over two hours to get round this hill. On the other hand, a Kaszub, asked the same thing, will say that it is a long way and difficult to get there on foot – and it will take 15 minutes!

It is not easy to find authentic elements of folk culture outside the museums. The most one can expect to see is an old cottage battered by the wind, the brightly-coloured woollen skirt worn by a countrywoman, or perhaps the traditional white costume of south Poland. A beautifully preserved traditional house will often turn out to be the

country dominated by agriculture into one dominated by industry.

For decades it was possible to convince country people that it was a mark of progress when their children went to live and work in the town. The government encouraged this thinking – rural origins were an advantage when applying for university or college places or grants – and soon there was a shortage of labour in agriculture. This aggravated the social situation since those who remained on the land had to work harder and harder, but were not valued by society. The farmers felt they were being exploited by the government, since they could only get fair prices on the very limited free market.

second home of a doctor or engineer from a nearby town.

Many old traditions have been preserved, but in order to become acquainted with them it is necessary to live in the community and be included in the everday life of a family.

The village community was thoroughly put to the test after World War II when the whole country was transformed by the processes of resettlement and socialist industrialisation. The communists counted it a success that within 10 years they had turned a

This was how the seeds of Solidarność Wiejska, "Farmers' Solidarity", were sown. Wałęsa was well aware that it was not only the industrial workers whose support he had to win if he was to be successful. And it was in fact primarily the farmers' sons who began the strikes in August 1980 in the Gdańsk shipyards and thus paved the way for the fall of the government. Wałęsa himself was born in a small village in Popówo near Toruń. His family still lives in the country and works on the land. The farmer's son became an electrician at the shipyard because he needed a job.

Solidarność Wiejska has not been as effective as Solidarity in the towns, and it cer-

Left and above, mechanisation of agriculture is slowly developing.

tainly does not have a leader of the same charisma as Wałęsa. Before the war, however, there was such a person – Wincenty Witos. This country aristocrat became the leader of a strong farmers' party and later prime minister.

Solidarność Wiejska was an opponent the communists could deal with more easily. It is simpler to corrupt and intimidate a farmer than a worker. If a worker is imprisoned for illegal agitation it means upset for his family; if a farmer is imprisoned for the same thing it means the ruin of the farm.

Terrible things began happening in the country after 1980. One of Solidarność Wiejska's leaders was found drowned in a ditch, and "unknown persons" attacked a priest who supported Solidarity. Popieluszko, the priest who was tortured and murdered by members of the secret service, was also a farmer's son. A Solidarity sympathiser was not allowed to have a tractor, and could buy neither fertiliser nor coal.

But it was precisely for these reasons that Solidarity developed as a close-knit neighbourhood organisation which was resistant enough to withstand the repression. It is from this that Solidarność Wiejska drew its strength. The result of the local elections in May 1990 has increased its strength even further, but it still has to play its political trump cards.

The Polish farmhouse: The houses are rarely attractive to look at and their interiors are also frequently merely a reflection of the styles popular in the towns. Progress in the country came with the arrival of the television set. Farmers' sons and daughters aspire to the youth culture of the towns: clothing, music and attitudes that are radically different from those of the older generation. Sadly, children are often ashamed of the rustic behaviour of their parents and grandparents.

A farmhouse, whether traditional or modern, is the home of several generations, a home founded on family ties and hospitality. Christenings, weddings and funerals provide an opportunity for family get-togethers. Several dozen members of the family may assemble on these occasions and drink together for two or three days, which unfortunately often involves the imbibing of excessive quantities of hard vodka.

Vodka flows like a stream through the average Polish village. The appeals of the priest, the teacher and other figures in authority fall on deaf ears. A celebration without vodka would be interpreted as inhospitality, or even a sign of poverty on the part of the host. This is the disastrous legacy of the past, when hopelessness was drowned in alcohol, and it is in marked contrast with the traditions and religion of the people.

There are similar contradictions concerning attitudes to sex, where puritanism and intolerance on the part of parents and the priest conflict with daily sex on the TV, in the cinema and on video. With a few drinks inside them the young men soon forget their manners and gentlemanly courtesy is abandoned for crude behaviour.

There is no pity for the girl who gets pregnant before marriage and she is invariably turned out of her home. If the man responsible is identified, he will be set upon by her brothers and cousins: vendetta Polish style. Country people in Poland have a highly-developed sense of honour. Business agreements in the market place are often sealed with a handshake. The code of honour includes completing military service and appearing at celebrations in uniform, and the most important pictures on the living-room wall are the photo of the man of the house in uniform and the couple's wedding photo. This sense of honour is handed down from generation to generation; only in recent years have breaches begun to appear.

On public holidays it is evident that the traditional customs – a mixture of Catholic and pre-Christian rituals – are still very much alive. At Easter, brightly-painted eggs are knocked against each other in the manner of the English game of conkers. The person whose egg proves most resistant wins the next Easter egg. An equally old custom is the drowning of the "Marzanna" on the first day of spring. The "Marzanna" is the symbol of winter, and is an ugly, scarecrow figure. Christmas has its own set of tratitions. Hay is placed under the white tablecloth when families eat their Christmas meal; afterwards

Rural Poland in the towns: Social changes brought the rural population into the towns, and many farm children became doctors, engineers, professors, politicians and artists. One of them is a winner of the Nobel prize for peace and state president.

Once in the towns, children from the country often lose any sense of identification with their village and home district, especially after having made a considerable effort to shed the rural elements of their language, their rural traditions and everyday culture. However, not all the ties are broken. It is fashionable to have something rustic at home, whether in the form of furniture, ornaments or pictures. A second home in a village is

they predict their own health and fortune on the basis of the length and quality of the stalks. On Christmas Eve many country people still share their food and homes with the animals, because on this night all creatures should share each other's fate; the animals are said to understand what the people say.

Whoever has been a guest in a Polish farmhouse on a public holiday will remember the occasion for years; it will also take him a few days at least to recover from the orgy of eating and drinking.

Left, the face of innocence. **Above**, villagers indulge.

becoming increasingly popular; this is called a *dacza* in imitation of the Russian custom. Owners of *daczas* go there at weekends for a bit of country life. Town-dwellers are becoming increasingly aware that although life in the village might have been harder, it was at least quieter and more healthy. The carefully tended allotments are a substitute for country roots.

The airline stewardess announces that we are leaving Poland and a completely different landscape with different houses inhabited by different people unfolds below. Rural Poland bids goodbye with a hearty "*Szczesc Boze*" – "God bless you".

CATHOLICISM

If on a Sunday you are anywhere near where there is a church – and there is no shortage of churches in Poland's towns and villages – it is as well not to be in a hurry. The roads and squares are full of families dressed in their Sunday best making their way to mass. And on special religious holidays the procession of brightly-coloured flags extends for miles as the miraculous picture of Mary the Mother of God is carried for several hours from house to house. In the living room of every family a picture of the Virgin Mary or a portrait of Pope John Paul II occupies pride of place. There is hardly a meeting of the militant Solidarity that is not accompanied by the singing of a hymn, if indeed it is not actually held in a church in the first place. For years the Sunday mass in the church of St Brigitte in Gdańsk has deeply impressed visitors, not as a celebration of the Eucharist but as a political manifestation.

Religious origins: Christianity was introduced in Poland in the 10th century. It was primarily for political reasons that the first kings had themselves baptised and took the country from the pope as a fief. They did not consult their subjects and followers, members of the Slavic tribes and adherents of a very different religion based on ancestor and nature worship, and resistance to Christianity continued for two centuries. The first Christian missionaries did not have it easy and many, like Bishop Wojciech of Prague (who died in 997) met a martyr's death.

In spite of this, at around the turn of the first millennium the archdiocese of Gniezno proceeded to expand its sphere of influence. Gradually the rulers imposed their will. Polygamy and working on religious holidays were prohibited, times of fasting and contributions to the church were made compulsory. The Cistercians established the new religion in the towns. By the middle of the 12th century all newborn babies were being christened and from this time on the synthesis of the old faith with the new proceeded without conflict. The church made concessions to the traditional cult by allowing me-

<u>Left</u>, **Mary the Mother of God and protectress of Poland through the centuries.**

morials to be built to ancestors, tolerating ancient peasant customs and introducing new festivals involving intercessions for good weather and rich harvests.

With the breakdown of central secular power in the 13th century, the church was able to escape secular domination. From then on it followed the doctrine of St Thomas of Aquinas, according to which it was the duty of the church to admonish tyrants and protect the rights of the faithful. The Cracow metropolitan Stanisław was the first church leader to publicly oppose a prince. This resulted in the fall of the ruler, which strengthened the authority of the clergy as defenders of justice, and the Polish church has taken

Calvinists. Frantic activity by the Jesuits halted these movements. In later years, with misfortunes falling upon the country from Protestant Germany and Orthodox Russia, the maxim "to be a Pole is to be a Catholic", overruled all else.

Bond between church and people: At the beginning of the Reformation the Catholics lived in the western half of the enormous Polish-Lithuanian state and the adherents of the Orthodox church in the eastern half. In order to establish a counterweight to an increasingly powerful Moscow and to the Orthodox church, the national Roman Catholic church, based on the Greek Catholic tradition, was founded in 1596 after the Union of

this role seriously ever since.

Although Poland is, and always was, a Roman Catholic country, religious toleration has always gone hand in hand with national belief. There was never any religious persecution in Poland. Indeed Protestant Scots, fleeing the Counter-Reformation in Scotland, were given sanctuary in Poland. Scottish sounding names crop up in Polish telephone directories to this day.

The Reformation nearly got a hold in Poland (as it did in neighbouring Bohemia and Morovia). Calvinism and Lutheranism had their followers, and a radical group, the Arians or Polish Brothers, separated from the

Brześć. In the 17th century the church turned to the worship of saints – at the same time as living standards were falling. The Mother of God, the mother and queen of Poland, was the chief object of veneration. While the state fell apart, religion and superstition flourished: there were over 400 local cults based on miraculous manifestations and pictures that were supposed to deliver people from their need. While the nobility of Western Europe were inspired by philosophy and art, relics and miracles were the subject of conversation amongst their Polish counterparts. It was at this time that the idea of "Catholicism under siege" became part of the church's ideology, the idea of the one true faith in an heretical world.

Although the high-ranking clergy – who were after all principally aristocrats from the ruling Polish families then fighting for power and influence – were not entirely blameless when Poland was split up, and quite frequently made deals with the occupying powers, the bond between the church and the people was never destroyed. Aided by the uprising against Russia and the Vatican's defence of Polish independence, the church was soon able to win back the complete trust of the nation. Numerous orders also settled in Poland and improved the image of the church through their ministering work. It

The church went along with this, at first tentatively, and then more consciously and actively, and did not betray the trust of the Polish people even in the darkest days of recent history. Throughout the occupation by Nazi Germany and the terrors of the Stalinist regime, as well as the persistent endeavours of the communist leaders to change Poland, the church held firm. We will only mention two of the countless heroes who confronted these troubled times: the Franciscan friar Maximilian/Raimund Kolbe, who in 1941 went voluntarily to the gas chamber to save the life of a man who was father of a family although he did not even know him; and Jerzy Popieluszko, a young

was thus that Poland – beginning in the western part of the country that was under Prussian occupation – came to be equated with Catholicism. It was no more accurate a representation of the situation than it is today, but it developed a momentum of its own and became something for the people to hold on to: the idea that the cultural identity of Poland, including its freedom and religious tolerance, was guaranteed so long as the Catholic national church continued to exist – even if state sovereignty was a long way off.

Left, finding solace in the Church. **Above**, many Polish people put their hopes in the Pope.

Warsaw priest who was abducted by the secret police and murdered as a consequence of his defence of his community and the political goals of Solidarity.

Spokesman of the nation: When in 1976 the Polish conference of bishops published a pastoral in which the Catholic church was portrayed as the legitimate representative of the people and the nation, it received the people's unanimous approval. The election of Cardinal Karol Wojtyła as Pope in 1978 strengthened this claim still further. In 1979, on his first journey home, the Pope encouraged millions of his countrymen with the words: "Do not be afraid!"

The Second Republic of Poland (1918–39) was a multinational state: out of 35 million inhabitants only 24 million were of Polish origin. After the Poles came the Ukrainians, of whom there were an estimated 5–7 million. They were followed by the Jews, who numbered 3.3 million, the Belorussians, of whom there were 1.5 million, and the Lithuanians and Germans, totalling some 500,000. With such a mixed ethnic structure, conflicts were only to be expected. Although a multicultural society could have been constructed by means of decentralised structures and incorporation of the rights of the minorities into the constitution, the government never took advantage of this opportunity, and the internal stability of the state was constantly under threat from Greater Poland nationalism on the one hand and separatist resistance on the other. This was possibly also one of the reasons for the rapid decline of Poland in 1939.

The new Poland within the borders that had been established at the conferences of Yalta and Potsdam was to be an ethnically homogeneous state free from conflict between different nationalities. It soon became apparent, however, that the alteration of the borders and the mass resettlements – under the pompous and misleading name of "repatriation" – did not heal the old wounds but, on the contrary, inflicted newer, more painful ones. Added to this was an atmosphere of hostility between the individual nationalities who were all reproaching each other for their behaviour during the war: the Ukrainians were accused of having collaborated with the Gestapo, the Belorussians of having sympathised with Stalin's secret service and the Poles of having blackmailed the Jews and denounced them to the Germans. There was no mention of the fact that it was often only individuals who had been guilty of such behaviour, and the prejudices were merely reinforced with the encouragement of the nationalists of every group.

The shifting of the border between Poland and Russia to the west, and the annexation by

Left, the German-Silesian minority demonstrates for autonomous rights.

the USSR of regions that were formerly east Poland meant that most of the Lithuanians, Belorussians and Ukrainians now also lived outside the boundaries of the Polish state. Those who remained in Poland – in accordance with the agreement – were resettled.

The tragedy of expulsion: The resettlement process varied tremendously, but those who suffered the most tragic fate were the Ukrainians. Even after the border was shifted in 1945, there were still 700,000 Ukrainians living in Poland. Some of them moved voluntarily to the Ukrainian Socialist Soviet Republic, but many refused to leave their homeland. In southeast Poland a war broke out between the Polish army and the UPA (Ukrainian Army of the Uprising) and finally, in 1947, the Polish authorities decided to distribute the remaining 200,000 Ukrainians over the whole country.

What this meant in practice, however, was resettlement in that part of the country that had formerly been eastern Germany, since it was the only area where there were still unoccupied farms, farms that had been abandoned by the Germans. We therefore have the paradoxical situation whereby the voivodships of Wrocław/Breslau, Szczecin/Stettin, Koszalin/Köslin and Olsztyn/Allenstein are now the focus of the Ukrainian population in Poland.

However, there are still no large or concentrated groups of Ukrainians in any of these places, since the authorities saw to it that no more than two or three Ukrainian families ever settled in any one village, and no more than 10 percent of the population was Ukrainian in any one district. Some exiles took advantage of the political thaw of the 1950s to return to their homeland, the Bieszczady mountains in southeastern Poland, but most of them were refused permission to go back there. The Polish government's fear of having a well-organised group highly conscious of its own nationality concentrated in this part of Poland was and is still very much alive.

Ukrainians: Today there are around 300,000 Ukrainians in Poland. They have only one primary school (in Biały Bór, voivodship Koszalin) where the children are taught in Ukrainian, and two high schools (in Legnica and Gorów Ilawecki), where, although the children are taught in Polish, Ukrainian is also on the timetable. The Department of

Ukrainian at Warsaw University takes only a few students each year. The only museum of Ukrainian culture, in a wooden hut in the small village of Zyndranowa near Dukla (voivodeship Krosno), was founded by a private individual, Teodor Gocz, in spite of official prohibition.

The Ukrainian churches around Przemysl and Krosno were either handed over to the Catholic church, and in the process stripped of all signs of their past, or they were allowed to fall into disrepair. On the official "Map of Polish Confessions", the Ukrainian Catholic church does not appear at all. There is a Ukrainian language newspaper, *Nasze Slowo*, but this is only published at irregular inter-

vals. One established event is the Festival of Ukrainian Culture which takes place every other year in Sopot and brings together Ukrainian choirs, music ensembles and dance groups. The most famous of these are *"Zurawie"*, composed of Ukrainians from all over Poland, *"Polonina"* from Legnica and *"Lemkowyna"* from Bielanka near Gorlice. In Bieszczady hikes and integration meetings lasting several days are organised to keep Ukrainian national consciousness alive. To facilitate such activities, the Society of Ukrainians in Poland has acquired property in Zdynia, near Gorlice, on which it plans to build an amphitheatre and a hostel –

there is no doubt that better times are ahead.

Lithuanians and Belorussians: Fate was kinder to the Lithuanians and the Belorussians. The several thousand Lithuanians who lived around Suwalki on the Lithuanian border were left more or less alone after the war. In Punsk there are a primary school and a high school, several folk ensembles and an ethnographical museum, and the Lithuanian Social and Cultural Society has its headquarters in Sejny.

Of the over 200,000 Belorussians who were still in Poland after the war, 36,000 had resettlement forced on them. Those who remained in the country lived in concentrated groups in their home villages and

ing to counteract this development. It is assisted in this by the Orthodox Church, and the Holy Mount of Grabarka near Siemiatycze has once again become very important as a place of worship for Belorussians and other Orthodox believers. At the festival of Corpus Christi the Belorussians make a pilgrimage to the summit of the mountain with penitential crosses on their backs. These are later set in the ground next to the church; there are already tens of thousands of crosses there. In June 1990 the church was plundered and set on fire but the perpetrators were never identified.

Germans: The situation on the west border of Poland has been quite different from that

towns in the area of Bialystok, Bielsk Podlaski and Hajnówka. In spite of this the Belorussians are one of the best integrated minorities. Their relatively good position, the fact that they participate in local government but also the decreasing number of Belorussian schools have resulted in a weakening of their national consciousness.

The Belorussian Democratic Union, which was founded in 1990 and is the first party representing an ethnic minority, is attempt-

Left, a friendly smile from the Tatra. **Above**, minorities in Podhale are well practised in preserving their cultural identity.

in the east. At the Potsdam Conference it was decided that the Germans should be resettled. Some had already fled from the advancing Red Army, but there were still around 3 million who were subsequently resettled; by the early 1980s there were only a few thousand Germans left in Poland. The problem of the German minority can only be understood in connection with the fate of the Silesians, a fate which illustrates only too well the grave errors of the Polish government's policy with respect to minorities. For over 600 years the Silesians lived outside Poland and absorbed much of the German culture, while at the same time retaining the

Polish language and Polish customs. Nevertheless, after the war even the Silesians, the majority of whom saw themselves as Poles, were treated as Germans. They were forced to submit to the "repolonisation" process, and suffered discrimination and harassment. The Polish state's incorporation of Silesia was characterized by Stalinistic despotism. After 600 years of resistance to Germanisation it took only 45 years of communism for a quarter of a million Silesians to enter themselves as German on the German minority list. Only after the change of government and the visit of Federal Chancellor Kohl in 1989 did the situation change.

On the St Annaberg, a mountain which is

senate elections, who only lost to the Solidarity candidate by a margin.

Jews: The fate of the Polish Jews in the postwar period was as complicated as that of the Germans. Only a few thousand had survived the Holocaust in Poland, but in the first half of 1946 alone at least 137,000 who had fled or been deported to the Soviet Union returned to their home country. In the next few years, however, around 120,000 left again and emigrated to Palestine. It is not known how many also emigrated to other countries because they found themselves unable to live in a country that had become the graveyard of their people. The involuntary exodus of the Jews is a reflection of the

considered holy by both Poles and Germans, Mass is now also read in German; it is now perfectly legal to attend German classes and new music ensembles and choirs have been founded, while the Social and Cultural Association of the German minority has established its headquarters in Gogolin. In Kemielnica/Himmelwitz the first sign in German has appeared in a bar, and the letterbox also bears a German label. The German minority is concentrated around Strzelce Opolskie/Gross-Strehlitz, Glogówek/Oberglogau, Gogolin and Krapkowice/Krappitz. Krapkowice is the home of Henryk Król, the German minority's candidate in the

tragic postwar history of Poland: it reached record levels during the periods of political crisis, which were always accompanied by anti-Semitism: 1950, 1956–57, 1968–69. In spite of this, however, the Jews of postwar Poland were always able to preserve and develop their cultural identity and religious independence. They have their own organisations, schools, magazines, folk ensembles, a theatre and a Jewish Historical Institute with a library and a museum in Warsaw.

There are currently around 5,000 Jews living in Poland. The three Jewish high schools had to be closed for lack of pupils, and it even became necessary to fly in a

Rabbi from the USA to serve the Jewish community. In the Jewish theatre it is becoming increasingly rare to find members of the audience who can still follow the text in Yiddish and do not have to resort to using headphones.

The Polish government's policy with respect to minorities in the postwar period was self-deceptive right from the beginning. Failing to grasp the true facts of the situation, the government was as it were taken in by its own propaganda that glorified a "homogeneous Poland". The annual statistics contained no information about minorities, since the powers-that-be proceeded according to the assumption that if something is not mentioned it does not exist. The minorities, whose insecurity was compounded by the ambivalent attitude of the Catholic church, could only take this as a declaration of war and thus refused to cooperate with a state which was highly suspicious of independent cultural activities of any kind.

The constitution of 1952 – on paper perfectly democratic – guaranteed the minorities equal rights in every respect. In practice, however, the aim of this totalitarian state was "polonisation" and the uprooting of the other nationalities. The state executive bodies interpreted the constitution to suit themselves. In the face of such despotism every attempt on the part of a minority group to preserve and develop its culture naturally came up against bureaucratic obstacles.

The mutual mistrust that had been thus reinforced for decades was one of the reasons why, after the change in 1989, only the German minority showed any interest in putting forward candidates for election and the minorities in general did not take the opportunity of securing representation in local government. There are already signs that this was a mistake, since, as has often happened in crisis situations in the past, strong nationalistic tendencies are once again making their appearance in Poland. This time, however, they are not the result of encouragement from above, but are being generated in the middle classes which – in Poland as in other countries – have an almost traditional susceptibility to racism.

In his inaugural speech in September 1989 the new prime minister Tadeusz Mazowiecki said, "Poland is our homeland, but it does not belong only to Poles. We share this country with people of other nationalities. It is our wish that they should feel at home here, keep their own languages alive and enrich our community with their culture."

Left, Silesian bandsmen play. **Above**, even today, colourful costumes are part of the Polish scenery.

THE JEWS

How long have there been Jews in Poland? The earliest reliable source of information mentions the arrival of Jewish exiles from Prague towards the end of the 11th century. For centuries Jews converged on Poland from all over Europe, fleeing from political or economic persecution in their home countries. However, there were also many who came, not as a result of any external threats, but drawn by the opportunities in the most tolerant country of the continent. It was not without justification that Poland was called "a paradise for the aristocracy, heaven for the Jews and hell for the peasants".

The Jewish name for Poland was "Polin" (etymologically "po" = "here" and "in" = "peace"). This feeling of security was derived from the laws of the country and the policies of the Polish rulers: Jews were subject only to the king's own courts or those of his representatives; the murder of a Jew was punishable by death, and even failure to help a Jew who was attacked was punished with a fine. Towns which did not step in quickly enough to quell anti-Jewish riots also had to pay a fine, ritual murders could not be brought to court, the sale of anti-Jewish literature was forbidden, and so on.

What happened in history: The Jewish Council of Four Lands, founded in 1581, was a political institution unique in Europe. It was responsible for the countries of Great Poland, Little Poland, Lithuania and Russia, and mainly dealt with internal Jewish affairs, also liaising with the authorities.

During the time of the First Republic (1569–1795), there were hardly any anti-Jewish excesses by comparison with the rest of Europe. The few government directives that really were anti-Jewish were hardly ever put into practice. This is only partly explained by the weakness of the state executive organs, and the pragmatism of the Polish aristocracy: the real reason was rather that in Poland there was simply no general hatred of the Jews.

The aristocracy was not inclined to harass

Preceding pages: a young Jew pays his respects to the victims of the Ghetto. **Left**, the old grave-yard in Cracow is testimony to the enormous importance of the Jewish community up to 1939.

the Jewish communities for the simple reason that these two sections of society had close economic connections. Although these connections were advantageous to both sides, they nevertheless resulted in misfortune for the Jews on two occasions. In the violent uprising of Bohdan Chmielnicki in the Ukraine (1648–54), which was actually directed against the Polish rulers, the Jews were massacred in their thousands as suspected allies of the Poles. The tragedy was repeated during the popular uprising in the Ukraine and Podolia in 1768 – on this occasion thousands of Polish aristocrats and Jews suffered terrible deaths.

The Catholic church in Poland was am-

true to their faith, for centuries the Polish culture was enriched by specific Jewish characteristics. They made major contributions to scientific development and frequently occupied leading positions in medicine, mathematics and astronomy as well as in cultural areas such as architecture, painting and goldsmithery.

Jews were very industrious and usually worked as craftsmen, merchants, doctors and bankers, but seldom as farmers. They were often very wealthy. The basic unit of Jewish autonomy was the community, which was run by a governing body called the *kahal*. The *kahal* was responsible for the judicial system, administration, religion,

bivalent towards the Jews. While on the one hand the Jews were regarded as "the chosen people", on the other they were also "the murderers of Jesus". The church accordingly announced that they should not therefore be persecuted and killed, but that they should live together in a separate community.

The anti-Jewish resolutions passed by many church synods were often moderated in practice. The unique position of the Jews in Poland is illustrated by the fact that a Jew who had been converted to Catholicism could even be elevated to the nobility.

The Jewish contribution: Although or precisely because the Jews usually remained

education and welfare.

The Jewish way of life in Poland by no means remained unaffected by the religious and social trends of the times and came variously under the influence of the mystic *cabbala*, Sabbatarianism with its strict observance of the Sabbath, Frankism, a mystical cabbalistic sect which emerged in Podolia in 1755, the *haskalah* of the enlightenment and in particular Hasidism, a popular movement of both a religious and mystic nature based

Above, In 1939 the Jewish population of Poland was 3.5 million. In the 1990s only about 5,000 remain.

104

on the cabbala and Judaism, which also had its origins in Podolia in the 18th century. The founder of Hasidism, Baal Schev Tov, was born in Poland.

The Jews in particular were badly affected by the weakening of Poland as a consequence of wars and internal anarchy in the 17th century. Gradually their economic and political situation deteriorated. In 1764 the Polish parliament, the Sejm, dissolved the Council of Four Lands for economic reasons, but it did not touch the communities. Although the government was aware that the status of the Jews in Poland was in need of fundamental reform, no substantial changes were made before Poland finally lost its independence. Some 900,000 Polish Jews thus automatically became citizens of the three occupying countries.

In the 19th century Polish-Jewish relations underwent considerable change, and the occupying powers also abolished many of the regulations that had been designed to protect the Jews. Their motto was "divide and rule", and there is evidence to show that they deliberately provoked anti-Jewish campaigns and riots.

It is perhaps for this reason that the majority of the Jews supported the Poles in their struggle for independence. They fought with them in the Kosciuszko uprising (1794), the November uprising (1831) and the people's spring (1848–49). The first incidence of real cooperation between national Polish and Jewish independence fighters, however, occurred during the January uprising of 1863. On this occasion, it was for the first time a Pole of the Mosaic faith who formulated the ideals which inspired his countrymen to pursue their struggle.

Growing aggression: The defeat of the January uprising slowed down the progress of the Poles towards their national ideal, especially in the areas annexed by Russia. The idea of a reuinified joint state slowly faded. Other forms of integration, however, gradually developed to take its place. The liberal elite in particular began to concentrate their attentions on social questions and frequently on socialism itself. At the same time they also campaigned for the revival of Polish tradition and culture – in spite of all the attempts made by the occupying powers to assimilate the Poles into their own countries.

The decline of the aristocracy also plunged their traditional partners, the Jews, into massive economic difficulties. The increasing part played in occupied Poland by the bourgeoisie, the long-standing competitors of the Jews, who were now fast becoming the leading social power, dealt the final blow to the "status quo" of the independence era.

Poland naturally did not remain unaffected by the wave of nationalism that swept Europe at the turn of the 20th century. The Jewish community reacted by turning increasingly to Zionism.

The constantly worsening economic situation, the politics of the occupying powers and growing signs of anti-Semitism amongst the Polish population led many Jews to seek their safety in emigration, and large numbers went to North America.

Increasing alienation: During the Second Republic (1918–39), the National Democracy Party, which had strong right-wing leanings, became increasingly radical in their attitudes towards the Jewish population. The party had placed a high value on the "national cultural community" and from this perspective the independence of the Jewish culture could easily be interpreted as the alienation of the Jews from the Polish people.

Once again it became fashionable to make the Jews responsible for every social evil. They were accused of communism, association with the Freemasons, economic parasitism and of an inability to assimilate themselves into Polish society. The pressure to emigrate increased considerably. Occasionally the hostility did not stop at verbal attacks – there were pogroms, harassment at the universities and economic boycott.

The sections of society that supported Marshal Piłsudski (in power from 1926 on) did not share these attitudes. Many Jews had fought for the independence of Poland under the leadership of Piłsudski, and their loyalty to the state was much more important to the political realist Piłsudski than their forced assimilation.

After the death of the marshal (1935), however, the programme of his followers gradually began to bear closer resemblance to that of the nationalistic right. Although the state condemned the use of force of any kind, statements made by various politicians now more frequently indicated approval of an economic boycott of the Jews. The Catholic church criticised the use of force, and expressed its approval of certain features of Jewish life, but nevertheless held that Catholics should not associate with Jews.

The aims of the Zionists were emigration and formation of their own state. They had a good relationship with the government of Poland – the left wing of the Zionist movement under the leadership of Wlodzimierz Zabotynski was even supplied with weapons and money, and was also offered military training. The Orthodox Jews, represented by the party Agudas Israel, were also on perfectly normal terms with the state administration. The Jewish socialists on the other hand acknowledged only one homeland: Poland. Understandably, however, the right-wing rulers did not approve at all of their political programme.

During the period between the world wars the mood of the Jewish minority in Poland alternated between hope and resignation. There was frequent conflict, but the climate was conducive to socio-political change.

The leading contributions made by the Polish Jews to the country's culture and the major part that they played in shaping the ideology of national rebirth are undisputed. The wealth of literature produced by this community is a particularly good example of its cultural involvement. Many 19th-century authors and their successors, among them Icchak Lejb Perec, Mendele Mojcher Sforim, Schalom Alejchem, Schalom Asch, Icyk Manger and Izrael Jehoschua Zynger, achieved world fame; Polish poets of Jewish origin such as Julian Tuwim, Antoni Slonimski, Bolesław Lesmian and Bruno Schulz occupy a prominent place in the literary history of Poland.

The Polish Jews always retained their unmistakable cultural independence however. It was a separateness that made them vulnerable to racist and religious harassment, a problem nowhere more obvious than in the *stetl*, the Jewish quarter that existed in almost every Polish town. This Jewish world in miniature, with its characteristic architecture and its dense network of social and cultural relationships against the background of a deep-rooted religious tradition, was the starting point for the rich contribution the Jews made to the culture and science of Polish society.

Opinions differ greatly when it comes to evaluating the attitude of the Poles to the Jews during the occupation and the Holocaust. Jakub Karpinski remarks: "So much has already been said on this subject, that a quote, book or film can always be found that will cause great offence to either the Poles or the Jews".

If we just look at the problem in terms of statistics, there is no doubt that the attitude of the vast majority of Poles was either one of passivity or indifference towards the fate of the Jews. The reasons for this lay in fear of reprisal (any kind of assistance was punishable by death, and this also included the family of the individual concerned), the anti-Semitic resentment of the prewar period, and also in fresh evidence of disloyalty on the part of the Jews, since one section of this community had greeted the Red Army's invasion of Poland in September in 1939 with enthusiasm.

The solidarity of the persecuted: There were nevertheless many Poles who took the risk of helping Jews. Sometimes in this altered situation people even overcame their own pronounced anti-Semitic prejudice. It is, for example, known that Jews were hidden and saved from the Nazis by National Democrats. The Christian community was also very much involved in rescue operations, above all the clergy themselves; nunneries were particularly active and saved many Jewish children. An important part was played by the "Council for Jewish assistance" ZEGOTA, an organisation which the government in exile helped finance.

Of course there were also those on the other side, a small but notable number of individuals. It is known that there were sporadic cases of collaboration with the Germans, when, for example, the inhabitants of the ghettoes in Bilgoraj and Szczebrzeszyn were liquidated. There were many cases of denunciation, and some Poles enriched themselves unscrupulously through the appropriation of Jewish possessions.

One of the most evil practices was that followed by the blackmailers, who threatened their Jewish fellow-citizens with betrayal, but then delivered them up even if they paid up. These, however – it must be stressed again – were only isolated cases. Of the 3.5 million Polish Jews only approximately 250,000 survived the war, mostly because they were able to escape from the Nazi sphere of influence. Many of those who returned home after the war felt as if they had come back to live in a cemetery.

The new government was anything but charitable towards the survivors of the Holocaust and were in many cases active in preventing the Jews from reconstructing their communities. There were even isolated cases of pogroms (the most well-known of which took place in Kielce), but the true background and the people responsible have never come to light. As a result of this climate, many Jews therefore finally decided to emigrate, and left Poland for good.

Immediately after the war the communist leadership of Poland was still hoping that the new state of Israel that was just coming into

conflict between the different factions of the communist party resulted in a campaign against artists, scientists and students. Many of them were of Jewish origin, and the rulers found that the simplest thing to do was to make the Jews the scapegoat, since these were the people likely to offer the least resistance.

A policy was pursued of making the Jews once again responsible for the deficits accrued under socialism, that had reduced the economy to a state of vegetation. In order to stir up the population against them, attention was drawn to the inglorious part some of them had played during Stalin's reign of terror. This all took place against the back-

being at the time would be socialist-oriented or would at least sympathise with the countries within Moscow's sphere of influence. For this reason a military training camp offered training to volunteers who belonged to the Zionist Haganah movement. These friendly feelings soon evaporated when it became evident that Israel was developing along the lines of a bourgeois society.

If emigration in the 1940s and '50s was of a more voluntary nature, the waves of emigration in the wake of the events of March 1968 were a different matter entirely. The

Above, eating together cements family life.

ground of the Arab-Israeli war, when the whole of the Eastern bloc was vociferous in its condemnation of the Israelis. The repulsive campaign led at least 20,000 Poles of Jewish origin to turn their backs on the country they had been born in and considered their homeland and seek a new life in Israel or overseas.

Today the Jewish minority in Poland consists of a mere 5,000 people. They have their own cultural, religious and scientific institutions and produce their own publications. The reduction of 3.5 million to 5,000 represents a dramatic and irreplaceable loss to Polish society.

"MAŁA KOMEDIA"
(II scena Państwowego Teatru Komedia)

Krakowskie Przedmieście 21/23

Felicien Marceau

J A J K O

PRAPREMIERA STYCZEŃ 1958 R.

109

Every Pole has two weak spots: one is his religion, the other is the literature produced by his people. Religion and literature are the two main pillars on which the whole of the Polish heritage rests: throughout the turbulent history of the country they have been the symbol of the continuity of the Polish national identity and culture.

National heritage: The tragedy of the partitions and the loss of national independence determined the developments of Polish literature in the 19th century. Literature as-

literature. Its leading representatives were living and writing in exile – in Dresden and Leipzig, in Rome, London and Brussels, and above all in Paris. Their work expressed the Messianic idea of national mission, uniting the watchword of Poland's liberation from the tyranny of the Partitioning Powers to that of a fight for social justice and the liberty of all peoples.

Adam Mickiewicz, author of the national epic poem Pan Tadeusz, was also an outstanding playwright and political writer.

sumed the role of the nation's spiritual leader and upheld a feeling of patriotic community up to the moment of the recovery of Poland's independence after the First World War. It also faithfully followed the armed uprisings and all Polish efforts in the fight with despotism. The Polish National Anthem, the so-called Dabrowski's Mazurka was composed towards the end of the 18th century in Italy, where Polish Legions were fighting at the side of Napoleon.

Polish Romanticism, born in close contact with the philosophy, social ideas, and literature of Germany, France and England, made its own special contribution to European

Juliusz Stowacki, a lyric poet of great subtlety, created Polish Romantic drama, in the tradition of Shakespeare and Calderón. Zygmunt Krasinski, in his drama *Nie-Boska Komedia* (The Undivine Comedy) gave a penetrating vision of a great social revolution. Cyprian Kamil Norwid, poet and playwright, underestimated in his lifetime, is now gaining fame as the forerunner of modern Polish poetry.

Under such circumstances it is no wonder

Preceding pages: Polish posters are famous. Above, writers such as Barbara Wachowicz (here autographing her books) are respected people.

that the literature of Poland is full of elaborate allegories, allusions and symbolism and is always very closely connected with local political and historical events. In order to escape the attention of the oppressors, the messages which the authors wanted to convey and the true meaning of their works had to be in symbolic form, which of course does not make it easy to follow for readers of other nationalities today. Without a more detailed knowledge of the country's history and customs and the Polish character it is very hard to understand the literature of this nation, let alone appreciate it.

Nevertheless the main works of Polish literature have been published with overwhelming success in numerous foreign languages and have been received with understanding and enthusiasm.

Western European heritage: This success can be explained by a second characteristic of Polish literature that has not yet been mentioned, and that is its European heritage, the western traditions in which it had its roots. By contrast with the Russians, whose "openness" to Western influence was never the same after Peter the Great and always had something artificial about it, the Poles, a Slavic people living in a country positioned on the dividing line between east and west, had almost always kept their gaze fixed firmly on the West.

To discover the reason for this it is necessary to go right back to the beginnings of Eastern European culture: while Russian culture was influenced from the start by the doctrines and traditions of the Greek Orthodox Church and dominated by Byzantium, which had little in common with Western Europe, the origin of Polish culture was firmly rooted in the Latin tradition of the Roman Catholic church.

Poland as a consequence felt right from the start that it was part of Western Europe and took all its cues from there. Polish literature featured importantly in every epoch of European cultural development, the Renaissance and the Baroque age, the Enlightenment and Romanticism, realism and modernity, and Polish writers were influenced by their counterparts in France, Germany, Italy and England.

Polish literature belongs decisively to the main body of European literature; its forms, contents and themes thus pose no serious problems for the Western reader. Even if now and then he stumbles over a metaphor that is particularly full of allusions, by and large he will feel perfectly at home with the general form and subject matter of the works he takes up.

What follows is little more than a brief survey of the most important names and trends in Polish literature. The limited space available here does not permit more than a short description of a very generalised nature in each case.

Medieval roots: The Christianisation of Poland took place in the 10th century. From then on Poland came under the influence of the universal Latin culture of the Catholic Church and entered the arena of European history, although it was another two centuries before Polish literature was also playing a part on the European stage.

One of the first outstanding writers in Polish literary history, in the second half of the 16th century, was a poet by the name of Jan Kochanowski, who was fully the equal of the Western European poets of his day. His masterpiece *Treny* (1580) is a collection of poems reflecting on the grief he experiences at the death of his young daughter and his struggle to regain inner harmony. The powerful language of these poems set high standards which were to influence all subsequent Polish poetry.

The following century was characterised by constant military conflict with Russia, Sweden and Turkey, and by internal unrest and disputes over constitutional reforms. Polish baroque literature is correspondingly dominated by the epic. One particularly interesting example is the collection of letters written by the Polish king Jan III Sobieski to his wife. In this remarkable series of writings, major battles, court intrigues and the cabals of high diplomacy are described and accounted for on an almost daily basis.

Romanticism and foreign rule: The Enlightenment, which began in Poland in about 1750, followed more or less the same pattern as the European Enlightenment, with strong cultural influences from France and England. Romanticism on the other hand, which reached Poland relatively late, was a much more independent movement, and, through the achievements of a star trio of unusually gifted poets, Adam Mickiewicz, Juliusz Slowacki and Zygmunt Krasicki, was transformed into one of the greatest epochs of Polish poetry.

Polish Romanticism coincided with the loss of national independence. Given the bad situation that the country was in, the Polish Romantic poets saw it as their duty to keep the spirit of Polish independence alive; their strengths and visionary powers were founded on their attempts to keep the torch of Polishness burning even under iniquitous foreign rule.

Adam Mickiewicz is without a doubt the best-known of all the Polish poets, with a reputation that has spread far beyond his own country. One of his works, *Dziady* (1832), is a Messianic vision of the past history and the future of Poland, in which he portrays his native country, suppressed by foreign powers, as the Christ amongst the peoples, destined to rise in glory. It is certainly no coincidence that the student unrest in the spring of 1968 erupted immediately after a controversial production of *Dziady*.

Outside Poland Mickiewicz is best known as the author of the nostalgic epic poem *Pan Tadeusz* (1834) in which he evokes the idyllic life of the *szlachta*, the Polish landed gentry. The heroic nationalism of the Polish romantic poets reached its climax with the uprising of 1863; this was crushed by the army of the czar and Poland became a Russian province.

The individual and society: The literary period which followed this unsuccessful rebellion was radically different and has been interpreted as a reaction against the romantic movement: this was the epoch of Polish positivism. The lonely hero motivated solely by ardent patriotism was no longer the centre of interest in literature. The rise of a new social class, the town-dwelling intelligentsia, resulted in a shift of emphasis to urban life, with all its social problems. The new form of literature dealt with the relationship between the individual and society and the responsibility each individual had to society.

A vivid picture of life as it was lived by the Warsaw bourgeois in the late 19th century has been drawn for us by Boleslaw Prus in his novel *Lalka* (*The Doll,* 1890). Also amongst the positivist writers is the Nobel prize winner Henryk Sienkiewicz, the author of the all-time best seller *Quo Vadis* (1896). This symbolic novel, which deals with the persecution of the Christians in Rome at the time of the Emperor Nero, has been translated into numerous languages and also made into a film.

Literary experiment: The movement generally referred to as "Young Poland" consisted of a number of different groups and literary trends which emerged in the period between 1890 and 1918. What all the authors involved had in common was the desire to put poetic imagination back into literature, with the result that there was also a noticeable preoccupation with theories and manifestoes during these years; a development that reflected similar tendencies in the rest of contemporary Europe.

The prose of this period is either experi-

mental, as illustrated by Władysław Reymont's *Chlopi* (1904–09), the lengthy novel for which he was awarded the Nobel prize in 1924, or realistic, as illustrated by the works of Stefan Żeromski, the writer who was a passionate advocate of social justice and national freedom.

The genius of this epoch is undoubtedly Stanisław Wyspianski, a painter and dramatist without equal amongst his contemporaries in Europe, with the exception perhaps of Alfred Jarry, the creator of *Ubu Roi. Wesele* (1901) is a masterpiece full of evocative allusions, a tragicomic parable of Poland's past and future in the form of a puppet show.

While many of the ideas of the Young Poland movement were based on what was going on elsewhere in Europe, Wyspianski is entirely original in that, in his search for visionary forms, he goes back to the Polish romantics to find a literary means of expressing the plight of Poland.

New freedom: In 1918 Poland regained its independence after almost three centuries of foreign rule. The enthusiasm of the population knew no bounds. With their new-found freedom to express themselves as they wanted on the subjects they chose, Polish writers produced a wide range of distinguished literary works.

Poetry remained experimental, and was

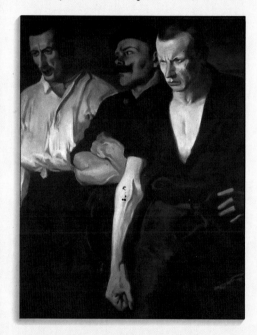

represented in this period by such masters of the language as A. Slonimski, J. Lechon and J. Tuwim. Polish prose now focused primarily on the new society with all the possibilities it presented, as illustrated by the works of J. Kaden-Bandrowski, A. Strug, S. Żeromski and Z. Nalknowska.

One particularly famous writer of the period is Witold Gombrowicz, although at the time he was not known much outside Poland, and he did not achieve world fame until after World War II. Only the grotesque aspects of

Left and above, painting has greatly influenced the historical consciousness of the Poles.

reality interested him, and his taste for the exceptional and the unusual first found expression in his novel *Ferdydurke*, which was published in 1937. The experimental prose form in which it was written is generally acknowledged to have influenced the development of modern prose on an international scale; later it led him in the direction of the Polish theatre of the absurd, of which he became one of the country's best-known representatives.

The theatre of the absurd generally owes a great deal to the Polish avant-garde; alongside the French version of this art form as represented by Artaud and Boris Vian there is a very distinct Polish variety, which was introduced by the brilliant S.I. Witkiewicz and later represented by Slawomir Mrozek.

After World War II Witkiewicz, like Gombrowicz and later Mrozek achieved international fame: his works were translated into many different languages and given numerous performances abroad. His obsession with the idea of the "dissolution" of Europe, the dangers of mass society and the cultural levelling that this inevitably entails, make him a writer whose work will always be relevant.

Experiences of death: The reconstruction of an independent Polish state was harshly interrupted by the invasion of the Germans and the Soviet Russians with whom at that time they were in alliance. Eastern Poland was lost to the Soviet Union, and the rest of Poland was subjected to five years of German occupation.

The rich literary harvest of these very painful years was naturally only fully revealed after the end of the war. One of the most outstanding works of this period is Tadeusz Borowski's *Prosze Panstwa do Gazu*, a collection of short stories based on the author's personal experiences in the extermination camp at Auschwitz-Birkenau. This critically-acclaimed book was translated into almost all European languages and caused a sensation in all the countries where it was published.

As well as the numerous books dealing with the experiences of World War II, works soon started to appear that focused on the establishment of the new socialist state. The most outstanding of these is Andrzejewski's great novel *Popiol i Diamant* (*Ashes and Diamonds*, 1948), the tragic story of a young

man who conspires against the new regime. The film of this novel made by the young Andrzej Wajda brought him his first international success as a director.

The collective hero: From 1949 onwards the literary scene in Poland was dominated by socialist realism. The factory worker or collective farmer was now the main literary hero. Blindly committed to the revolution and constantly on the hunt for imperialist saboteurs, he hung on irksomely in a multitude of books not worth mentioning until the onset of the "thaw" in 1955–56, when he was replaced by more human protagonists. In place of the heroism of the war years and the immediate postwar period came the more moderate atmosphere of the "stabilisation" that took place in the 1960s and 1970s.

Polish literature from now on concentrated on the nuances and contradictions of everyday life in communist Poland. The most important authors of this epoch are T. Konwicki, J. Iwaszkiewicz, M. Hlasko, T. Rózewicz, M. Nowakowski and S. Mrozek, and Zbigniew Herbert is one of the best modern lyric poets in Europe.

Martial law and revolution: When in the late 1970s and 1980s tension, political unrest and economic crises were the dominant feature of life in Poland, the nation's writers were also among those who most vociferously challenged the government. Many were still forced to resort to foreign publishers if they wanted to be published, but gradually independent publishing houses began to make an appearance. As the decade when on, works of Polish literature which had only featured in catalogues and bibliographies until this time, including books by emigrants such as Gombrowicz and Milosz, were distributed all over the country.

The events of those years are now the centre of attention, together with an analysis of their significance for Poland. In *Miesiace* (1981), a Warsaw diary, a veteran of Polish literature, Kazimierz Brandys, reflects with a certain irony on Poland's present turmoil. The revolutionary events that took place in 1989 and the long-awaited re-establishment of democracy have undoubtedly been a powerful stimulus for Polish literature. It will be interesting to watch how it treats these developments in the future.

Left, bargain buys for the art lover.

POLISH ART

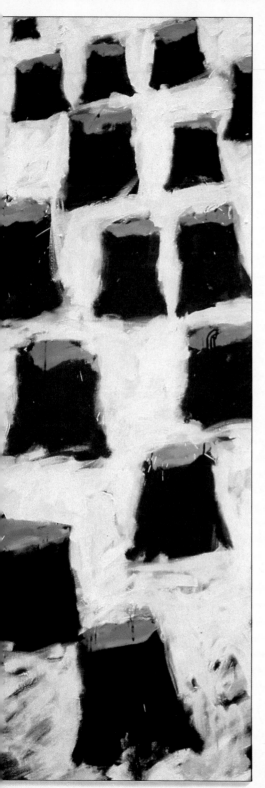

As a consequence of its geographical position and the value orientation of Polish society as a whole, since the time of the Napoleonic wars Polish art has had more in common with the west than with the east. As might be expected of a nation that had been divided against its will, Polish art dwelt in a world of hope and dreams rather than one of political and economic realities. It is therefore probably correct to say that romanticism is at the heart of all modern Polish art. This is particularly true of the initial period, from 1830 to 1918, but it is applicable afterwards as well.

In Poland "romanticism" is not just a definition of a limited period in the history of art and a specific style, it is also a philosophy of life and possibly even the determining force behind Polish art as a whole, as a result of the country's history.

Sense of mission: In keeping with the tradition of all Slavic peoples, the literature of Poland, in particular the great national poetry of the romantic period, had a strong influence on art, music and theatre. The monumental verses of Mickiewicz, Slowacki and Krasinski were still a model for art in general, with its sense of social mission, even in the 20th century. The prestige of romantic poetry as a "national message of salvation" so dominated the whole of the 19th century that in 1857, in a magazine for Polish exiles, it was seriously suggested that Poles, like other northern peoples, had no natural talent for the fine and visual arts.

This was how, from his exile in Paris, the author Julian Klaczko denied the art of his country its right to exist, and this just at the time when Piotr Michalowski (1800–58) was producing works that were on a level with those of Géricault and Delacroix, and even Goya. Michalowski's new interpretation of cavalry romanticism put this genre on a different plane. In his scenes of horsemen from the Kosciuszko uprising and the Napoleonic wars (now in the Cracow museum), this Polish patriot demonstrates an even more lively and explosive temperament than the

Left, a painting by the internationally famous Leon Tarasewicz (born 1957).

Paris artists, trained in the tame classical tradition, who had been his examples.

Michalowski's work also contains numerous elements which anticipate both impressionism and the expressive style. In the allegorical and historical pictures of his successors Juliusz Kossak (1824–99), Artur Grottger (1837–67) and in particular Jan Matejko (1838–93), the Central European interpretation of realism and academicism makes its appearance. Polish artists were now taking their cue from Munich and Vienna rather than from Paris. With its depiction of history, the national fate and the fight for independence and freedom, Polish painting fulfilled a patriotic and visionary mission

tic painters in their efforts to represent the history of their nation were no philosophic idylls. National emotiveness is a much more likely product of the the struggle for human truths and individual expression than ecstasy and fantasy. The work of art that focuses on the past is a means of self discovery and allows the artist to embark on a subjective analysis of reality and aesthetics.

It was not only realism that developed in a perfectly natural fashion from Poland's romantic heritage; the same process was also evident with respect to symbolism and expressionism. By contrast, for example with their German counterparts, Polish artists do not portray landscapes as a mirror of inner

and was enthusiastically received by large sections of the population. The Poles still see historic figures and events primarily through the eyes of the 19th-century romantics. During his lifetime Matejko was presented with a sceptre as a token of honour, symbolising his spiritual leadership of the Polish people at a time when they had no king. *The Battle of Grunwald* and other large panoramas depicting major historical events painted by Matejko, as well his vivid allegories, e.g. the picture *Polonia* (1863), influenced the traditionally oriented Cracow School until after World War I.

The best pictures produced by the roman-

life and its tumults. The all-pervading calm of Poland's traditional landscape painting, with its absence of problems and its deep roots in the home country, originates exclusively from the workshop of the late impressionists.

Music lovers: The development of Polish music echoed that of art in that it too had certain patriotic foundations. At a time when the concept of "national music" was still unknown anywhere else, Chopin was already using light-hearted elements of folk music in his works. In the compositions of his contemporary Stanisław Moniuszko (1819–27) these elements were elevated to the status of the national Polish musical style. While the popularity of Moniuszko is due more to the musical inoffensiveness of his creations, at the hands of the representative of Young Poland, Karol Szymanowski (1882–1947), the fresh sounds of Polish folk music were translated into the symphonic drama of the contemporary avant-garde. Rather along the lines of the composers on whom he modelled himself (Stravinsky, Bartok and Janacek) Szymanowski tried to find a new way of combining ancient traditions with the exciting new spirit of the analytic modern age.

"Synthesis of the arts" and "shared inspiration" – these were the new mottoes dominating Polish aesthetics around the turn of the century. Matejko's most important pupil, the painter, dramaturg, theatre reformer, architect and man of letters Stanisław Wyspianski (1869–1907), may be regarded as both the symbol and the chief representative of this new tendency. The tragedy of the Polish Middle Ages and the dreamlike visions of whole generations take on a new tone in Wyspianski's interpretation, an interpretation that is both critical and eerie at the same time. In Malczewski's picture *Melan-*

choly (1894), which hangs in the National Museum in Poznań, all the demons of the country's past are translated into the alienated present. As a result of this new, highly realistic imagery, the romantic tradition of the art world acquired an undreamt-of expressiveness. European symbolism was enriched by some new and original features displaying a psychoanalytical penetration of humanity that had never been encountered in painting before.

The independence achieved by Poland in 1918 resulted in a considerable simplification of the functions of art. The younger generation was no longer prepared to be conscripted into patriotic duty, and in Cra-

cow a group which went by the name of the "Formists" was founded. The members of this group supported the idea of the autonomy of aesthetics.

The nihilistic programme of the futurists and late expressionists made a clean break with all that had gone before. It declared war on all varieties of regional art, whether this was the "retrospective" orientation of neoromantic and historical painting, the "imagery" of the symbolists, or academic "colourism".

After the war Mieczyslaw Sztuka's Cracow-based group "Blok" emerged on the scene with an Eastern European interpreta-

Left, J. Matejko: *Copernicus in the Tower of Frombork*. **Above**, J. Malczewski: *Self-portrait*.

tion of constructivism. Architecture, sociology and the new technical civilisation were the reference points of a generation that was not by coincidence located in Lódź, the industrial centre of Poland. Malewicz's fellow-artist Wladyslaw Strzeminski (1893–1952); his wife, the sculptress Katarzyna Kobro (1898–1951); and Henryk Stazewski (1894–1988), had a charismatic influence on the constructivist avant-garde with their particular approach to art, which they called "unism".

The suicide of their opposite number from the rationalists, the fantast and protosurrealist Stanisław Ignacy Witkiewicz, on 18 September 1939, is symbolic of the irreparable

pictures: they have to be topical, admonish and uncover what has been concealed. Memories of the war and the critical observation of everyday life are predominant in the works of a whole generation of expressive realists in the early 1950s.

The new music of the modern Polish composers also drew its inspiration from the same source. The *Funeral Music* (1958) by the veteran of them all, Witold Lutoslawski (born in 1913), was followed by the *Strofy, Oratorium, Dies Irae* and the *Threnody for the Victims of Hiroshima* by Krzysztof Penderecki (born 1933) and finally by the *Exorta,* which was the work of Tadeusz Baird (1928–81).

damage done to Polish culture by World War II. Unworldly aestheticism, whether of a traditional or an avant-garde nature, was shown to be utterly old-fashioned and useless in the face of the brutal realities of the war. Art had to find another way of expressing itself.

The *Memories of Auschwitz* of Xavery Dunikowski (1875–1964), who had himself been a prisoner there, the drawings of the Warsaw ruins by T. Kuliseiwicz, which he completed in 1945/46, and the surrealist visions of Bronislaw Linke are characteristic of the change. The aesthetics of the new realism reinforce certain functions of the

The Warsaw Autumn Festival of Contemporary Music has been organised on a regular basis since 1956, but the focus is not all on classical music and the annual jazz jamboree that takes place in October is an event attracting equal interest.

Film and theatre: The films made since the war are also characterised by tragedy inspired by memories of the recent past, but in addition show a surprising convergence of lyricism and the grotesque, dreaminess and humour. A. Wajda's *Kanal* (1957), A. Munk's *Eroica* 1958), and the "black series" of the Polish documentary makers (1949–55) are typical examples. One inspiration gave rise to another, and it was not by chance that the new revolution in the fine arts was symbolised by the comprehensive vision of the painting *Symphonic liturgy of Arthur Honegger* (1955) by Marian Bogusz, a forerunner of the Polish neo-avant-garde in the early 1950s.

There was a direct connection between Polish theatre and the activities of the fine arts. The balanced, inward-looking style of the most outstanding representative of pre-war theatre, Leon Schiller (1888–1954), is a thing of the past. In recent decades Polish theatre has been characterised by its ability to present highly topical messages using direct images that have an almost physical effect on their audiences.

What makes it unique amongst all the European theatrical traditions is the complex visual stimulation of almost all the productions, since most Polish producers have studied art and are hence capable of designing the set themselves, and often even the very elaborate costumes and props as well. The outstanding names in this field are Grzegorzewski, Wajda, Swinarski, Pankiewicz, Sartkowski, Szajna and Kantor. Generous subsidies for the theatre, in accordance with the traditional conception of the stage as a "School for the education of the nation" (W. Boguslawski) have enabled some experiments of extraordinary intensity to be made – experiments which are unique in all Europe – whereby not only the stage but also the public and the auditorium are included in the action.

The pedagogical and psychological experiments of Grotowski, in which he has attempted to change the function of the theatre, have been very well received, not only in his home country but also abroad. Grotowski began his work in the provincial theatre in Opole, and later continued in his own "laboratory" in Wrocław; he concentrated in particular on training his actors in mime and gymnastics and developed a separate new concept of what he called "poor theatre". The audience is included in the improvised "happenings" on the stage while the actors function rather like helpers and psychotherapists. The mystery play tradition revived by Grotowski, where ecstatic rites are used to

bring out the significance of archetypal stories, has been developed by other producers, in particular Szajna: *Replika, Witkacy* and *Dante* (1970–74) in the "Studio" Theatre in Warsaw, and Kantor in the "Cricot 2" theatre in Cracow.

The animated prop, which, in the interpretation of Kleist and Craig, can replace the living person in that it puts him on the same level as inanimate things, and the abolition of the difference between life and death and between dream and reality in the action on stage, has spread from the theatre productions of Kantor and come to influence the whole art scene of Poland. The associative human creations of M. Abakanowicz, which

underline the anthropological ambiguity of all forms through the indefinite nature of the materials that are used, have been brought to life by W. Hasior, J. Benes, J. Lukomski and other late expressionists. There is a fluid transition from the concentration on the surrealist object, which had been a characteristic of Polish art for years, to the intimate performance.

At present the trend in Poland is towards neo-rationalism, whereby a conscious distance is maintained from romanticism of every kind. The indefatigable H. Stazewski has become the central figure of the younger generation of art analysts and representa-

Left, Krzysztof Penderecki conducts. **Right**, the late theatre director Tadeusz Kantor at rehearsals.

tives of concrete art – among whom are K. Sosnowski, Z. Gostomski, R. Winiarski, Z. Dlubak and R. Waszko. Painting has recently taken on spatial dimensions: instead of pictures there are now "environments". The projection of slides, films and videos are now all used to supplement the traditional media of art.

New censors: When the country was put under military law in 1981 the experimentation which had been embarked upon with such enthusiasm came to a halt for several years. As a consequence of the artists' withdrawal from public life, and their deliberate boycotting, not only of all official exhibitions, but also of museums, theatres and private galleries, Polish culture soon found itself in a state of crisis. Although the church offered asylum, this soon turned out to be less of a blessing than it had appeared to be at the outset. On the one hand, exhibitions which were held on church premises were the source of a number of new ideas, which were then taken up in particular by the new museums founded by the dioceses. On the other hand the intervention of priests with little knowledge of the world of art meant that in practice the "red" censor was merely replaced with the "black" one.

The situation can now be described as having stabilised. In keeping with the tradition of the leading galleries of the past such as Krzywe Kolo and Foksal in Warsaw, Krzysztofory in Cracow, Akumulatory in Poznan and Pod Mona Lisa in Wrocław, private initiatives on the part of the artists are attracting the attention of the public. New means of access to the public are being sought, but also new means of access to the international art market. In Poland, as in Western Europe, the artists of the younger generation are returning from their high-flying intellectual expeditions to the cosy familiarity of the home atelier. The current reactions of the representatives of the post-modern era in the theatre, music and the fine arts in Warsaw, Cracow and Poznan are no different from those of their contemporaries in the art and theatre schools anywhere else on the continent.

The paintings of L. Tarasiewicz, T. Ciecierski, W. Pawlak and J. Modzelewski are equal in every respect to the well-known works of their western contemporaries. The common leitmotif of all the artists, whether they come from the West or the East, is the campaign against the deceptiveness of pure aesthetics as a guiding principle.

In the process of confronting their own artistic tradition, Polish artists have also taken a hard look at the idea of never-ending progress. The creed of emotion and nostalgia, even banality and aggressive fragmentation, that runs like a thread through the great but deceptive general visions of the avant-gardists, is now placed high on the new scale of values.

Even the sacred topic of nationality and similar subjects which no-one was allowed to attack before are not spared sceptical and sarcastic treatment, as demonstrated by W. Pawlak with his red-and-white flags, produced with mocking attention to detail. The deliberate naïvety of E. Dwornik's narrative style has attracted many imitators.

One characteristic of the current trends that we are now witnessing in Poland, is the surprising uniformity of inspiration evident in all areas of art. The purpose of the artists who occupy whole rooms with their works and flood the world of art with allegorical objects is not merely to make the materials and production techniques of their creations more visible; they are also attempting to demystify art.

In addition, these artists are making complex allusions to the realities of the consumer-oriented society that is also beginning to emerge in Poland. The works that are currently installed in Polish galleries, and the films, videos and theatre productions, such as Wisniewski's *Blendung,* that are now being presented on the country's stages and screens, are full of such elements.

Thus the post-modern trends are continuing in the Polish tradition of making the most important existential questions of the nation clearly visible to all. "The autonomy and universality of current Polish painting is based on the direct experience of drama that has been a characteristic of Polish life," writes Adam Brincken (born 1951), one of the leading representatives of the younger generation.

Modern Polish art is worth watching closely, not least by the West.

Right, the Poles are renowned for their jazz. The cream of the international jazz scene converges on Warsaw for the annual festival.

THE ENVIRONMENT

In Poland a sign prohibiting swimming in a particular stretch of water should be taken very seriously, even if it does not seem at all convincing when the water in question is sea of a splendid blue with crystal-clear waves breaking on a picture-book beach. As a result of untreated sewage pumped straight into the sea, excessive – often invisible – quantities of bacteria are common.

On the other hand, a report by Greenpeace revealed that Polish food has fewer harmful substances in it than food in most other countries. The reason for this is simply that the ground is less frequently fertilised, because the farmers cannot afford it. There is also no money for the anabiotics that are so often used by farmers in the West to fatten their calves.

No tourist need therefore have any qualms about going into a restaurant in Poland and ordering a tasty piece of veal. However, tourists who visit the splendid Renaissance market square in Cracow on a cloudy day when there is no wind should resist the temptation to open their mouths in admiration. If they do, they will swallow excessive quantities of smog from the chimneys of the largest communist industrial project, Nowa Huta, the iron and steel works, which is only 12 miels (20 km) upwind of the city.

Power of the people: At every turn, visitors are likely to encounter contradictory evidence regarding Polish attitudes to the environment. There is not a single nuclear power plant in Poland and the only project that was started has now been officially abandoned as a result of persistent blockading by the population. Even basic awareness, however, is often hopelessly limited. Witness, for example, the farmer who positions his manure heap right next to the household well; as a result of this thoughtlessness, he is slowly poisoning his family.

For years the damage done to Poland's environment was ignored by the people and covered up by the state. If a party leader declared in a speech that the state of the environment was improving every year, eve-

Left, industrial pollution, a major problem, has led to the birth of green movements.

ryone was expected to believe it, even if the fish in the Vistula simply refused to swim normally with their bellies down and the children in Silesia were constantly being ill.

Now this state of affairs has changed completely. Everyone knows what the situation really is; the minister for environmental affairs has taken up arms against the industrial barons and the government has been endlessly discussing where it is to get the money from to try and remedy wrongs of many years' standing.

Of course, pollution is no respecter of borders. Nor does it bow down to the superiority of one ideology over another. Environmental problems are global. In spite of this

turn exports its pollution to Belorussia and large areas of the Ukraine.

The situation on the Baltic Sea is far worse, with the water polluted on a vast scale by the former GDR, Poland and the USSR. This is primarily caused by the rivers which flow into the Baltic, such as the Vistula and the Oder, carrying with them enormous quantities of untreated sewage and waste from residential areas and industry. To remedy this will take decades.

Problems are compounded by the immoral practice of siting "dirty" industries on international borders. This was the case with the nuclear power plant in Greifswald (former GDR), the iron and steel work complex

the individual countries have difficulties communicating with one another about their common environmental problems. In central Eastern Europe generally, a critical analysis of environmental policy was additionally hampered by the hypocrisy of the politicians and the repeated hushing up of important environmental data.

The current situation: The pattern of pollution in this part of the world is as follows: the air in the western and southern part of Poland has a high content of dust and carbon dioxide, blown across from neighbouring countries. The Ruhr, the industrial area of Germany, is one of the main offenders. Poland in

"Eisenhüttenstadt" (former GDR) and the coking plant in Stonawa (Czechoslovakia). The catastrophe of Chernobyl demonstrated how real the threat of such technology is, even when it is a long way away.

These negative trends were only reinforced by the planned economy of Poland. The fact that Poland is producing almost twice as much untreated industrial waste as the Federal Republic of Germany is alone evidence of this. With production policy as it is, the reduction of waste is proceeding at a snail's pace by comparison with the way other countries are dealing with the problem – e.g. Canada, which in the course of five years has reduced its industrial waste to a third of the original quantity.

Not every area of the environment, of course, is in such a sorry state. There are still numerous regions where nature is unspoiled; there are huge tracts of forest and national parks, lowland plains full of lakes, mountain ranges and agricultural areas where the soil is still in its natural state. However, the fact remains that over a third of the population of the country lives in regions that are hazardous to health and heading for an ecological crisis. According to official statistics, there are 27 regions in Poland with a combined area of 13,600 sq. miles (35,200 sq. km) where the environment is endangered. Here the rate of illness and the number of deaths due to environmental causes – especially among new-born babies – is significantly higher than elsewhere, and the public has long been aware that living in one of these regions means a marked reduction in the quality of life.

It is paradoxical that the former minister for environmental affairs refused for two years to accept the term "environmentally endangered area", arguing that this was "enemy propaganda". The map showing the environmental situation in Poland is a clear indication of the extent to which the doctrine of intensified industrialisation modelled on the Soviet pattern was followed. The whole of southern Poland was a victim of this concept, although their neighbours, in this case Germany and Czechoslovakia, have also contributed to the pollution.

As a consequence the town of Bytom can be reckoned amongst the 10 most polluted towns in the world. The splendid pine forests of the Izerski mountains are dying, and it is scarcely more beneficial from a health point of view to take a holiday in the Karkonosze than to remain in the town. In the north the ecological situation is governed by the state of the Baltic. There has recently been some improvement on the coast: the water is somewhat cleaner than it used to be and there has been a gradual reduction in the number of beaches unsafe to use.

The tracts of forests and the lakes in the north of the country comprise one of the

country's most unspoiled environments and it is no coincidence that this area is called the "green lung" of Poland. Attempts to industrialise it were resisted, there is no intensive farming here and there are no rapidly expanding towns. If the forests of this region do not fall victim to acid rain from the West, a large, relatively clean enclave will be preserved for the benefit of the whole of the European continent. Fortunately it is being actively protected.

Water, water everywhere?: In spite of the apparent abundance of water, Poland is still one of the most arid countries in Europe. This is connected both with the climatically unfavourable position of Poland and the

marked variations in precipitation, from season to season and region to region. With its unregulated and extensive utilisation of ground and surface water, which is generally regarded as common property available free of charge to everyone, Poland is slowly but surely approaching the point where it will have exhausted its water supplies.

In central and southern Poland the shortage of water during periods of low rain has already reached a critical point. Over one hundred large towns, thousands of smaller towns and almost the whole of agriculture are affected by temporary shortages of water. The main causes of water shortage are

Left, game parks and nature reserves provide sanctuary to all manner of animals. **Above**, a harbinger of spring.

waste, losses in the water distribution network and pollution of surface water and of the sea.

In a report for a conference in Bergen that took place in 1990, only 4 percent of the flowing water examined and 1 percent of the stagnant water was described as "clean". Almost 40 percent of the flowing water and 53 percent of the stagnant water was classified as "considerably polluted". Polluted, salty water from hard-coal mining flows into the Vistula and the Oder. To make the whole situation even worse, the mining areas are located in the upper reaches of the rivers.

The situation is even more alarming as far as sewage and waste water are concerned,

land's energy is obtained from coal, which is a very plentiful and easily accessible commodity in this part of the world. As a result the emission of sulphur dioxide compounds – which are extremely harmful both to human health and to the environment – has reached frighteningly high levels. A further unfortunate consequence of this emission is the deterioration of cultural monuments (for example in Cracow). The permissible norm in Poland has long been exceeded and fundamental changes to the whole economy would have to be made in order to bring about a substantial reduction in the quantities of harmful substances in the air.

This would include the restructuring of

and the water in the sewerage system is as good as untreated. Of the over 800 towns of Poland, more than half have no sewage or waste water purification plants and all waste is allowed to flow untreated into the sea; the plants that do exist are to a large extent inoperable.

It is only now that the proper management of water is slowly being introduced. As a first step the price of water was radically increased and the country was divided into 12 water management regions. Such changes however cost a great deal of money; Poland is having to pay dearly for the sins of the past.

Air pollution: Around 80 percent of Po-

industry and a complete change of policy with respect to the production of energy. Equally imperative is the improvement of public transport in the larger towns, since this is the only way traffic, which is responsible for a large proportion of the harmful emissions, can be limited. There are currently 212 private cars registered for every 1,000 inhabitants in Poland, but as yet there are no signs of any plans to introduce lead-free petrol. (The bicycle has yet to be reintroduced as a means of transport in Poland.) One small but positive step that has been taken is the reduction of the speed limit to 55 mph (90 kph).

Back to the land: The main causes of soil contamination are the high concentration of atmospheric pollution and the recent use of fertilisers and chemical pesticides. In 1990, in the course of the relief action for Poland, chemical products were imported for use in agriculture that had been taken off the market long ago in the EC because of their harmful consequences.

The alarm was sounded by Greenpeace, who conducted a sensational campaign against this practice and argued that because it had previously made little use of artificial fertilisers, Poland was therefore in an ideal position to become an important producer of whole food. The prerequisite for this, how-

inhabitant is twice as high as in neighbouring Germany or in Denmark, somewhat lower than it is in France, but six times higher than it is in Great Britain. The forests are relatively young, their average age being 45 years (as compared with 52 years in the Federal Republic of Germany, 35 in England and 38 in France). Most of this, 79 percent, is pine forest, and, as in Germany, these trees are suffering as a consequence of the acid rain. Monitoring experiments revealed that in 1987 only 24.4 percent of the pine forests and 46.6 percent of the deciduous forests consisted of healthy trees.

An important biological factor indicating the state of the forests and the water is the

ever, was that it should stop harming the food chain, e.g. by letting untreated waste and sewage into the rivers.

Even the allotment holders can no longer safely enjoy their produce, since their little plots of land are often situated close to large factories and traffic arteries: in some areas the situation is so bad that the fruit and vegetables grown in this way are not suitable for consumption.

Poland's forests are its greatest treasure. The number of trees the country has per

Above, there is a wealth of fauna along the banks of rivers and streams.

occurrence of white-tailed eagles (*haliaetus albicilla*) and ospreys (*pandion haliaetus*). These birds are found in large tracts of forest comprising old trees and with clean water somewhere in the vicinity. Both species are threatened with extinction in Europe. At present it is estimated that there are only 100 to 120 pairs of white-tailed eagles and 30 to 40 pairs of ospreys left in Poland. If you spot a white-tailed eagle or an osprey, you can be sure that you are in an unspoiled part of Poland.

The changes that are taking place in post-communist Poland must include protection of the environment. Conversions from one system of government to another take a long time however and are extremely expensive. The government's programme includes the reduction of sulphur and nitrogen emission, an improvement of river water to a level of second-degree purity and an ambitious recycling programme for industrial and community waste.

An important element of current environmental policy is the concept of a chain of protected areas. Poland has areas which are particularly rich in biological resources, the preservation of which is vital if the ecological balance of the country is to be maintained. In 1987 these areas made up 9.2 percent of the country, and the target for the year 2000

is 15 percent. The protected zones consist of national parks (e.g. Tatrzański, Białowieski), where tourism is limited and industrial activity prohibited, of nature reserves under particularly strict protection and scenic parks with limited tourism and controlled farming practices.

The realisation of such concepts depends to a large extent on the environmental consciousness of the local and regional authorities. Environmental parties and organisations are also beginning to play an important role: free green parties have emerged in Poland, and the Polish Ecology Club, which has a high degree of scientific and moral authority, is very active. There are also numerous local organisations, such as the Ecology Club run by the Franciscans.

Most important of all, however, is that all those who enjoy the benefits of nature treat it with respect.

Europe's last bison: Stag, elk and wild pig abound in Poland. In some wilderness areas there are even wolves. This range of natural history is an achievement for a European state, but what makes it unique is the addition of one animal – the wild bison.

Most people are surprised that bison ever existed in Europe. Plains bison everyone knows about: staple food of the American Indian and a resource from which he built his shelter and sewed his clothes. But a European bison sounds almost primeval.

By the end of the 1920s only a few breeding pairs of bison were left in Europe, in captivity in Lithuania. Some of these animals were re-introduced to the Białowieża forest on the Polish eastern marches, where prior to World War I they had lived since the Ice Age. Under protection in Białowieża they soon multiplied and became established as semi-wild animals.

The bison reserve is over 195 sq. miles (500 sq. km) in total and it is an integral part of the forest area, which is the last fragment of the primeval forest that once covered virtually the whole of Europe. For this reason the hardwood is as carefully preserved and protected as the wildlife. Though sometimes fed artificially, the bison mostly browse on oak, elm, willow and other deciduous matter. In winter they eat mainly acorns and shrubs.

About 170 *bison bonassi* are at large in Białowieża, and from this breeding reserve surplus animals have been shipped to other countries and to other areas within Poland. One particular journey made by a reserve-bred bison became famous. Having been transported several hundred miles to a new home in another part of Poland, the beast became homesick and set off back to Białowieża. Its progress was followed by press and radio. If it passed a country cottage and found the shutters open, it would poke its bovine head inside for a look, much to the consternation of the inhabitants.

Left, air filters are not commonplace in Poland. **Right**, hunting in winter.

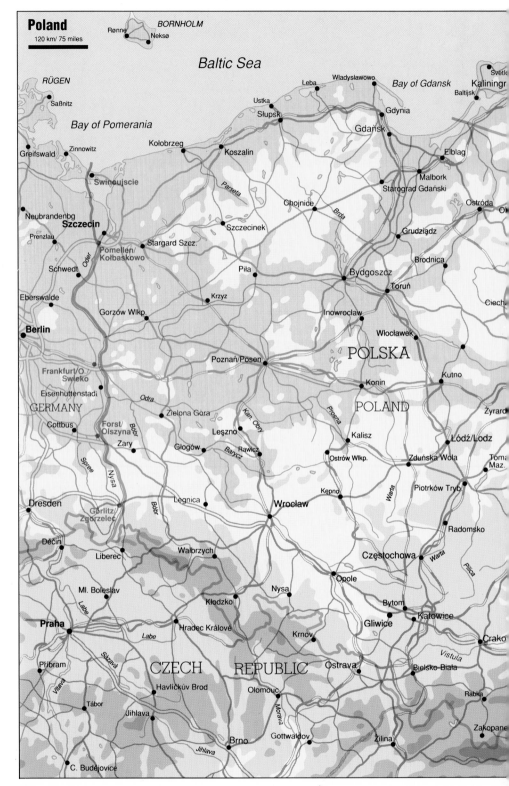

Poland

120 km/ 75 miles

Baltic Sea

Bay of Pomerania

Bay of Gdansk

RÜGEN

BORNHOLM
Rønne
Neksø

Svetl
Kaliningr
Baltijsk

Saßnitz

Zinnowitz
Greifswald

Leba
Ustka
Słupsk
Wladysławowo
Gdynia
Gdańsk

Kołobrzeg
Koszalin
Elblag

Swinoujscie
Malbork
Starograd Gdański
Ostróda
O

Neubrandenbg
Szczecin
Prenzlau
Chojnice
Szczecinek
Grudziądz

Stargard Szcz.
Pomellen/
Kołbaskowo
Piła
Brodnica

Schwedt
Ciech

Eberswalde
Krzyz
Bydgoszcz
Toruń

Berlin
Gorzów Wlkp.
Inowrocław

Włocławek

Poznań/Posen
POLSKA
Kutno

Frankfurt/O.
Świeko
Konin
Żyrard

Eisenhüttenstadi
POLAND

GERMANY
Zielona Gora
Prosna
Łódź/Lodz

Cottbus
Forst/
Olszyna
Leszno
Kalisz
Toma
Maz.

Zary
Głogów
Rawicz
Ostrów Wlkp.
Zduńska Wola

Legnica
Kepno
Piotrków Tryb.

Dresden
Görlitz/
Zgorzelec
Wrocław
Radomsko

Děčin
Liberec
Wałbrzych
Częstochowa

Ml. Boleslav
Nysa
Opole
Bytom

Kłodzko
Gliwice
Katowice

Praha
Hradec Králové
Krnov
Crako

Přibram
CZECH
REPUBLIC
Ostrava
Bielsko-Biała
Vistula

Havlíčkův Brod
Olomouc
Rabka

Tábor
Jihlava
Morava
Zakopane

Brno
Gottwaldov
Žilina

C. Budějovice

Oder
Odra
Ken. Obry
Barycz
Bobr
Nysa
Spree
Warta
Pilica
Warta
Parseta
Brda
Labe
Labe
Sázava
Vltava
Jihlava

132

PLACES

When the world thinks of Poland, certain names and events spring to mind: Lech Wałęsa and "Solidarity", the suffering of World War II, Treblinka and the Warsaw Ghetto. But for most people Poland itself is something of an unknown quantity. The following chapters aim to unveil the many facets of a country which the Polish-born writer Joseph Conrad referred to as "that advanced outpost of Western civilisation".

In 1939, addressing Britain's parliament, Sir Winston Churchill said: "The soul of Poland is indestructible... she will rise again like a rock, which may for a spell be submerged by a tidal wave, but which remains a rock." But even he could not have imagined how much the Polish soul would have to endure over the ensuing decades. Now the flood waters have finally receded, however, the rock is still there.

On a journey through Poland one often has the feeling of having stepped back in time. Ancient groves of trees – lindens, maples and poplars – line the roads. Farming continues to rely on the horse-drawn cart. As fertilisers are little used, produce is "organically" grown and invariably tastes much better than in the so-called developed countries.

Poland is famous for the breeding of top-quality Arab stallions on huge stud farms dotted around the vast plains. But the country is not all flat. High mountains rise in the south, and in the north thousands of lakes nestle between undulating hills. The country has some of the most unsullied natural beauty to be found anywhere in the world. The Bieszczady wilderness in the southeast corner is the last natural habitat of the European bison and the Białowieża forest in the east is Europe's only surviving area of primeval forest.

WARSAW

Warsaw is a city that is much more than the country's capital, the headquarters of industry and a major traffic junction. Warsaw is first and foremost the cultural centre of Poland; it is the home of the Academy of Sciences and the National Library, the International Chopin Competition is held here every five years and the *Warszawska Jesień*, a festival of modern music, and the International Book Fair take place in the city every autumn.

The saddest period in the city's 700-year history was World War II. Over 700,000 citizens lost their lives and the city was razed to the ground. The centre has been rebuilt true to its original, but most of the 1.7 million inhabitants now live in the new estates built on the outskirts of Warsaw.

The city lies on the River Vistula. A very long time ago, so the legend goes, this stretch of water was the home of the **Warsaw Mermaid**, a being half woman and half fish. Today her image graces the capital's coat of arms. The river splits the city into two halves, but only the left bank has features that will be of much interest to the visitor. Approximately 82 ft (25 metres) above the gently flowing water are the old and new towns, the Royal Castle, the commercial centre, modern hotels and splendid parks. This is the real heart of the city.

The old town: Although it has a history that dates back to the Middle Ages, the **Stare Miasto** (Old Town) part of the city has been completely reconstructed from the rubble left by World War II. Today however there are no longer any signs of the tragic destruction that took place; the new "old" town has already acquired a historical patina of its own and has become the elegant, lively centre of the capital. Its faithful reconstruction has earned it the UNESCO designation of "World Cultural Heritage".

The **Old Market Square** has been the centre of town life since Warsaw's beginnings in the 13th century. Today this square and the streets leading off it comprise one of the most picturesque parts of the city. Artists and craftsmen sell their works on the pavement and the magnificent town residences house numerous antique shops and galleries.

In summer the brightly-coloured umbrellas of the coffee houses transform the old market square into a sea of colour and hackney-cabs roll across it taking tourists on a leisurely tour of the old town.

Gourmets will find some of the country's best restaurants in this part of Warsaw: **Bazyliszek**, **Świętoszek** and **Rycerska**. The speciality of the coffee house **Kamienne Schodki** is the famous "Warsaw duck"; also to be recommended are the **Café Krokodyl** and the wine bar **U Fukiera**.

The main church in the old town is **St John's Cathedral**, which is also the oldest church in Warsaw and was rebuilt in the Gothic style. The Nobel prize winner Henryk Sienkiewicz is buried here.

On summer evenings the old town is enchanting with the red tiles of the city walls and towers glowing under the spotlights.

A **Barbakan** or city gate leads to the **New Town** (Nowe Miasto), which was built 100 years after the old part. The house at **ul. Freta no. 16** is the birthplace of Marie Curie, originally Maria Sklodowska-Curie, the woman who twice won the Nobel prize. An exhibition in its rooms illustrates the work of this brilliant scientist.

At the edge of the old town is **Plac Zamkowy** (Castle Square) featuring the **Zygmunt Pillar**, the oldest monument in Warsaw. On this high pillar is a statue of King Zygmunt or Sigismund III bearing a cross and a sword. It was this king who moved the capital of Poland from Cracow to Warsaw.

The **Zamek Królewski** (Royal Castle) was destroyed at the end of the war by the German Wehrmacht, the interior was plundered and the walls blown up. The decision to reconstruct it was only taken in 1971, and the whole castle has now been accessible to the public since 1984. All the architectural fragments

Preceding pages: Warsaw old and new; a street in the old city. Below, the Zygmunt Pillar at the entrance to the old city.

remaining from the original building were integrated into the new one, which was reconstructed in the style of the early 17th century – and given a splendid 18th century interior.

During its 700-year history the castle served as the residence of the dukes of Mazovia and the Polish kings, and later became the seat of the country's parliament. In 1791 the Constitution of 3 May was drawn up, the first constitution in Europe based on the principle of liberty.

Most of the works of art housed in the castle are from the few collections which survived Nazi occupation. Among them are views of the city in the 18th century by Bellotto, otherwise known as Canaletto.

In the former castle chapel is the urn containing the heart of the Polish and American freedom hero Tadeusz Kościuszko (1746–1817), who led the Polish troops against Russia in a last desperate struggle to assert the country's independence.

The **Trakt Królewski** (Royal Way) is the Varsovians' favourite place for a stroll because of its historic significance and imposing character. It begins on **Plac Królewski** (King's Square), continues under various other names – **Cracowskie Przedmieście, Nowy Świat** and **Aleje Ujazdowskie** – to **Łazienki** and **Belweder** and comes to an end in **Wilanów**.

Ranged along **Cracowskie Przedmiescie** are historic palaces, churches, town residences and monuments from Poland's past as well as its present. The palace of the Radziwiłł family today houses the office of the Council of Ministers. It was here that the Warsaw Pact was signed in 1955 and here, at the round table, that the talks between Solidarity and the government took place in 1989. In the **Church of the Holy Cross** are the urns of Frédéric Chopin and the writer Władyslaw Reymont, who won the Nobel prize for literature in 1924. The monument to Nicholas Copernicus is a work by the well-known Danish sculptor Bertl Thorvaldsen.

Adjacent to Cracowskie Przedmiescie are two of the most interesting squares

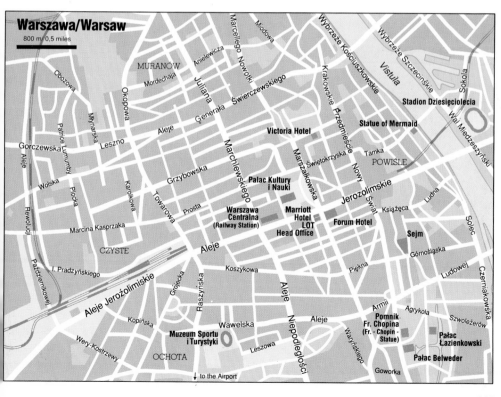

in the Polish capital. **Plac Zwycięstwa** (Victory Square) is still awaiting completion. The **Ogród Saski** (Saski Gardens) date from the baroque period: the first official public gardens in Warsaw, they have been accessible to all the inhabitants of the city since 1727. Of the former Saski Palace only the colonnade remains, which since 1925 has been the site of the **Tomb of the Unknown Soldier**. Every Sunday on the stroke of noon the ceremonial changing of the guard is performed before a host of visitors. At the edge of the square guests and casual visitors can enjoy the stylish atmosphere of the modern **Victoria Hotel** with its restaurants, cafés and casino bar. The classical hotels **Europejski** and **Bristol** have both been renovated and are also recommended for a relaxing drink.

The adjoining **Plac Teatralny** (Theatre Square) is named after the large theatre originally dating from the first half of the 19th century that was rebuilt in its old form after destruction in World War II. The monument to the heroes of Warsaw, popularly known as the "Warsaw Nike", that stands in front of the theatre is in quite another style.

Not far away, on **Plac Bankowy** (Bank Square), is the **Gallery of European Painting**. Particularly worth seeing in this gallery is the collection that was donated by Janina and Zbigniew Porczyński.

The street bearing the name of **Nowy Swiat** (New World) was rebuilt in 19th-century style. It is a typical shopping street in the truest sense of the word. The cake shop **Blikle**, famous far beyond Warsaw for its cakes and tarts, should not on any account be missed. A further landmark in this street is house no. 45, where the famous modernist writer of Polish origin Joseph Conrad, originally Konrad Korzeniowski, spent his childhood (at the age of 17 he left Poland for Marseille).

The **Aleje Ujazdowskie**, the most elegant avenue in old Warsaw, has now become the street of the diplomats, with one embassy after another ranged along it. This is also where the **Sejm** and the

A medical student does an on-the-spot check-up.

Senate of the Republic are located. In the adjacent park is the monument to the well-known pianist and politician Ignacy Paderewski.

Rising above the expressway **Trasa Łazienkowska**, which crosses the **Aleje Ujazdowskie**, is the **Water Palace**. This former summer residence of the Vasa kings is now a museum.

Adjoining the Botanical Gardens of the University of Warsaw is Lazienki, a splendid palace complex which has one of the most attractive parks in Europe. This complex was once the summer residence of the last Polish king, Stanisław August Poniatowski, who had the palaces and pavilions built to suit his requirements at the end of the 18th century. The central point of the park is a classical palace in a picturesque setting by the water. Like the other Warsaw buildings, it was carefully reconstructed from the ruins of World War II, and furnished with the works of art that were once in the possession of the king. The theatre in the old Orangery is one of the few authentic 18th-century court thea-

tres in existence and today houses a museum. At the foot of the Chopin Monument regular piano recitals are held during the summer.

At the edge of Lazienki is **Belweder** (Belvedere), a palace dating from the early 19th century. This is the official residence of the President of the Republic of Poland.

Wilanów is some way out from the city centre. It was once the residence of King Jan III Sobieski, the monarch who defeated the Turks outside Vienna. Many people called it the "Polish Versailles", as it was designed in imitation of the French Baroque residence of that name. The oldest part of the palace is the main building, which dates from 1681–96. In 1804 one of the first museums in Poland was opened within its walls by the then owner of Wilanów, Stanisław Kostka Potocki. During the German occupation the most valuable objects of art were stolen, the park was destroyed and the gardens ruined. Today, however, the whole complex is once again in use as a museum, and boasts the largest portrait collection in Poland. In the historic Orangery there is a display of arts and crafts, and in 1968 the first **Poster Museum** in the world was opened in the former riding school.

The nearby restaurants **Wilanów**, **Kuźnia Królewska** and the **Café Hetmańska** all offer excellent cuisine.

In the district known as **Śródmieście** is the largest square in Warsaw, **Plac Defilad**, with the capital's highest building towering above it. This **Palace of Culture and Science** was built in the years 1952–55 as a present of the Soviet Union to Poland. In spite of its not very attractive appearance it nevertheless plays an important part in the scientific and cultural life of the capital. Among the institutions and facilities accommodated within its walls are scientific institutes, cinemas, theatres and even a Technical Museum. From the observation terrace on the 30th floor there is a splendid view over the city itself and the surroundings of Warsaw.

Opposite the main entrance to the palace, on what is referred to as the west side, are a number of department stores.

Polish good ooks.

The names of all of them are easy to remember: **Sezam**, **Junior**, **Sawa** and **Wars**. Also in this part of the city is the slim building of the **Forum** hotel.

At the other end of the shopping street is the **Central Station** and opposite this the headquarters of the Polish Airline, **LOT,** and the luxury **Marriott** hotel. The Marriott is the most likely address of anyone who is in Warsaw for business purposes.

Before World War II Warsaw was the city with the largest Jewish community in the world. One particular street, the **Trakt Pamięci Męczeństwa Walki Żydów**, has been named in remembrance of the sufferings of the Jewish population of the Warsaw Ghetto in the years 1940–43, and also their courageous resistance in the uprising of 1943.

This street leads to the monument to the heroes of the Ghetto and the commemorative wall; it was here that the Jews were assembled before being transported to the extermination camp Treblinka.

Among those buried in the Jewish cemetery in **Okopowa Street** is the inventor of Esperanto, Ludwik Zamenhoff. The only synagogue which survived the war and is still open today is in the nearby street of **ul. Twarda**.

The **Cmentarz Powązkowski** (Powazkowski Cemetery) dates from 1790. Many of its gravestones are works of art in themselves, and a number of celebrated writers, scientists and artists are buried here. The **Communal Cemetery**, not far away, is primarily the burial ground of soldiers who lost their lives in the two world wars, most of them victims of the regimes of terror under Hitler and Stalin. On All Saints' Day the people of Warsaw remember their dead and bring flowers to this cemetery.

On the **Żoliborz** estate along **Krasiński Street**, is the modernistic church dedicated to **St Stanisław Kostka**, a building that attracts many visitors. Near this church is the grave of the priest Jerzy Popiełuszko, the outspoken supporter of Solidarity who was murdered by the Polish secret service in 1984; it is now a national memorial.

Since 1989 life in Warsaw, as in the rest of Poland, has undergone considerable change. One of the most noticeable differences is the improvement in the supply of goods in the shops; now everything is available, although prices are not exactly cheap.

Unfortunately, however, this has not been matched by a parallel improvement in the city's public transport facilities. During the rush hours, from 6–8 a.m. and 3–5 p.m., trams and buses are full to overflowing and in the city there are long traffic jams.

Saturday morning is the time when most Warsaw families do their shopping. On Saturdays, but now to some extent also straight after work on Friday, many Varsovians pack up their cars, leave the city and go to spend the weekend in the country. On Sundays the streets are almost empty; most people who have stayed behind in the city leave their cars in the garage and make their way unhurriedly to early morning mass. After an hour or so of spiritual refreshment the trend is to go for a walk in one of the many parks.

The numerous cafés are very popular as places to go for a relaxing hour or two and a chat with friends. This is certainly the case on public holidays, with only one exception: on Corpus Christi almost everyone takes part in the festival processions.

The right-hand bank, the flat side of the river with the district known as **Praga**, suffered relatively little damage during the war. This is where many of the city's large industrial works are located, among them the car factory which produces the **Polonez**, and the well-known confectionery factory **E. Wedel**. On this side of the river there are also the Greek Catholic church, **Cerkiew**, which dates from the 19th century, and the German embassy.

The particular local flavour of this part of the city is best reflected by the **Różycki Bazaar**. The most interesting view of the old town is also obtained from this point.

Warsaw, a city that has risen from ruins of war, has once more become a lively metropolis.

The individual touch.

144

IN MAZOVIA

The historic region that surrounds Warsaw is known as Mazovia. From 1138–1526 it was an independent princedom, but after this it was divided up. Because of its geographical situation, this region functioned as a bridge between the two capitals of the Polish-Lithuanian crown – **Cracow** and **Vilnius**, and it was inevitable that eventually the town in the middle, Warsaw, would be elevated to the status of capital of Poland. The landscape of Mazovia is generally either flat or gently rolling, and was formed by Ice-Age moraines. The river valleys are of particular scenic beauty.

Immediately adjacent to Warsaw is **Kampinowski Park Narodowy** (Kampinowski National Park), which, with an area of 86,385 acres (35,000 hectares), is the largest national park in Poland. Moors, dunes and large areas of woodland in the Vistula flats still provide an ideal environment for elks and other big game. During World War II many Poles were brought here secretly and shot by the Nazis. The most notorious location of such executions is **Palmira** in the *Puszcza Kampinowska*. After the war a proper cemetery was constructed, which contains the graves of 2,500 such victims.

Not far from Palmira, where the River Narew flows into the Vistula, stands the gigantic **Modlin Fortress**, made of earth bricks and constructed in 1806 by order of Napoleon. Later it was reinforced and extended; the barracks alone has a circumference of 10,500 ft (2,800 metres) and is the longest building in Europe. It accommodated the entire garrison of the fortress, which numbered 26,000 men. East of Modlin is the **Zegrzyński Lagoon** that was formed by high water and the water pressure of the Narew. Many people come here from Warsaw at weekends.

Further down the Narew is **Pułtusk**, an old town situated on an island. This town has twice achieved world fame: in 1806 through the battle that was fought here between the Napoleonic and Russian armies, and in 1868 when an enormous meteorite, the Pułtusk meteorite, landed nearby. The former **Bishop's Palace** is today the headquarters of Polonia, a non-profit-making organisation that looks after Poland's cultural heritage. The longest marketplace in Poland, a cobbled square dominated by a Gothic town hall tower, extends as far as the collegiate church. This dates from 1443, with a splendid Renaissance nave added in 1554. Pułtusk also boasts a number of other attractive old churches worth visiting and parts of its original town wall.

The road which leads out of Pułtusk in a northwesterly direction passes next through **Gołymin**, which is famous for its Gothic church. Not far from Gołymin is the town of **Ciechanów**, with venerable old Gothic buildings that testify to its long history. The impressively large castle and two churches, are striking examples of Masovian brick Gothic architecture. The countryside north of Ciechanów was the scene of a massive battle in September 1939, when the Germans attempted to march straight through it to Warsaw. The many military cemeteries that are to be found in this area are a reminder of this particular conflict, in which numerous soldiers lost their lives.

Close to Ciechanow is the little village of **Opinogóra**. In the crypt of the church is the tomb of one of the greatest Polish romantic poets, Zygmunt Krasinski. The small local palace houses a museum documenting his work, and in the splendid park there is a monument to the poet.

Further to the east is the expanse of wooded countryside known as **Kurpie**. The wooden houses here are some of the most beautiful in all Poland. The best place to stay and admire them is **Nowogród Łomżyński** where the River Pisa flows into the Narew, which has an attractive open-air museum.

Not far from Nowogród, in the small village of **Łyse**, folk artists and local people congregate on Palm Sunday every year when a prize is awarded for the most beautiful **Easter Palm**. These palms can still be seen after Easter, as

they are kept for a long time in the church and the belltower. The wooden church is the work of carpenters from Kurpia; the impressive interior was decorated by local artists.

From Łyse the road continues to the "Capital of Kurpia", **Myszyniec**. Every year on the Thursday after Trinity Sunday the Corpus Christi procession sets out from the square in front of the neo-Gothic church. It is a very colourful occasion, with all the participants dressed for the occasion in the old national costumes.

A similarly colourful procession can also be seen in nearby **Kadzidła**. This is also the place to watch the women skilfully producing the traditional silhouettes made from coloured paper. In the town's church there is an exhibition devoted solely to this form of folk art.

Continuing eastwards, **Łomża** on the River Narwia, has an interesting permanent exhibition of amber, which was once mined in Kurpia. Also in Łomża is an attractive Gothic cathedral with a beautiful interior.

150

The lower reaches of the banks of the Vistula are lined by many interesting towns with long histories. In **Czerwińsk** a church displaying both Romanesque and Gothic features towers high above the river valley. In the adjoining monastery a church ethnographical museum is housed.

Further down the Vistula we come to **Płock**, which is the capital of Northern Mazovia. The ruins of a castle, many churches from all epochs and in all styles and the oldest grammar school in Poland (founded in 1180) are the dominant features of this historic town. In the crypt of the cathedral are the tombs of two Polish kings, Władysław Herman and Bolesław Krzywousty. The **Museum of Masovia** is especially worth a visit; it houses the best Art Nouveau collection in Poland.

According to the *Guinness Book of Records*, the 2,099-ft (646-metre) high transmission tower of the radio programme *Warszawa I* in **Konstantynowo**, close to Płock, is the highest tower in the world. Opposite Płock, near

Siepiec, is a picturesque open-air museum with examples of the typical architecture of Northern Mazovia; this can be combined with a visit to the centre for folk art sculpture in nearby **Zawid Kościelny**. Further south, on the right bank of the Vistula, lies **Maciejowice**. In the year 1794 Tadeusz Kościuszko led the Polish troops into battle against Russia: their defeat was to seal the fate of the Polish state.

Warka, on the opposite bank, attracts many visitors. The suburb of **Winiary** is well-known as the birthplace of General Kazimierz Pułaski, the freedom hero of Poland and the USA, and, as might be expected, it contains both a museum and two monuments named after him. Continuing in the direction of Warsaw, we come to the town of **Góra Kalwaria**, which was modelled on the city of Jerusalem and is the destination of many Catholic pilgrims. Later on in its history it also became a religious centre for Orthodox Jews and the home of a rabbi who was said to perform miracles.

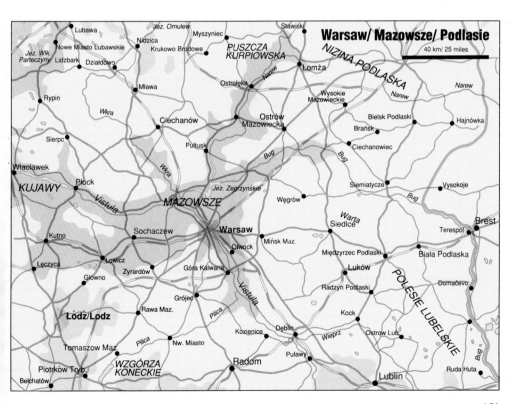

East of Warsaw – Podlasie: The open countryside of the region known as Podlasie begins east of Warsaw and extends right to the eastern border of Poland. In the Middle Ages this area was uninhabited and separated the Polish tribes from the East Slavs. Settlement was hampered by the constant invasions of the Jadzwingers, who lived further to the north.

When in the 13th century the danger subsided, Poles settled the heathland region from the west and Belorussians moved in from the east. Even today there are places which contain both a Russian Orthodox church and a Catholic church.

Until 1939 every town in this region also had a synagogue, and in addition there were many Protestant churches and even two mosques in the area. Podlasie was always a melting pot of many different cultures and peoples, a region where the Latin culture of Western Europe met the Byzantine culture of Eastern Europe.

Podlasie is characterised by the Ice-Age moraines typical of lowland landscapes. Many charming wooden houses have been preserved, and large wooden crosses in the vicinity of churches and cemeteries still exert a sobering influence on passing travellers.

The town of **Węgrów** is typical of the Podlasie region. Next to the market square is a Gothic **Parish church**, which was rebuilt in baroque style and decorated with frescoes by Michael Angelo Palloni in the early 18th century. In the sacristy hangs the famous **Magic Mirror** dating from the 17th century. The **Church of the Reformation** was built by a Polish architect of Dutch origin, Tylman van Gameran. It also has frescoes by Palloni and the splendid tomb of Jan Krasiński which dates from 1703. Among those buried in the Protestant cemetery are Scottish weavers who settled in this area. The Jewish settlement has long since vanished – in the Piski district of Węgrów there was an extermination camp for Jews that was known as "Little Treblinka".

The village of **Liw**, west of Węgrów

Vernacular architecture in Podlasie.

and already within the borders of Mazovia, is dominated by a massive castle. It was built in the 15th century but was destroyed twice by the Swedes and was only partially reconstructed. A later building dating from the baroque era, the **Starostwa**, houses a museum of weaponry.

Siedlce, the capital of the voivodeship, is predominantly an 18th-century town. The figure of Atlas bearing the globe crowns the **Town Hall**, which is also called the *Jacek*. The former prison, which dates from 1841–44, is today a museum, and the town possesses many monuments reminding the visitor of its turbulent history, of the persecution of the community's Jews and the advance of the Soviet army in 1944.

Biała Podlaska, a town which like Siedlce is situated on the railway line between Warsaw and Moscow, was founded in the 15th century and for a long time belonged to the Radziwiłłs, one of the richest aristocratic families in Poland. During the occupation there was a camp to which Polish and later also Russian, French and Italian prisoners-of-war were taken. The cemetery in ul. **Łukaszyńska** testifies to the inhuman conditions prevailing in the camp, where thousands died of hunger and exhaustion.

The **Radziwiłł Castle** only partially survived the upheavals of Polish history. A pavilion with towers and a chapel, surrounded by a parapet, are all that has been preserved.

The churches of Biała Podlaska date back to the 16th and 17th centuries, although the new Greek Orthodox church was only consecrated in 1989. The monument to Jozef Ignacy Kraszewski (1812–87) recalls that this was where the famous Polish writer went to school. The museum dedicated to his memory is located in **Romanowo**, the picturesque village in which Kraszewski spent his childhood, which is approximately 30 miles (50 km) southwest of Biała.

Lying north of Biała, close to the border with the Soviet Union, is Janów Podlaski, famous for its large stud farm.

The Narew haff (lagoon).

There is an international demand for the splendid Arab horses which are bred and reared here.

The upper reaches of the **River Bug** are dominated by the walls of the town of **Terespol**, an important border crossing. On the other side of the river, in the USSR, is the former fortress town of **Brest**. Still further upriver is **Koden**, destination of many pilgrimages on account of the miraculous picture, the **Virgin of Koden**, that is kept in the town's church. Koden has a special significance for the Catholics of Podlasie and Belorussia, similar to that of Częstochowa for the rest of Poland. On the site of the former castle is a Gothic church that was once Greek Orthodox; it contains a wooden sculpture, well worth seeing, which depicts the martyrdom of the Polish people and the stations of the cross.

Jabłeczna, not far from Koden and also on the River Bug, is the centre of the Greek Orthodox faith in Poland. The most important buildings in the town are the **Church of St Onufrie** (1840) and the only Greek Orthodox monastery and seminary for priests in Poland. Every year in June there is a lively country fair held here.

The most interesting town on the Bug, however, is **Drohiczyn**. Today a place of no particular significance, it was once the scene of a coronation when Prince Daniel crowned himself King of the Ukraine. The barrows in the area surrounding the town date from the 7th to the 9th centuries and the settlement itself, with a history which goes back to the 7th century, was once the customs post between Poland and the Ukraine. Archaeological excavations carried out here brought to light thousands of lead seals from all over Europe, some of which are now on display in the town's museum. A dominant feature of the town is the castle hill, which towers over the river.

On the river itself there is a concrete Soviet bunker dating from the time of the 1939 Ribbentrop-Molotov Pact; at this time Drohiczyn belonged to the Soviets. A series of similar bunkers, **Poland's stud farms are world famous.**

also known as the "**Stalin Line**", is ranged along the Bug. Drohiczyn also has a notable Orthodox church and three notable baroque churches, which unfortunately suffered severe damage during World War I.

Northwest of Drohiczyn is the little town of **Ciechanowiec**, with a fascinating agricultural museum that is well worth visiting. The best part of this museum is the open air section with its exhibition of wooden buildings from Podlasie – houses, silos, taverns, mills and windmills. The section which covers veterinary medicine is also extremely interesting.

Not far from Ciechanowiec is the village of **Treblinka** (*see box*). In the work camp Treblinka I (1941–44) and the extermination camp Treblinka II (1942–43) approximately 800,000 people were murdered.

The **Białowieska Heath**, the most unspoilt forest in Europe, runs along the eastern border of Poland. Once the hunting ground of Lithuanian princes, Polish kings and Russian czars, this national park is now a world reserve under the special protection of UNESCO. It is here that primeval bison may still be seen roaming at liberty, and other species of animals and plants threatened with extinction are also protected. Wild horses (tarpans), reindeer, red deer, wild boar, wolves and rare species of bird are all to be found living in the wild in this park. In order that the animals are not disturbed and the natural surroundings are preserved in their present unspoilt condition, the park may only be visited in the company of a guide. In the village of **Białowieża** the former palace has been converted into a hotel, next to which is the informative natural history museum. On the way to Hajnowki there is a show reserve for bison and wild horses. In **Hajnowki**, on the western edge of the park, stands an imposing Greek Orthodox church, the combined work of artists from Poland, Greece and Bulgaria.

The largest town in northeast Poland is **Białystok**. The massive baroque palace of the Branicki is a particularly interesting piece of architecture; it is also called the "**Versailles of Podlasie**". Today it houses the Medical Academy. The adjacent arsenal, built in 1755, is used for exhibitions. In the town hall is an exhibition of Polish art that is well worth seeing, with an unusual section dealing with the art of the Jadzwingers. The Greek Orthodox cathedral dates back to the 16th century: the modern **Church of St Roch** provides an interesting contrast. The former summer palace of the Branickis in **Choroszcz**, 7½ miles (12 km) away, is worth a detour for anyone with a keen interest in interior design.

Twenty-six miles (42 km) northeast of Białystok is **Sokółka**. It was in this region that Jan III Sobieski halted the advance of the Tartars, and a whole section of the local museum is given over to this event. In the villages of **Bohoniki** and **Kruszyniany** are the only two remaining mosques in Poland, and there is an active Islamic community here. Certain characteristics of Slav architecture are also evident in these wooden Islamic buildings, which date from the 18th and 19th centuries, and in the Islamic cemeteries.

Nature lovers will be enchanted with the little River **Biebrza**. Along its banks the largest marshy area in Poland, and almost certainly one of the largest in Europe, has been preserved in its original state. Here there are still reindeer, beavers, wolves and thousands of waterfowl. The Biebrza is an ideal area for trying out water sports. Photo safaris are organised on the river and in the surrounding area with local guides who are expert in Biebrza's natural history.

Between Warsaw and Łódź: There are two possible routes that can be taken in a westerly direction from Warsaw. The northern one of the two runs along the edge of the Puszcza Kampinowska and passes through the village of **Kampinos**. Here the little wooden church dating from the 18th century is a good example of how the craftsmen in the villages made use of the simple building materials available to them to imitate the stone baroque churches in the towns.

Further along this route is **Żelazowa Wola**, the birthplace of Frédéric Cho-

CHOPIN

Ask a Pole what music touches him most deeply, or what music immediately suggests itself to him when he contemplates the melancholic landscape of Mazovia, and it is almost a hundred percent certain that he will say Chopin.

Frédéric François (Franciszek) Chopin is Poland's most famous composer. It is somewhat paradoxical that the man who created the romantic musical style of Poland was half-French on his father's side and spent the largest part of his life outside its borders as an emigrant.

Chopin was born in the year 1810 in the village of Żelazowa Wola, where his father was employed as a tutor at the house of Count Skarbek. He spent his youth in Warsaw and in the villages surrounding the capital made the acquaintance of the folk songs and dances that he later drew on in almost all of his works. He made his debut when he was still a small boy, appearing in charity concerts, and he played in the elegant salons of the aristocracy, who praised him most effusively as "Mozart's successor".

His first attempts at composition, primarily polonaises, also date from this period.

In autumn of 1830, immediately before the outbreak of the November Uprising, Chopin left Warsaw – as fate would have it for ever. Via Dresden, Vienna, Salzburg and Munich he finally arrived in Paris, and it was here that he achieved world fame. During his first few years in Paris he was still giving numerous piano recitals, at which he mainly played his own works, but later on he concentrated almost exclusively on composition. He was friends with many of the famous musicians of his day, including Franz Liszt.

In 1836 he met in Paris the novelist George Sand – a complicated lover but also a caring friend who looked after him during the long years of his illness. In the autumn of 1838 he journeyed with her and her two children to Valdemosa on Majorca, in the hopes of at last finding a cure for his weak lung. Among the pieces that he composed in this wild and romantic landscape were the famous *Preludes*, the splendid *Polonaise in A major* and the sonata which includes the funeral march. To his contemporary detractors this second sonata in B minor was nothing but a mass of confused sound – the ultimate in dissonance.

In spite of the mild climate on the Mediterranean island, Chopin's health steadily deteriorated. As a result, when he returned to Paris, he had to abandon composition altogether and earn his living by giving piano lessons to the wealthy. He took up composition again during a summer that he spent at George Sand's country estate in Nohant: among the pieces he wrote here was the *Polonaise in A flat major*. In 1847 George Sand, his companion for so long and the undoubted bedrock of his emotional life, finally broke with him and the composer was left lonely, increasingly ill and pretty well penniless.

In an attempt to escape from his painful memories he decided to flee to London, where he was introduced into high society by his pupil Jane Stirling. He gave numerous concerts at court, performing, for example, for the Duchess of Sutherland, Queen Victoria and Prince Albert.

But the composer himself felt empty and burnt out. "Where have my abilities gone, what has happened to my heart? I can hardly remember how they sing at home. The world is sinking round me in a strange fashion," he lamented. In 1848 he gave his very last public concert in London, where he had become gravely ill.

Even after his return to Paris he did not regain his strength, and he died in 1849 in his home at Place Vendôme 12.

At his funeral ceremony Mozart's *Requiem* was played, in accordance with a wish he had expressed. He was buried in the Père-Lachaise Cemetery in Paris, and his heart is kept in the Church of the Holy Cross in Warsaw.

With all his inner inconsistencies, Chopin managed both to irritate the music world and – as is still the case today – also to enrich it. His music is perhaps best described in the words of Franz Liszt: "The forms he created could only be free forms; he did violence to his genius as soon as he tried to submit it to rules and regulations not of his own making and not in accordance with the requirements of his creative spirit."

pin (1810) (*see page 157*). In the inn – his childhood home – is a museum documenting the life and work of the man who is Poland's most famous composer and pianist. It is especially worth coming here in the summer, when piano recitals are held almost every day in the park. This park was only created this century, between the two world wars, and provides a wonderful setting for Chopin's imaginative music. In **Brochowo**, which is where Chopin's parents were married, Chopin's baptismal certificate is kept in the late medieval fortified church. The formidable towers and walls of this building make it look more like a place of defence than a place of worship.

The second route from Warsaw to the west, which runs south of the one just described, leads through **Paprotnia**, which has a classical inn and a smithy, both of which are at least 200 years old. Napoleon himself is said to have once feasted in the restaurant, hence the name **Kuźnia Napoleońska**. The Franciscan monastery and church were built in 1927 by St Maximilian Kolbe. Monk and abbot of the monastery, Kolbe, died to save the life of a fellow-prisoner in Auschwitz in 1941, and was canonised in 1982. The church of **Niepokalanów** was built between 1948 and 1954; it also contains a Maximilian Kolbe memorial hall. In the cellar are exhibitions entitled "One thousand years of Polish history" and "The mystery of the sufferings of our Lord".

The two routes leading out of Warsaw in a westerly direction meet in **Sochaczew**, which contains the ruins of the palace of the princes of Mazovia and a museum devoted to the **Battle of the Bzura**. This was the biggest defensive battle fought by the Poles in 1939. It also contains a unique **Narrow-Gauge Railway Museum**.

From Sochaczew there is also a road branching off to the south in the direction of **Bolimów**. This community has no buildings of particular architectural interest, but is well-known for quite a different reason: it was here that on 31 December 1914, the Germans first used tear gas as a weapon. When this did not prove quite as effective as they had expected, they used chlorine instead, first in Belgium near Ypres in 1915, and then again in Bolimów in 1915, when 11,000 Russian soldiers were killed. It was not until much later that the use of gas was internationally banned by the Geneva Convention.

Not far from Bolimow is **Nieborów**, one of the most magnificent palaces in a parkland setting in Poland. The palace, designed by Tylman van Gameren and built from 1690–96, today houses a museum with valuable exhibits, among them a Roman sculpture of Niobe, portraits of European monarchs and a giant Italian globe dating from the 17th century. These works of art were collected by the Radziwiłł family, who owned Nieborów until 1945. Among the sculptures dotted around the beautiful park are the *Stone Women*, brought here from the steppes on the shores of the Black Sea. A second romantic park known as **Arcadia** is also located in Nieborów.

The old trading city of Łowicz forms the centre of the region. Here the beautiful, brightly-coloured national costumes have been retained, and the traditional folk arts and crafts have not yet degenerated to the level of mass-production for the tourists. The wood carvings, silhouettes and colourful hand-woven materials of Łowicz are famous and much in demand all over Poland.

The processions that take place at Corpus Christi are particularly colourful affairs. Anyone who is particularly interested in traditions of this kind should pay a visit to the museum housed in a baroque palace located right on the market square. The nearby church contains the tombs of the Polish primates, the princes of the church who took over the leadership of the state between rulers, until the new king was crowned.

Not far from Łowicz is a monument from the world of technology. The road from Warsaw to Poznań passes over a steel bridge that was the first in Europe to be electrically welded.

South of Łowicz, close to the railway line, is the village of **Lipce**. The famous Polish writer and Nobel prize winner

Władysław Reymont lived here from 1889-91, and set the story of his best-known novel *Chlopi* in this village.

Łódź: With its 850,000 inhabitants Łódź is today the second largest town in Poland, with light industry and 50 percent of the Polish textile industry located within its boundaries. Łódź was granted a town charter as long ago as 1432, but in 1820 still only had 800 inhabitants – a place of no significance whatsoever. Things began to change in 1823 with the building of **Nowe Miasto**, the first textile workers' estate. The removal of the customs barriers between Poland and Russia led to an enormous increase in the export of textiles to Russia, and in the second half of the 19th century Łódź became the most important textile centre in the world.

During World War II the Germans opened two large transit camps in Łódź for Polish prisoners-of-war, as well as a camp for Russian airmen, a camp for 5,000 gypsies from Germany, Austria and the Balkans and also a camp for 4,000 Polish children. Approximately 260,000 Jews were murdered here, and the people of Łódź itself were also affected; of its 600,000 inhabitants only around half survived the war.

After the war new estates grew up around the original districts of the town. In addition to the traditional textile industry, electrical engineering and chemical industries also came to Łódź. The first institutions of further education were founded, the most famous being the State College of Cinematic Art, Drama and Television (*see page 159*). The University of Łódź now also has a Department of Polish for foreigners.

Typical of Łódź are the ensembles that have remained from the 19th century; the industrialist's villa, the factory and the modest little houses of the textile workers. They were built in imitation of previous architectural styles, especially the Gothic and baroque styles, as were also the interesting town residences in **Piotrkowska** and **Moniuszko** streets. At least 30 houses in the Art Nouveau mode, in Polish "*Secesja*", have however also been preserved.

There are three museums that are particularly worth visiting:
● The **Art Museum** in the palace once owned by the Poznanski family, where Polish and international art from the 19th century onwards is exhibited. The main emphasis is on modern art, an area where further discoveries may be expected, especially in Poland
● The **Historical Museum of Łódź**, accommodated in another of the Poznański family's palaces, which has a surprisingly varied interior
● The **Central Textile Museum** in the White Factory: in 1838 this was the first spinning mill in Łódź to be fitted with a steam-driven engine. There is a fascinating portrayal of the development of technology in the textile industry and its social consequences in Poland and the subject is rounded off with a collection of 16th to 19th century textiles from all over the world.

Before the war over 30 percent of the inhabitants of Łódź were Jewish. Artur Rubinstein, the famous pianist and composer, was also born here, and the excellent philharmonic hall of Łódź has been named after him. The Jewish community was wiped out during the war and both synagogues and the old Jewish cemetery were destroyed. Only the new cemetery survived, with around 120,000 gravestones and the imposing **Izrael Poznański Mausoleum** erected during the period from 1893 to 1939. Today it is the largest Jewish cemetery in Poland and one of the largest anywhere in the world.

The surroundings of Łódź: North of Łódź is **Łęczyca**, which in the Middle Ages was one of the most powerful towns in Poland. In the nearby village of **Tum** is a Romanesque church dating from 1141–45, and adjacent to it the ruins of an old castle. Łęczyca itself has a number of monuments: a Gothic castle with an ethnographical museum, well-preserved town walls and a classical town hall. Not far from **Kutno** is **Oporów**, which has a charming Gothic castle museum situated on an artificial island.

East of Łódź, in **Rawa Mazowiecka**, is a Gothic castle. It unfortunately suffered severe damage in both world wars,

THE FILM SCHOOL OF ŁÓDŹ

"It was through a mere whim of history that Łódź became the film capital of Poland. In the years immediately after the war the capital, Warsaw, lay in ruins, and it was for this reason that the government chose the nearest suitable town when looking for a place to establish a centre of cinematography. It was common sense to site it where there was already a film institute: the choice was Łódź, and so it has also remained," says Roman Polanski (photo) in his biography *Roman by Polanski*. Two years after World War II the film course was also transferred from Cracow to Łódź and from then on it was here that filmmakers received their training. The communist authorities appropriated a small palace belonging to an industrialist, and by 1948 they had already promoted the school to the status of a college.

Łódź was an industrial town. By contrast with Cracow, writes Polanski, it was devoid of all charm, to such an extent that the joy experienced by applicants at being accepted by the school was tempered by doubts as to whether they could really stand living in such a dump for five whole years.

Right from the beginning the school was totally oriented towards the production of an elite. Although the country had been devastated by the war, the school was very well equipped and had excellent teachers.

The authorities did not spare any costs. The reason why they went to so much trouble is probably summed up in the quote by Lenin that is displayed, carved in marble, in the main hall: "Of all the forms of art we have, film is the most important one."

In the 1950s the Polish filmmakers were bound by the socialist style and there was no room for originality and freedom of thought. Only after Stalin's death did it become possible to make films that did not have to reflect the propaganda clichés of the communist government.

There emerged in Łódź what came to be known as the "Polish Film School". Its founders portrayed the past war and the heroism of this time in a new light. For the first time they were able to concentrate in their films on the problem of human loneliness. *Kanal* (Sewel) (Silver Palm in Cannes in 1957) and *Ashes and Diamonds* (FIPRESCI in Venice in 1959) by Andrzej Wajda and *Eroica* by Andrzej Munk – the best-known postwar productions – all date from this period.

A few years later Jerzy Kawalerowicz made *Mother Jeanne of the Angels* (Silver Palm in Cannes 1961) and Roman Polanski made the film that was nominated for an Oscar, *Knife in the Water* (FIPRESCI in Venice 1962).

The school trains directors and cameramen. Its curriculum includes the humanities and technical subjects as well as practical training, since its aim is to combine the qualities of a university, a polytechnic and an academy of fine arts. It has its own film studios where students can make practice and diploma films. Feature films are made in conjunction with professional film institutes.

Almost all contemporary Polish directors are graduates of the film school in Łódź, among them Andrzej Wajda and Roman Polanski, who have both become world famous.

Wajda (born in 1926) has been positively heaped with prizes: for *The Promised Land* (Moscow 1975; Valladolid 1976; Cartagena 1978; nomination for an Oscar), *The Iron Man* (Grand Prix Cannes 1981) and *Danton* (Prix Delluc 1983; Cezar 1983) – to name but a few. Today Wajda is the undisputed authority as far as young directors are concerned. In 1989, in the first free elections in Poland, he also became a member of the Senate.

Polanski on the other hand left Poland at a much earlier stage and made films abroad that enjoyed a huge international success: *Rosemary's Baby*, *Repulsion*, *Chinatown*, *The Tenant* and *Dance of the Vampires*.

Towards the end of the 1980s the films being produced by the younger directors dwelt with almost painful precision on the sad social realities of this decade, whilst at the same time attempting to establish a new manifestation of human solidarity. Krzysztof Kieslowski's 10-part series *Dekalog* about the Ten Commandments is a good example of this development.

so that much of the present building is a reconstruction. The village of **Boguszyce** near Rawa seldom attracts visitors, but is well worth a detour for its splendid wooden church. This church was built in 1558, and although not much to look at from the outside is magnificently decorated inside with paintings in the Renaissance style.

South of Łódź, in the area of **Bełchatów**, there are large deposits of brown coal. Further to the east is the industrial town of **Piotrków Trybunalski**, which has a well-known glassworks. The former royal palace, which was built from 1511–19, now houses a museum: other historic sights in Piotrków are the remains of the town walls, some valuable churches and the synagogue. The municipal station dates from 1850, when the railway line was built from Warsaw to Vienna. Brickwork stations like this are typical of this particular area.

A favourite place for weekend excursions is the River **Pilica** with its romantic villages and medieval castles surrounded by water. In **Inowłódż** is a Romanesque church founded by the Polish king, Władysław Herman, with a high stone tower that dominates the surrounding countryside. Close by is **Spała**; a popular spa which has a beautiful wooden church.

In the suburb of **Tomaszów Mazowiecki** there is a national park, **Niebieskie Źródła**. Its name, which means "Blue springs" is a reference to the blue sheen of the water, derived from the minerals it contains. Further upriver from Pilica is an artificial reservoir which supplies Łódź with drinking water. Here, in **Sulejów**, is an old Cistercian monastery, which is one of Poland's most important architectural monuments. It was founded and financed by Prince Kazimierz the Just in 1177. The well-fortified complex, still very imposing even today, includes a church, the ruins of a monastery, defensive walls with bastions and farm buildings. Today it houses a hotel.

Southwest of Łódź is **Zduńska Wola**, where, in 1894, the holy abbot Maximilian Kolbe was born (*see also*

Niepokalanów). As long ago as the 6th century a castle was built in the meadows by the River Warta not far from **Sieradz**, of which the round church is one of the remaining buildings. The Gothic parish church of Sieradz dates from the 14th century and the **Jagiełło House** is today the location of the regional museum.

In **Wieluń** the fortified walls with the Cracow Gate have also been preserved; the classical town hall was built on to these older constructions in 1842. The **Pauline Church**, which was originally a Gothic church and also has a splendid baroque interior, is the most outstanding of the churches and historic buildings in this town.

There are 37 old wooden churches in the vicinity of Sieradz which have survived the ravages of time. One of them, the **Church of the Holy Spirit** which stands in Sieradz cemetery, was built after the victory over the crusaders near Grunwald in 1410.

The church in **Grębień**, near Wieluń, is also particularly interesting: the interior is decorated with Gothic-Renaissance wall paintings which date from 1500–31. In **Ożarów** is an interesting ancestral seat, built of wood and dating from 1757. It is now a museum of interior design. Also well worth seeing is the 14th-century walled manor in nearby **Trubadzin**.

Between the Vistula and the Pilica: In the past this area was part of Little Poland. In the north it is mainly flat, but towards the south it becomes hilly. The wooded hills known as the **Góry Świętokrzyskie** or Holy Cross Hills are particularly attractive.

Close to Warsaw is **Czarnolas**, the village where Jan Kochanowski (1530–84) lived. This poet was one of the first to write in Polish, the usual written language in Poland in those days being Latin. He is buried in the church of nearby **Zwoleń**. Further to the west a monumental Gothic-Renaissance palace, now in ruins, towers above the town of **Drzewica**.

This region was the scene of the fiercest partisan battles in Poland and in the whole of Europe during World War

II. The commander of the Polish freedom fighters, Henryk Dobrzański, generally known as "Hubal", fell not far from the village of **Studzianna**, which is well-known for its baroque church. In revenge for Hubal's resistance many of the surrounding villages were burned down by the Germans and all men over 15 years of age were murdered. The village which suffered the most was **Skloby**, where 265 people lost their lives and 400 buildings were set on fire.

The surroundings of Drzewica and Studzianna are referred to by the ethnologists as *Opoczyński*. Here traditional costumes are rather like those of Mazovia, with different striped patterns. Wood is still frequently used as a building material in this region and there are many folk artists dedicatedly continuing the silhouette tradition.

The largest town in this region is **Radom**, which is today an important centre complete with metal industry, leather and tobacco factories. The oldest monument in Radom is the **Church of St Waclaw**. The medieval town centre has also been preserved, and there is an open-air museum with examples of the various building styles of this particular area. The old beehives of many shapes and sizes that are on display here are especially unusual.

South of Radom on country road E 77 is the village of **Orońsko**, where a centre of Polish sculpture has been established at Heimstatt, the former manor that once belonged to the famous painter Józef Brandt (1841–1915). The sculptures by modern artists in stone and ceramics are visible from the road.

A little further along this route, in the local palace of **Szydłowiec**, is the **Instrument Museum**, the only one of its kind in Poland. Other features of Szydłowiec are a Renaissance town hall, a large Jewish cemetery and a well-known sandstone quarry.

An alternative route leads from Radom to Sandomierz. Immediately after Radom we come to **Skaryszewo**. The horse market held here on the Monday six weeks after Easter attracts large numbers of gypsies, farmers and horse-lovers from all over Poland. It's an event well worth catching if you can.

Somewhat further along this road is **Iłża** – the scene of a major battle in 1939. The tower of the palace of the bishops of Cracow, a building that is now a ruin, was used in the battle as an observation point by the Polish army. A few miles from **Ostrowiec Swiętokrzyski** in **Krzemionki Opatowskie** is a quartz mine which is known to have been in existence in the Neolithic period when it was one of the largest in Europe. One section of it can be visited.

On the Kamienna between the industrial town of **Skarżysko-Kamienna** and **Starachowice** is **Wąchock** which has a Romanesque-Gothic church and a Cistercian monastery dating from the beginning of the 13th century. The monastery contains the most beautiful examples of Romanesque art in the whole of Poland. Another famous partisan leader from World War II, Jan Piwnik "Ponury" is buried here.

Further to the south runs a line of rocky mountains known as **Góry Swiętokrzyskie**. Amidst their wild and romantic scenery there are many places worth visiting. In **Samsonowo** are the ruins of a metalworks dating from the beginning of the last century and now a technological monument. Nearby is "Bartek", one of the largest and oldest oak trees in Poland. The trunk has a circumference of over 29 ft (9 metres). Another well-known place is **Oblęgorek**. This was where Henryk Sienkiewicz, the author of the novel *Quo Vadis*, lived until 1914.

The capital of this mountainous region is **Kielce**. Its bishop's palace was built in the 17th century, and now houses the National Museum: this includes a gallery of Polish art and a section dealing with the interior decor of palaces. Just opposite the palace is a baroque cathedral with an interior preserved in its original style and a beautiful sculpture of the Virgin Mary made of galena, a lead ore.

Northeast of Kielce rises the **Łysa Góra** (Bare Mountain) with its forbidding scree slopes. Situated on this mountain is the **Łysa Góra** or **Holy Cross Monastery** belonging to the Benedictine order, where a relic of the Holy Cross is kept. Before the monastery came into existence there was a pre-Christian sanctuary on this spot.

Today the countryside is unfortunately marred by a television broadcasting tower. The whole area surrounding Łysa Góra is a national park which extends over a total of 15,000 acres (6,054 hectares). The heath has splendid pine and larch woods and there are numerous clearings and deforested areas which are dotted with large boulders.

At the foot of this range of mountains is the attractive village of **Nowa Slupia**. There was already an iron industry here in the second century and it is perfectly possible that iron was exported from this area to the Roman Empire. Remains of the old furnaces are on display in the local museum.

All these mountains are composed of sandstone, and it is only north of Kielce that limestone begins to predominate. Here magnificent marble is also to be found, and even semi-precious stones such as malachite and azurite are relatively common. On the way from Kielce to Chęcin it is very worthwhile making a detour to see the most beautiful Polish grotto, known as **Paradise**. This grotto is open to visitors from 1 June to 30 November.

The ruins of an old castle tower above the little town of **Chęcin**, once a place of considerable wealth. For centuries the town was the centre of the lead ore mining industry.

The next place of importance on the road towards Cracow is **Jędrzejów**. Its Romanesque-Gothic church and the Cistercian monastery are interesting places: the monastery was rebuilt in baroque style. The town is, however, best known for its museum, which is named after the local Przypkowski family and includes their fascinating collection of sundials.

In the region east of Jędrzejów lies **Szydłów,** a sleepy little village that once had a town charter. It's a pleasant place to stop for a wander; its town walls and church have survived the upheavals of the ages undamaged.

A girl in typical traditional costume.

162

MAŁOPOLSKA/ LITTLE POLAND

Małopolska has been an important historical region of Poland ever since the 15th century. Stretching as it once did all the way from Cracow to Kiev, it was during all the centuries of division and foreign rule that Małopolska developed into the most loyal defender of Polish culture and tradition.

Today Małopolska covers the southeastern corner of Poland between the Soviet Union and Czechoslovakia. The southern part consists of the Carpathian mountains and their foothills which run along the Czech border. This is followed in the centre by the low-lying **Kotlina Sandomierska Basin**, to the north of which rise the **Wyżyna Małopolska** (the Małopolska Highlands). These are made up of a number of separate low ranges of hills in the centre of which stand the **Wyżyna Krakowsko-Częstochowska** (Cracow-Częstochowska Highlands). To the east the **Wyżyna Lubelska** (Lubin Highlands) jut out above the surrounding plains. The region is dissected by a number of rivers and streams such as the **Vistula**, **Dunajec**, **Wisłoka** and **San**, creating a landscape of great variety.

Particularly in the southern and eastern parts of Małopolska there still exist large areas of virgin forest, such as the **Puszcza Niepołomicka**, **Puszcza Sandomierska** and **Puszcza Solska**. Both mixed and pine forest flourish and provide home to deer and stag, packs of wolves, linx and even European bison and brown bears. Seven national parks as well as a dozen natural preserves and several hundred nature reserves have been established.

The city of Cracow lies right in the middle of all this countryside. It has been the historical capital of Poland for almost 1,000 years, and because of its architectural compactness and variety it has the title "world cultural city". Cracow's historical splendour provides an urban museum with few rivals and it rates as the most beautiful – and quaintest – of all Polish cities.

CRACOW

The city of Cracow (population 800,000) lies nestled in the valley of the River Vistula which runs between the Wyżyna Krakowsko-Częstochowska to the north and the foothills of the Carpathians to the south.

Although the origins of the city are lost in the darkness of antiquity, local archaeological findings confirm that man already dwelt in the area as long as 50,000 years ago.

In the early Middle Ages, the city existed as a fortified castle on the Wawel Heights above the river, on the spot where the royal palace now stands. The first written mention of the city was in 965 when it was documented as being an important trading centre. By the year 1000 it had become a cathedral town and in 1038 Wawel Castle became the seat of the Polish kings. The steady development of Cracow was halted twice (1241 and 1242) by Tartar invasions from the east.

In 1257, under the duke and later king Bolesław Wstydliwy, the settlement was expanded and came under the municipal law of Magdeburg. About 100 years later, the two new cities of Kazimierz and Kleparz were established in the vicinity. Today, they are separate districts of Cracow.

By the 15th century, Cracow had become a sizeable town of some 30,000 inhabitants, surrounded by fortified walls and turrets. One of the oldest universities of Central Europe, the Jagiełłonian University, had been established by King Kazimierz Wielki in 1384, so giving the town additional splendour and importance.

But the Cracow of the Middle Ages was not totally ruled by the academics; trade and handicrafts flourished as well. The city was situated at the junction of trade routes from western Europe to Byzantium and southern Europe to the Baltic. There were as many as 60 registered guilds and it was their fat profits, together with the hefty sponsorship of the citizenry and nobility, that secured lucrative contracts and a carefree existence for a multitude of master builders, painters and artisans who flocked in from all over Europe. The unmistakable countenance of this world culture city was created during this epoch.

When King Zygmunt III shifted the capital to Warsaw in 1609, Cracow lost much of its importance and suffered again through the wars that ravaged Poland in the 17th and 18th centuries. From 1815–46 Cracow was a free city and the capital of a mini-republic. In 1846 it was incorporated into the province of Galicia and so became a part of the Austrian Habsburg empire. The relatively liberal attitude of the Austrian authorities enabled Polish culture and science to progress, and even the activities of the independence movement were tolerated.

It was in this period that the painters Jan Matejko, Jacek Malczewski and Loen Wyczółkowski created their masterpieces and the forerunners of Polish Art Nouveau Stanisław Wyspiański and Jóseł Mehofer found the right environment for their work in Cracow. Józef Piłsudski, who later became Poland's head of state, also organised his legions from Cracow.

It must be mentioned that during its period under Austrian rule the city was metamorphosed into a powerful fortress which even managed to hold out against the Russian offensive of 1914. During the German occupation in World War II, Cracow was the capital of the General *Gouvernement*, whose governor general Hans Frank took up residence in the erstwhile royal palace on the Wawel.

Present-day Cracow, the third largest city in Poland, is an industrial as well as cultural centre. It was more for political reasons rather than any economic considerations, that the Sendzimir steelworks were established within the city area in 1949. The resultant wave of proletarian immigrants was intended to break the hold of the traditional elite families and impose the socialist spirit upon the royal city.

Fortunately these aims were only partially achieved, although a depressing

Preceding pages: the university city of Lublin; the trumpeter of Cracow. Left, the Wit Stwosz altar in the church of St Mary.

legacy remains in the clouds of dust and poison which bellow forth from the smoke stacks of the industrial part of the city and continue to make life rather uncomfortable for its inhabitants – whether patricians or proletarians.

Cracow is a city full of historical monuments. The centre has remained largely unchanged since the Middle Ages when it was built. The city walls were left standing until the 19th century, when they were replaced by a green belt, the so-called *Planty* which today surrounds the entire city centre and since very recently also marks the border of the no-traffic zone.

The heart of the city is the large Market Square, dominated by the Cloth Hall, which has remained a market hall in today's terms. Small shops have been installed in this large early-Renaissance building, and upstairs on the first floor there is a branch of the **National Museum** which houses a collection of Polish painting, including several works by Jan Matejko. The old Town Hall Tower/ **Wieża Ratuszowa** (11th century), the small Church of St Adalbert/**Kościół Św. Wojciecha** (10th century) and the memorial of the Polish poet Adam Mickiewicz (1898) complete the architectural ensemble on this side of the square. In the corner the spires of the Church of St Mary of the Assumption/ **Kościół Mariacki** (13th–15th century) soar heavenwards. The richly designed interior of the church contains a masterpiece of late-Gothic art, the carved high altar created by Wit Stowz from 1477–89. The craftsman's original German name was Veit Stoss, a man closely associated with the artistic heyday of his home city of Nuremberg. Every hour for the past 700 years, a trumpeter has played his tune from the church tower. It is strangely moving to listen to the mournful sound; the original watchman is said to have been struck by a Tartar arrow. Cracow is full of such quaint details and legends.

Painstakingly-restored houses and palazzi surround the market square. Many of them now house shops, lively cafés and restaurants, including the very **An art gallery beneath the city walls.**

special "**Wierzynek**" (*see page 172*).

When the sun shines the market square is full of animation. It is the setting for a number of Cracow's cultural events including the "Lajkonik", the investiture of the champion marksman of the city, and the annual exhibition of Christmas cribs.

In the northeastern corner of the market square Floriańska Street begins, a part of the **Royal Way** which afforded the rulers entry into the city from the Wawel. At the end of the street stands the only remaining remnant of the Middle Age city walls. It consists of **St Florian's Gate**, a piece of the city wall, four turrets, the arsenal and the **Barbican**, a defensive bastion built in 1498 which is the largest construction of its kind in Europe. Students from the nearby art academy have established a temporary art gallery under the wall.

Beyond the Barbican on Matejko Square/**Plac Matejki** stands the **Pomnik Grunwaldzki**, the monument to the Battle of Grunwald which the famous Polish musician Ignacy Paderewski

commissioned to commemorate this victory over the knights of the crusade in 1410.

There are two other places well worth visiting along the Florianska: the museum of Polish painter of historical scenes Jan Matejko (1898–93), **Muzeum Matejki**, which is housed in his birthplace, and the wonderful café Jama Michalikowa – a meeting point for artists ever since the days of Młoda Polska, where even today excellent cabaret is occasionally performed.

On the other side of the Rynek Główny, adjacent to the streets Św. Anna and Jagiellonski lies the Jagiełłonian University and the oldest university building, the **Collegium Maius**, the **University Museum** and the baroque **Church of St Anna**. Nearby, on the *Planty* and in front of the Collegium Novum stands the monument to **Mikołaj Kopernik** – the great astronomer Nicholas Copernicus who studied at the Cracow academy from 1491 to 1495.

The Grodzka, a continuation of the old Royal Way, leads in a northerly

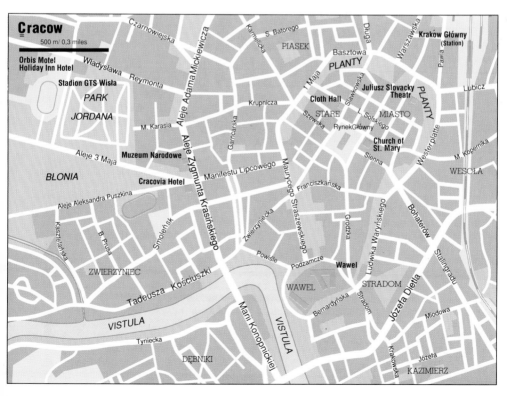

EATING WELL IN POLAND

On the market square in Cracow, where Grodzka Street begins, is Wierzynek, one of Poland's best restaurants. It is housed in three tastefully-restored buildings, and its tradition dates back to medieval times. One of the buildings, house number 16, belonged to the well-known patrician family of the Wierzyneks in the 14th century.

According to the chronicles of history, in the year 1364 Mikolaj Wierzynek organised, in the name of the town council, a celebration for all of the rulers in Europe. At the invitation of the Polish king, they came to Cracow to celebrate the reconciliation of Emperor Karl IV with the Hungarian King Ludwig and his marriage to Elzbieta.

Those in attendance at this festive banquet, presided over by the congress of rulers, included the above-mentioned Emperor Karl IV, King Ludwig of Hungary, the Polish King Casimir the Great, the Danish King Waldemar and King Peter of Cyprus, as well as princes of the Piast dynasty, Silesian princes and the rulers from Bavaria, Stettin and Mazovia.

Wierzynek, who was a merchant, banker and administrator of the king's court, presented each of the guests with a set of golden cutlery to demonstrate to them the generosity of the city of Cracow.

The tradition of this festive banquet lives on, not only in name but also in the superior cuisine of the Wierzynek restaurant.

The Renaissance rooms serve as a reminder of the golden age of Cracow. Here guests can enjoy cake and coffee in a refined atmosphere. One of the house specialties served by the native waiters is mulled honey; and the traditional old Polish dishes prepared in the restaurant can be especially recommended. The decor, from the cloakroom at the entrance all the way up to the Pompeii Room on the upper floor, is brimming with genuine hospitality. Guests should not, however, expect to find Milan design and *nouvelle cuisine* here. But, on the other hand, that is not the reason for your trip to Cracow, is it?

Anyone who has ever been lucky enough to be invited for a homemade meal in Poland was probably astounded by the wide variety of dishes found on the table. Economic crises and shortages of supplies seem to be forgotten when it comes to such a meal. The Poles have a rich tradition of hospitality and do not want to be outdone by anyone.

"When a guest is in the home, God is in the home" is an old Polish saying, and "Offer guests what you have, thereby revealing yourself" is another. Thus, the guest is king, not only in restaurants but also in the simplest homes. Even the poorest family will share with its guests all that it has to offer. This should not be seen as totally selfless, however, since the Poles themselves love to dine well and are always delighted to have an excuse for a festive meal: weddings, birthdays, saints' days, farewells, welcoming parties…

The national dishes of Poland date back to medieval times. Although they began as hearty and plain fare, they have, down through the years and under the influences of the Italians, French and Russians, become more refined. The typical meals of today are a combination of Polish and foreign traditions. Even the dining habits of the Poles prove how manifold and open to new and foreign ideas this land has always been.

On the important religious holidays, such as Christmas and Easter, the Polish people like to enjoy an especially grand meal. On Christmas Eve, the table is laden with a wide variety of sumptuous dishes. The typical meal begins with *Barszcz* which is a red beet soup. Carp or pike, prepared in a variety of ways, all of which are delicious, is served as the next course. Then comes the pasta, baked and sweet or savourily flavoured with home-grown herbs. For dessert, prune compote, pastries and poppy-seed cakes round out the meal. At Easter, the fish course is characteristically replaced by lamb baked in a dough crust.

But even on normal days nobody has to go hungry. The Polish women – emancipation is not exactly running rampant here and male cooks in the house are still relatively rare – display great ingenuity in creating delicious and hearty meals out of the simplest ingredients. It all starts with soup, and the Poles are great lovers of soup. *Żurek*, for example, is a soup made out of coarsely-milled rye. A generous helping of sour cream added to the soup gives it that extra something special.

Pierogi are square little pockets of dough stuffed with every imaginable filling: cheese, fruit, mushrooms or cabbage, to name but a few. The juicy pork or beef roast or the popular game meats – rabbit, wild boar or duck – are turned into gourmet dishes by the addition of the tasty mushrooms found throughout the woods in Poland. Chanterelles, yellow boletus, morels and the *Czernobyliki* are gathered in the forests and eaten fresh. Other popular methods of preparing these delicacies are baking, marinating or pickling.

While on the subject of preserving, it should be mentioned that the harsh winters have made the Poles particularly inventive in this realm. It would

flavour melts in one's mouth. In its juicy depths lies the most delicious of meats. Kitchen-boys then cook it; the heat results in a delectable juice and the *bigos* swells over the edges of the pot, filling the room with its aroma."

Bigos *(for 6 people) - Ingredients:*
1 kg fresh sauerkraut
250 grams cabbage, cut into fine strips
150 grams finely-chopped onions
250 grams pork
250 grams beef
250 grams smoked sausage
50 grams dried mushrooms
2 tbsp vegetable oil
5 pimentos
4 bay leaves, 1 garlic clove
salt, pepper, tomato paste

Cook the sauerkraut and cabbage separately in

be difficult to find a variety of fruit or vegetable which is not canned; and "grandmother's recipes" have not yet been bought out to be marketed by a supermarket chain. Where else in Europe can one enjoy tasty salt pickles from the barrel or scoop fresh sauerkraut from a keg? Not to mention the sour cherry jellies, cranberry jams, plum compotes…

To enable you to enjoy a Polish gourmet meal in your own home, here is a recipe for the most popular old Polish national dish – *bigos*, which is a sauerkraut and meat casserole. In earlier times, fresh game was prepared in this manner; today, beef or pork is used. One of the greatest Polish poets, Adam Mickiewicz, once wrote, "its basis is good cabbage, cut in strips and so sour that its

boiling water until tender but still firm. Cut the pork and beef into large cubes and fry in the oil along with the finely-chopped onions. Soak the dried mushrooms in water according to the instructions on the packet and then cook them. When finished, chop them finely.

Place all ingredients in a large casserole along with the sausage which has been cut into small pieces. Season with salt, pepper, crushed garlic clove, pimentos and a bit of tomato paste. Cover the casserole tightly and cook on the stove over a low heat for 90 minutes. Place the bay leaves in the pot for the first 20 minutes only (they must be removed after this time so that their bitter taste does not overpower the *bigos*). Serve the meal accompanied by a glass of Polish vodka followed by a robust beer or a hearty white wine.

direction from the Rynek Glowny. It contains the superbly preserved Romanesque Church of St Andrew (**Kościół Św. Andrzeja**), whose interior was converted into the baroque style, and the imposing Church of St Peter and Paul, whose portal is adorned by figures of the 12 Apostles.

The **Kanonicza**, which rates as the most beautiful street of old Cracow, runs parallel to the Grodzka. Here one can find the Stanisław Wypianski **Art Nouveau Museum** and Tadeusz Kantor's avant-garde theatre **Cricot 2**.

Perched on a limestone hill rising above the River Vistula, the buildings of the royal palace, the **Wawel**, stand sentinel over the southern part of the old city. It is protected by the Middle Age walls and towers as well as the more recent bastions and cannon. The whole complex consists of the royal palace itself, the cathedral, the vicarage and the servants' living quarters. The hill has been built upon ever since the 10th century, and it is therefore possible to discover every style of architecture here, from the Romanesque through Gothic to the Renaissance and the baroque and on to the bare functional barracks that characterised the time of the Austrian occupation.

The **Palace** is a large square building situated on the western part of the hill, with a beautiful cloister in the centre. The building has retained its outward appearance ever since the conversions undertaken by Franziskus Florentinus back in the 14th century. Today, it is a museum containing a number of interesting objects including the magnificent royal suites and chambers, the crown jewels and armoury, as well as the world famous collection of Flemish wall carpets, the so-called *Arrasy*, and one of the world's most important collections of Turkish and oriental *objets d'art*. The greatest treasure of all is the 12th-century Piast coronation sword, the "Szczerbiec". During World War II many of the exhibits seen here were given a safe temporary home in Canada.

The **Cathedral** on the Wawel is an impressive triple-naved building of

The cloth market and church of St Mary.

Gothic origin, built between 1320 and 1364. In the course of time a number of side chapels were added. The most interesting one is the **Sigismund Chapel** (1519–33). With its beautiful golden dome it is considered to be the finest Renaissance chapel north of the Alps. From the 14th century onwards, the cathedral served both for the coronation and the burial of the Polish kings. Depending on the spirit of the age from which they date, the design of the tombs varies from the ultra bombastic to the extremely plain, an example of the latter being the tomb of St Stanisław Szczepanovski in the central nave. The cathedral is crowned by three towers, one of which contains the famous **Dzwon Zymunt** (Sigismund Bell), which was cast in 1520. The bell still rings out when important state or religious events take place in the city.

The cathedral treasury is to be found in an adjoining building, and opposite the main portal is the museum which was established on the initiative of today's Pope, when, as Karol Cardinal Wojtyła, he was the metropolitan of Cracow.

In the south the old city borders on Kazimierz, historically an independent city with its own town hall, market place and churches. Today it contains a large number of protected buildings. Towards the end of the 15th century, around the present-day **Szeroka Street**, a separate Jewish quarter was established and governed according to its own laws. The Jews inhabited this part of Cracow until 1941 when the Nazis sent them to the ghetto and then on to the gas chambers. There are still seven synagogues to be found here, as well as two Jewish cemeteries. The **Jewish Museum** is located in the **Bóżnica Stara** (Old Synagogue) in Szeroka Street. Nearby, the smallest and most famous of all Cracow synagogues, **Remuh**, remains to this day a place of great cultural interest. Next-door is the only remaining Renaissance Jewish cemetery in Europe. The famous writer and philosopher Rabbi Moses Isseries was laid to rest here.

Market scene in the old city. Following pages: city festivals are celebrated with pomp and splendour.

Of the more recent buildings in Cracow, mention should be made of the fortifications dating from the Austrian Empire, including the mighty citadel-like building near the **Kopiec Kościuszki** (Kościuszki Hills), now a hotel and restaurant. From the top of the hills there is a wonderful panoramic view of the whole city.

The tour of Cracow can be wound up by paying a visit to the most modern part of the city, **Nowa Huta** (new hut). This massive district is a memorial to the postwar history of Poland; the architecture is typical of the kind created all over the Eastern bloc during the Stalin era. This model socialist city has become an especially regrettable example of bureaucratic planning ideology.

Lenin's statue stood in the Aleja Róż until the beginning of 1990 when the city inhabitants demanded that it be pulled down. In the neighbourhood of **Bieńczyce** stands the monumental **Church of the Holy Mother Queen of Poland** which is built in the shape of a ship. The building provided shelter for opposition groups during the period of martial law (1981–89). In Nova Huta there is also a **Cistercian Abbey** in **Mogiła** and the wooden 15th-century **Church of St Bartholomew** standing directly opposite.

But the heart of this part of the city is the gigantic mill which accounts for some 50 percent of Poland's total annual steel production and which, thanks to the absence of any filters, constantly belches out poison over Cracow and its surroundings. During the Round Table talks in 1989 the opposition, represented by the Ecological Club of Poland, pointed out the disastrous effects of this monstrous carbuncle. Finally, the State government and the municipal authorities are now taking the necessary and very expensive steps to reduce the emissions of poisonous gases and thereby increase the quality of life of the population. Some of the most polluting centres of production will have to be closed.

The area around Cracow: It is also well worthwhile to spend a bit of time exploring the area surrounding Cracow. The population here has taken special

care to preserve the characteristic folk-lore of the region, the so-called *folklor krakowski*. The most important elements of this culture are the traditional national costumes as well as the music and a dance known as the *krakowiak*. Additionally, the surrounding villages comprise a veritable treasure chest of architecture typical to this region. These structures were built by native craftsmen, working with traditional methods and tools, a custom which is still practised today.

A visit to the **Benedictine Abbey** in **Tyniec** is highly recommended. This former fortress, today partially in ruins, is located close to Cracow, on a romantic hill overlooking the banks of the Vistula. During the summer months, a series of organ recitals are held in the abbey's church.

To the east of the city, at the confluence of the **Vistula** and **Raba**, is the **Puszcza Niepołomicka** (the Niepołomicka) primeval forest, a former royal hunting grounds. At the edge of the forest, in **Niepołomice**, a small but charming hunting lodge, once used by the kings, enchants visitors. The arcades in the structure's courtyard are especially lovely.

Nearby, on the Sandomierz Road, lies the village of **Iglomia**, hometown of the Holy Albert Brothers. Painter and monk Adam Chmielowski founded the congregation of St Albertus, which devoted itself to the care of the poor. Numerous archaeological digs have also taken place in this region. One of the more important finds was a highly-refined manufacturing works dating from the 2nd to the 4th centuries AD.

The village of **Wiślica**, located about a one-hour drive from Cracow, was the main fortress of Wislanie between the 9th and 10th centuries. The town's Gothic college also displays some Romanesque elements. However, this is not all that this complex has to offer. A crypt with a handsome floor relief as well as the remnants of several Romanesque structures dating from the 10th to 12th century are found here. Among the latter are another church and a baptismal font which serve as testimony to the fact that the Christian religion played a role in this region long before it was officially recognised as the religion of the state.

While in the Cracow region, one should not miss the opportunity to visit the **Salt Mines** in Wieliczka. These are Poland's oldest working mines and have been in operation for the past 1,000 years. The salt lodes are 1 km wide and 6 km (3.7 miles) long, and the pit has now attained a depth of over 984 ft (300 metres). The mine contains a labyrinth of passageways, chambers and galleries with a total length of about 124 miles (200 km) of which 2½ miles (4 km) are open to the public. Three chapels with unique salt sculptures as well as a subterranean sanatorium for patients suffering from asthma and allergies are also located here.

To the northeast of Cracow, in the area of the **Wyżyna Krakowsko-Częstochowska** (Cracow-Tschenstochau Plateau), is the **Ojcowski Narodowy Park**. It is a typical erosion landscape with flat limestone hills, deeply-carved valleys and bizarre stone and cliff formations shaped like clubs, needles, towers and gates.

The most interesting part of this park is the valley of the **Pradnik River**, located near Ojcow, with its unique flora. The oldest traces of mankind in Poland, about 120,000 years old, were found in a cave here. The largest cave, the **Łokietek**, is open to the public. At the northern end of the park, in **Pieskowa Skała**, is a beautiful early-Renaissance style palace with a museum and adjoining restaurant.

Ruins of medieval fortresses are also found outside the park, perched among the Jura hills along the **Szlak Orlich Gniazd** (path of the eagles' nests). These ruins can also be visited by the public.

At the plateau's western edge is **Olkusz**, once known as "the silver city". This is Poland's oldest centre of mining. An abundance of lead-ore and zinc-ore, both with a high silver content, is found in the area around Olkusz. Nearby is a highly unusual landscape – the **Pustynia Błędowska** (Desert of Bledow). This is a relatively large (11½ sq. miles/30 sq.

The ruins of Rudno Castle.

km) area made up of sand and dunes.

East of Cracow: Travelling from Cracow eastward along the E 40 which leads through **Taranów**, **Rzeszów** and **Przemyśl** all the way to **Medyka** on the Soviet border, one passes through another region of Małopolska. Not far from the above-mentioned city of Wieliczka, in **Bochnia**, is a second salt mine, almost as old as that in Wieliczka, and which is also open to visitors. The next town along the route is **Brzesko**, justly famous for its excellent beer called *Okocim*. The brewery was founded in 1845 by the Czech industrialist Baron Goetz.

To the south of Bochnia, in the solitary village of **Nowy Wiśnicz**, is a lovely, recently-restored palace owned by the Lubomirski family. This palace has an interesting history. After the war, the property was confiscated by the state as part of the land reform policy, but the deed was never changed. Thus, when political events led to a change in the constitution of the government, the property was returned to its former owners.

It is an impressive structure with five towers, massive walls and a pentagonal courtyard. Formerly a Gothic fortification, the original castle was renovated by the renowned architect Maciej Trapole in the 17th century, giving it its present form. The walls and the inside of the palace are filled with splendid architectural details, wall paintings and stucco-works.

Not far from Brzesko, in the town of **Dębno**, is a small but interesting Gothic castle housing a museum of late-Gothic weapons, paintings and furniture.

The next important village along the route through Małopolska is **Tarnów**. This voivodeship city, with a charter dating back to 1330, was once the seat of the powerful noble Tarnówski family. The famous Polish general, Hetman Jan Tarnówski, is descended from this family. Today Tarnów is an important industrial centre with large chemical plants. Construction of these factories was initiated by Ignacy Moscicki, president of Poland before World War II. The city is the site of nearly 350

buildings now protected under the national monuments law.

Medieval Tarnów is built on two levels. The upper and lower cities are connected by means of picturesque stairways. The former defensive walls were removed and replaced in the late 19th century by a road around the city. This surrounds the old Polish city centre, thereby preserving the charm and character of this former county seat of the Austro-Hungarian empire.

The old town is especially interesting with its town hall decorated with a Renaissance attic, its arcades, patrician houses and a huge 15th-century cathedral containing precious tombstones of the Taranówski and Ostrogski families.

Not far from the old town is the **Plac Bohaterów Getta** (Square of the Ghetto Heroes), and just beside that is the former ritual bathing house of the Jewish community. It was from here, on June 14, 1940, that the first transport to Auschwitz, comprising 738 persons, took place.

While on the subject of the years of

A pilgrim in penitential robe.

Nazi occupation, the Church of St Joseph and the **Holy Virgin of Fatima**, erected in the 1950s, should be mentioned. A chapel in this church is dedicated to the suffering of the Polish people. Just as impressive as this chapel is the sculpture of St Maximilian Kolbe who voluntarily sacrificed his life in Auschwitz to save others.

The area around the city is also extremely interesting. The contemporary composer **Krzysztof Penderecki** lives in a classical villa in the neighbouring town of **Lusławice**. Nearby is the village of **Wierzchosławice**, birthplace of Wicenty Witos (1874–1945). This famous man was the organiser and leader of the peasant movement which took place between the two world wars.

Lovers of folk art will not want to miss paying a visit to the village of **Zalipie**, about 32 km (20 miles) from Tarnów. In this unusual village, all of the buildings are adorned with paintings. Folk artists have covered the walls, the insides of the houses, stables, barns, fences, furniture and even the doghouses with colourful and original paintings of plant motifs.

Zalipie, however, is not only famous for its lovely pictures. It is just as renowned for its embroidery, hand-cut silhouettes and straw dolls. Visitors can take time to marvel at these gems of art from the countryside in a museum located here. This museum is housed in the home of the late **Felicja Curyłowa**, a painter herself.

The village of **Ciężkowice**, with a history dating back to the 10th century, lies in the valley of the **Biała River**. The wooden structures along the marketplace, with their open galleries, present a particularly charming scene.

The nature preserve **Skamieniałe Miasto** (the Petrified City) is located near Ciężkowice. Here a fantastic cliff configuration, the source of numerous myths and legends, can be seen.

Kotlina Sandomierska/Valley Basin of Sandomierz: The central region of Małopolska is the site of a wide depression that is known as the Kotlina Sandomierska. This flat, typically rural

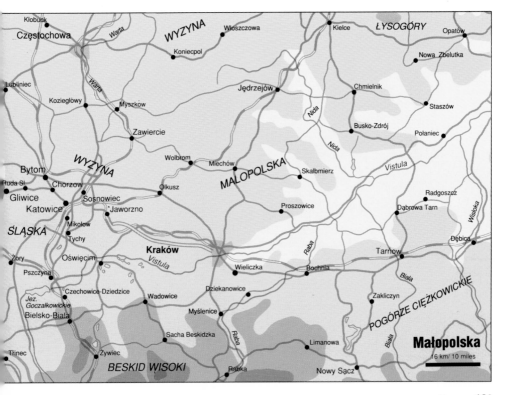

landscape is composed of fields interspersed with large wooded areas. The farms here are generally small, about 5–7½ acres (2–3 hectares), and the numerous narrow strips of cultivated land create colourful patterns.

The rural population here has always been radically oriented, often revolting against the ruling authority. The last revolt was in the winter of 1981 when the peasant uprising and strike led to the founding of the "Peasant-Solidarity".

The most important city of this region is **Rzeszów**. Founded in the 14th century, Rzeszów has always had merely a provincial character. Up until 1939, half of its population were Jews; during World War II almost all of them were murdered. Two synagogues, rebuilt from the rubble of the war, and a Jewish cemetery serve as memorials to this former Jewish community.

The cityscape is dominated by the magnificent **Royal Palace of the Lubomirski Family**, surrounded by bastions, walls and moats. The baroque **Church** and the **Bernardine Cloister**

have also been preserved. A regional museum is today housed in the former **Piarist Cloister**. Here one finds an extensive ethnological collection as well as an art gallery.

The city, normally so quiet and peaceful, comes alive with activity every other year in July. Ever since 1969, Rzeszów has been the site of the **World Festival of Polish Folklore Groups Living Abroad**.

Just like numerous other cities and villages in this region, Rzeszów has its own commercial tradition. In earlier times, markets took place here weekly and, on special occasions, huge fairs were also held. This custom has been preserved to this day: twice weekly, on Tuesdays and Fridays, a market takes place. This market has lost some of its traditional character, however, and today is more reminiscent of a bazaar.

Łańcut: Situated on the international motorway E 40, 10½ miles (17 km) east of Rzeszów, is the medieval city of Łańcut with its magnificent palace. This former residence of the noble families

The Benedictine abbey in Tyniec.

of **Lubomirski** and **Potocki** today houses a public museum.

The centrepiece of the palace is an almost-square structure with corner towers and a central inner courtyard. A bastion in the form of a five-pointed star surrounds the complex. Several out-buildings were added at a later date: the library, a greenhouse and a court building which is now a restaurant and hotel. The palace is encompassed by a park laid out on a grand scale. This park is the site of a small palace and a manège. The former stables and barns today serve as a coach museum housing magnificent carriages and sulkies.

The fortress was originally built on top of old foundations in the years 1629–41 by Stanisław Lubomirski. With the help of the Princess Elzbieta Lubomirska (1736–1826), a stunning-looking lady renowned throughout all the courts of Europe, the structure was expanded into a modern residential palace at the beginning of the 19th century. This renovation was carried out according to plans drawn up by the famous architect Piotr Aigner. Later, at the turn of the century, a facade in French new-baroque style was added.

The main building houses a 18th–19th century **Museum of Interior Design** with well-preserved original interiors. The unusual library contains over 20,000 valuable old volumes. The upstairs living apartments, the ballroom, large dining hall and theatre, as well as the Turkish room on the main floor, are all splendid.

A surprise awaits visitors to the former horse stables. Here a rich collection of old Russian icons is housed.

A **Music Festival** has been held annually in the palace since 1961. International celebrities and music fans gather here each year, carrying the reputation of the festival and the palace far beyond the borders of Poland.

In the small cities around Rzeszów, including **Sokołów**, **Kolbuszowa** and **Strzyżów**, traditional country fairs still take place. Here visitors can buy authentic arts and crafts produced in the surrounding area.

Folk art in the village of Zalinie.

A few of the villages in this region, in particular **Medynia Głogowska**, **Pogwizdów**, **Medynia Łańcucka** and **Zalesie**, are centres for the traditional craft of pottery. Here almost 120 potters are at work producing traditional crockery for everyday use as well as artistically-decorated ceramic dishes and sculptures.

To the south of Rzeszów is a range of hills known as the **Pogórze**. The **Wisłok River** meanders picturesquely through this landscape. Here the atmosphere is peaceful and quiet, almost pastoral.

Time seems to have stood still in this region – in the crooked peasant hamlets as well as in the numerous small villages. However, due to the expulsion of their former Jewish native population, these have lost much of their charm.

The villages of Małopolska were formerly constructed almost exclusively out of wood. Although many examples of this type of construction still exist, an exceptionally good one is the small church in **Blizne**, located between Rzeszów and Brzozow. Built in Gothic style from thick larchwood beams at the turn of the 15th century, it has remained unchanged to this day.

The portion of the Kotlina Sandomierska to the north of Rzeszów is covered with the rich forests of the expansive **Puszcza Sandomierska** (Sandomierska Wilderness Area). These woods are brimming with mushrooms, berries and wild game. The region is inhabited by the **Lesowiaki**, a tribe which has always nourished itself from the products of the surrounding fields and woods. Old, custom-made farms, quaint traditions and fascinating rituals can still be found throughout these woods.

Elements of the disappearing folklore can also be seen in the open-air museum in **Kolbuszowa**. This museum also serves as the venue for a variety of cultural events.

During World War II, the German army had two large military training grounds as well as test fields in **Puszcza Sandomierska**. Several prison and work camps were also included in this complex. The most notorious work camp **Traditional dolls.**

184

was in **Pustkowo**. Here about 15,000 people, mainly Poles, Jews and Russians, lost their lives.

In the nearby village of Blizna, experiments with V-1 and V-2 rockets were carried out. The conspiratorial military intelligence sector of the Polish home army (*Armia Krajowa*) decoded the secrets of this carefully guarded area, retrieved a rocket which had been fired by the Germans and, after dismantling it, smuggled its parts to London.

The dignified city of **Leżajsk** lies about 31 miles (50 km) to the northeast of Rzeszów, not far from the **San River**. Numerous historical buildings and other reminders of a distant past can be found here. Farmers markets and large church festivals take place weekly. In the northern part of the city is a fortress-like Bernardine cloister which dates from the 17th century.

The beautiful and richly decorated interior of this basilica is dominated by an organ, one of the largest in Poland. Built at the end of the 17th century, this instrument, with its 74 registers and 5,894 pipes, spans all three naves of the church. In recent history, organ concerts enjoying a far-reaching reputation have been held here annually in May. However, those passing through in other months need not miss out – the in-house organist will more than likely be willing to perform for those who particularly request it.

In the basilica one also finds *The Miraculous Image of the Virgin Mary with Child*, famous since 1634 as a painting which can work miracles. In August, on Assumption Day, large numbers of believers and unbelievers alike are drawn here by the magnificent processions and celebrations.

Economically speaking, the northern portion of this region, at the confluence of the Vistula and San rivers, is the most interesting. The centre of this area is **Tarnobrzeg**, poverty-stricken and forgotten in the past; recently, however, its sulphur deposits have brought much wealth to the district. This sulphur is principally found in the mines of **Machów** and in the Jeziorko pits. The mineral is exported in granular form via the harbour in Gdańsk. This export brings much-needed hard currency to the region.

Baranów Sandomierski is located at the eastern edge of this sulphur basin, on the right banks of the Vistula. The city is especially renowned for its palace, a structure which is reputed to be one of the finest jewels of Renaissance architecture. All that remains from the original 16th-century fortress, however, is a rectangular structure with corner towers and a gate. The courtyard with arched passageways, the unusual stairway and a romantic loggia were added at a rather later date.

The palace is richly decorated with murals and stucco-works and is today the site of a museum as well as a luxury hotel. The museum, housed in the cellar, has exhibits pertaining to the sulphur industry; fortunately, the excellent wines and food of the neighbouring hotel are not affected by this strange bedfellow.

A short distance to the east of Tarnobrzeg is **Stalowa Wola**, one of the youngest cities in Poland and an important centre of the metal industry. Stalowa Wola was built in 1937, in conjunction with a weapons manufacturing plant. Today, this factory produces steel and construction machinery.

Nearby, on the opposite side of the San, lies the old village of **Radomyśl nad Sanem**. This is the site of an unusual patriotic-religious play which is performed every year at Easter. A group of residents, dressed in the colourful robes of Turkish soldiers, holds a military parade in the city. Afterwards they go from house to house wishing the inhabitants luck and asking for a donation to pay for their costumes. They are accompanied by a marching band and a large number of spectators, many of whom travel great distances to watch this spectacle.

A bit further to the east of Stalowa Wola, along the road leading from Niska to Lublin, lie the villages of **Lazek Ordynacki** and **Lazek Garncarski**. These towns, nestling in the woods, are renowned for their creatively-designed pottery. The craftsmen still work in traditional family pottery studios: the father prepares the clay and forms the vessels, the women paint and decorate the objects and the children help wherever assistance is needed. These pottery workshops produce flowerpots, tiles and dishes which are very popular.

The small city of **Rudnik** lies half-an-hour's drive away from Stalowa Wola in the direction of Jarosław. This town is famous for its tradition of basket-making. Two manufacturing plants and several thousand helpers working in their own homes produce baskets which are exported to many different countries. However, it is rarely possible to purchase one of these baskets here in Rudnik – just one more bizarre example of the modern Polish state's thirst for hard currency.

Our route now brings us back to the north along the Vistula. **Sandomierz** is situated on a high terrace perched on the banks of this river. The city, a historical trading centre founded on the grounds of an ancient settlement, is one of the oldest and most picturesque in Poland. It was formerly the capital of an independent duchy.

Its strategically important fortress enabled it to become one of Poland's three largest commercial centres as early as the 12th century.

Sandomierz enjoyed an extraordinary golden age during the Renaissance. The old town is perched on an oval-shaped hill 98 ft (30 metres) above the river valley. It has managed to preserve much of its medieval character, including several narrow streets with romantic nooks and crannies.

One of the characteristics that makes this town, as well as so many other places in Poland, so charming, is that although much has been perfectly restored by talented craftsmen, a little bit of squalor still exists. Thus, instead of the scrubbed and sterile cleanliness that overwhelms the visitor in many of the medieval towns of western Europe, which put on a special face for the tourist trade and often feel more like theme parks, these old quarters relay the impression of old communities where ordinary people still live and work.

The remains of a royal palace can be seen at the southern edge of the city. Adjacent to these is a triple-nave cathedral dating from the 14th century. Its elements of Gothic architecture and the frescos painted in Byzantine style merit special attention.

Adjacent to the cathedral is the Gothic house of **Długosz**, a medieval historian and chronicler of Poland. Today, the Diocesan Museum, with its collection of art and art objects, is housed here.

Nearby is the **Church of St Jacob**, which formerly belonged to the Dominicans. This church is Poland's best remaining example of a Romanesque brick church. It serves as a memorial to the bloody Tartar invasion of 1259. Its lovely Gothic portal overwhelms the visitor with the charm of its elementary simplicity. Inside, one is impressed by the rich designs of the glazed bricks as well as the Byzantine frescos dating from the 15th century.

The marketplace in the centre of the city is surrounded by a number of stylish houses. The delicate gallery decorating the house of the Olesnicki family makes this building especially noticeable. The town hall dominates the middle of the marketplace. To the north, one finds the remains of the former city wall with its towering **Brama Opatowska** (Abbot Gate).

While in Sandomierz, visitors should plan to spend some time exploring the surrounding areas. This is a typical, non-wooded and arable landscape, renowned for its production of fruits and vegetables. There are several noteworthy objects in this region.

An old Cistercian abbey and a Romanesque church dating from the first half of the 13th century are found in **Koprzywnica**. In the small village of **Ujazd**, the impressive ruins of the **Krzyztopor** palace can still be seen. This palace was built in the 17th century by the Ossolinski family, but was destroyed soon thereafter by the Swedes. A bit further to the northeast is **Opatów** with its Romanesque college.

A far-reaching system of passageways, cellars and vaulted chambers winds its way under the streets and houses of Opatów. Five centuries ago, this served as a refuge for the inhabitants of this town; today part of it is open to the public.

Eastern Małopolska: The eastern portion of Małopolska, which is nestled in the valley of the San River, is a typical agricultural region. Those journeying eastward from Rzeszów should plan to stop in **Jarosław**. Here, beyond the three cloister hills, is the far-ranging tract of land forming Poland's eastern boundary. Situated on the banks of the river, Jarosław is one of the oldest cities in this area. Its commercial markets and fairs, which drew merchants from all over Europe, were renowned. The old town, with its wealth of interesting architecture, is a veritable paradise for photographers.

In the sector of town around the marketplace, the old houses with their characteristic passageways, covered courtyards, decorated stairways and galleries are particularly picturesque. The house of the Italian patrician family Orsetti, built in Renaissance style with an open gallery and attic, is especially noteworthy. This building is an ancient merchants' headquarters and today serves as a regional museum.

Other interesting sights awaiting visitors to Jarosław are the picturesque town hall, a number of older churches, among them Russian-Orthodox, and even a couple of synagogues. Entering the city from the direction of Cracow, one can see the late-baroque Dominican **Cloister** hidden behind the surrounding walls.

Outside of these walls is a small well. The water coming from here not only has a fantastic taste, but is also reputed to work magical powers on those who drink it.

According to legend, a sculpture of the Madonna was found here in ancient times. Soon thereafter, the sculpture was discovered to be a source of miracles. An exceptionally valuable work of art is the Gothic wooden sculpture of **Mater Dolorosa** from **Zbawiec** which is today found on the main altar.

Nearby is **Jodłówka**, where the Sanctuary of the Holy Virgin, with its chapel

Sandomierz stands above the Vistula Valley.

and well, is located. Legend has it that here, too, the Virgin Mary appeared and performed miracles.

In several of the villages around Jarosław, many old palaces and court-yards still exist. Among these villages are Pelkinie, Wysocko, Pawłosiow, Rozwienica and Rokietnica.

In **Sieniawa**, a visit to the recently-restored palace of the Czartoryski family is well worthwhile. Equally inter-esting are **Zarzecze**, with the Dzieduszycki Castle, and **Węgierka** with its ruins of a medieval manor house.

In the small city of **Pruchnik**, a few miles to the south, time seems to have stood still for several decades. Original wooden houses, with open galleries and precise, extremely complex decorative woodwork, are found at the market-place and in the surrounding streets. Many are extremely old and represent very rare examples of Polish architec-ture. Old traditions have also been pre-served: for example, it has been the custom for traditionally-dressed guards to hang an effigy of Judas as a public

ritual on the Saturday before Easter.

East of the San River Valley are the old Polish-Russian border regions, part of which have been inhabited by Ukrainians since the years 1946–47. This stretch of land has for centuries been the scene of confrontations be-tween the cultures of east and west; here two nationalities lived and fought with and against each other.

After the end of World War II, the Ukrainian partisans fought a bitter bat-tle for four years for the Ukrainians' right to autonomy and to establish set-tlements. In the end, having suffered enormous destruction, they lost their fight and were crassly resettled, mainly in the USSR.

After years of fighting, evacuated, burned-out villages dotted the landscape. Even today many regions are only thinly settled and settlements can be found that are almost totally grown over with vegetation.

Characteristic of this region is the wooden architecture of the Russian-Orthodox and Ukrainian churches fre-quently found in the old Ukrainian vil-lages. These are truly gems of folk ar-chitecture. Some of these are today used by the Roman Catholic church.

Some of the more beautiful eastern churches are found in Rudka near Jarosław and in Chołyniec (both 17th century), in Pazdziacz and Piątkowa near Dynowo (both 18th century) and in Radruz (16th century).

The traditional altar screen, the *iconostasis*, has been preserved in some of the churches. This wall has icons dating from the 17th–19th century, many of which have exceedingly great artistic value. The National and Diocesan Mu-seum of the city of **Przemyśl** houses an interesting collection of painted icons.

The Ukrainian population here has, for the past several years, once again celebrated its national holiday, the **Feast of St Jordan**. The faithful, bearing flags and crosses, congregate on the banks of the San on a winter morning and a deeply religious festival then begins, one which is intense and mysterious. **A typical** After the ceremony, the people wash **wayside** their faces and eyes with river water. **shrine.**

Freshly cleansed and with renewed strength, they are considered able to master their daily lives.

Przemyśl: The landscape surrounding this typical border town, a melting pot of various cultures and traditions since the 7th century, is enchanting. The heavily-wooded and hilly Pogórze Przemyskie (the foothills of Przemyśl) stretches out to the south of the city.

In nearby **Krasiczyn**, the lovely Renaissance palace of the Krasicki family is located. This seat of one of Poland's most powerful families is a large building with protective structures and a tower over the entrance. Stylish stucco-work and paintings decorate the tastefully-restored palace. Not far from Krasiczyn, in **Kalwaria Pacławska**, is a Franciscan cloister containing a miraculous picture of the Virgin Mary, which has enjoyed special veneration for the past several centuries.

In the area around the cloister, the stations of the cross are illustrated in 42 picturesquely-situated chapels. The wooden houses in the village which grew up around the cloister are also worth seeing. This is an extremely quiet and almost uninhabited area. Only in August, when the traditional annual fair takes place, do flocks of believers assemble here.

Those who would like to spend some time on the water, in peaceful solitude, should travel to the village of **Słonne**. It is about 18½ miles (30 km) west of Przemyśl, in the **San River Valley**. Visitors are sure to find room in one of the numerous small guesthouses here. A bit further to the south, in the woods around the former village of **Arłamow**, is a holiday hostel which formerly belonged to the communist party. **Lech Wałęsa** was kept prisoner here for a time. Today it is open to the public and, among other activities, hunts are organised in which foreigners can also participate. Anyone who enjoys horses and riding will want to visit **Stubno**, north of Przemyśl, where the state maintains a stud farm with English thoroughbreds, as well as a riding club.

The expansive woods of the **Lasy**

The youth of today.

Lipskie, the **Lasy Janowskie** and the **Puszcza Solska** begin at the northeastern edge of the **Kotlina Sandomierska** (Valley Basin of Sandomierz). These dense woods stretch from the Vistula River Valley to the Soviet border. The spruce forests, with their large game population, offer exceptionally good hunting, and numerous hunting lodges await the visitor.

Roztocze, which begins a bit further to the south, is also an extremely picturesque region. A unique mixture of flora and fauna blankets the rolling forest-covered hills. In the most beautiful portion of Roztocze, (in the centre), the **Roztoczanski Park Narodowy** (Roztocze National Park) has been established around the towns of **Zwierzyniec** and **Krasnobrod**. Large limestone cliffs can be seen on the peaks of the **Wapielnia** and **Kamienna** mountains. On the southern faces of the Roztocze hills, the remains of the **Molotov Line** fortifications, dating from World War II, are still evident. At the other end of the region, in the **Kotlina Zamojska** (Basin of Zamość), lies the lovely city of **Zamość**.

Zamość: This city, founded during the Renaissance (1579–1616) by the Chancellor Jan Zamoyski, and designed by the Venetian Bernard Morand, was a mighty fortress which was built so solidly that it was able to resist the attacks of both the Cossacks and the Swedes. The palace, renovated in the years 1821–31, gives a gloomy barracks atmosphere to the town. This is despite the fact that a large portion of the complex was turned into a pleasant park after a part of the fortifications was destroyed in 1866.

The **Rynek Główny** (Market Square), with its famous town hall and subsequently added stairs, is located in the centre of town. The square is surrounded by townhouses whose character has unfortunately been changed through countless renovations. Adjoining this central marketplace are two other squares: the **Rynek Solny** (the Salt Marketplace) and the **Rynek Wodny** (the Water Marketplace). The western part of the city is dominated by the palace of the Zamoyski family. This is a magnificent residence which has been altered many times throughout its history. Zamość was once a city with a multifarious population, including Poles, Russians, Jews and Armenians. Today the old orthodox church, the synagogue and an Armenian meeting house stand as testimony to those times.

Lubelszczyzna: The region of Lublin, in the northwestern part of Małopolska, is a forest-covered agricultural area with industry concentrated in the larger cities. The largest of these is **Lublin**, an important centre for industry, culture and science. It has five institutions of higher learning, including the KUL (**Katolicki Uniwersytet Ludowy/** Catholic People's University), the only Catholic university in all of eastern Europe.

Lublin has long been important both militarily and commercially. A fortress existed here as early as the 11th century, and in the 14th century a royal castle was built. In July of 1944, after the liberation, Lublin became the provisional capital of Poland and the seat of the transitional government which was installed by Stalin.

The small old town is full of interesting sights. The **Marketplace** with its old houses, the 16th/17th-century **Cathedral** and the Dominican **Cloister** dating from the 14th–17th century are especially noteworthy. The lovely church is decorated by 11 chapels. Two of the most magnificent are those of the Firlej family with its original two-storey grave and of the Tyszkiewicz family. The latter has a fresco depicting the Last Judgment in its dome.

Not too much is left of the former castle since a neo-Gothic prison has replaced a part of it. A tower and a chapel decorated with Russian-Byzantine paintings are all that remain of the original complex.

During the years of the German occupation, thousands of Poles were tortured and killed within the castle walls. And following the war, Polish freedom fighters and anti-communists were imprisoned here.

Near the castle is a **Russian Church**

with an *iconostasis* dating from the time of the Renaissance. In the middle of the city, the **Plac Unii Lubelskiej** (Lublin Union Square) serves as a memorial to the union between the Grand Duchy of Lithuania and the Kingdom of Poland, carried out in 1569.

The city suffered extensive damage during World War II. The Nazis kept 40,000 Jews imprisoned in the ghetto; they were later murdered in the **Bełżec** extermination camp. In 1941 the Nazis established one of their most terrible extermination camps in **Majdanek**, a suburb of Lublin. Here victims from 216 European countries were brought to their deaths.

Between Lublin and the Vistula is the region of **Płaskowyż Nałęczowski** (the Nałęczow Plateau), where the city of Nałęczow is also located. The golden age of this city began in the 18th century when mineral springs were discovered here. Today it remains a popular health resort for patients suffering from circulatory disorders or heart disease. Many famous Polish authors, including **Bolesław Prus** and **Stefan Żeromski**, often came to this spa. A biographical museum has been erected in their honour and a house built for Stefan Żeromski is also still standing here.

On the right banks of the Vistula is the lovely city of **Kazimierz Dolny**. Founded by King **Kazimierz Wielki** (who died in 1370), Kazimierz Dolny was the centre of the grain trade for many centuries, resulting in great wealth for the town. This is especially well illustrated by the noteworthy townhouses, six of which can still be seen. Built in Renaissance style and richly decorated, these are veritable architectural gems.

Several old churches also adorn the city. Although it was heavily damaged in 1944, Kazimierz Dolny was reconstructed thereafter with special attention to detail.

In the spring, orchards explode into flower all around this town on the Vistula. Here musicians and authors feel especially at home. In July of each year a traditional fair takes place. As a

The marketplace in Kazimierz Dolny. Following pages: historic Lublin, the cultural hub of Eastern Poland.

part of this fair, a folk music competition is also held.

A short way up the river from Kazimierz Dolny is **Puławy**. This city can look back on a rich tradition of culture. During the epoch of the disintegration of Poland, toward the end of the 18th century, a centre of Polish culture and political activity developed here on the estates of the Czartoryski family. It was because of these seditious activities that the Czartoryski family estates around Puławy were confiscated by the czarist authorities and the various members of the family were forced into exile. The authorities even went so far as to change the name of the city to New Alexandria.

During the time of Isabella Czartoryski, a fabulous palace was built with gardens in English style, as well as the **Gothic**, **Chinese** and **Alexander** Pavilions, the **Temple of Sibylle** and the small **Palace of Marynka**. This well-preserved complex still exists today.

The medieval city of **Chełm**, famous for many centuries for its chalk industry, lies at the eastern edge of the Lubelszczyzna. The city itself is perched on a 722-ft (221-metre) high chalk hill known as the **Chełmska Góra**, an easily defensible spot in the Middle Ages. At the point of highest elevation, an impressive architectural ensemble is clustered closely together. This includes a cathedral, bishop's palace, cloister and gate – remains of the original castle.

In order to mine the chalk for trade, lengthy passageways and deep shafts were carved out of the soft stone hills as early as medieval times. Today, a multi-level labyrinth exists here. It is 25 miles (40 km) long and up to 89 ft (27 metres) deep. These mines are open to the public. The entrance is found along the **Ulica Przechodnia**.

To the north of the line connecting Lublin and Chełm is the region of **Polesie Lubelskie**. This is a peaceful area, not yet developed for tourism. It is covered with woods, meadows and swamps. The variety of flora and fauna is protected by numerous nature preserves and parks. The most interesting of these are **Jezioro Biale** and the large **Krowie Bagno**.

KARPATY

The Carpathian mountain range, the largest chain of mountains in Europe after the Alps, runs through the whole of Southern Poland. Its highest massif is the **Tatra**, and adjoining this are the lower ranges, which are less alpine in character: the **Bieszczady** and **Beskidy**.

This unique mountain world was turned into a series of national parks as long ago as the 1920s and '30s in order to preserve it from the encroachment of industrialisation. This unusual foresight means that even today this is an area of virtually unspoilt nature, with rare species of animals and plants to be discovered in its dense woodlands which are one of its characteristic features. The healthy climate and numerous medicinal springs make it the ideal place for a health cure.

The western part of this area has been opened up to tourists with the provision of an extensive network of guesthouses, good paths and convenient rail connections. In the eastern part, on the other hand, only limited concessions have been made to tourism, and this thinly populated area will therefore appeal more to those who prefer to hike with a rucksack, tent and their own supplies and explore the wild beauties of nature independently.

Bieszczady, a jungle-like region in the southeastern tip of Poland, is one of the places that has scarcely been touched by tourism, and is a place that no nature-lover should miss. The long gentle slopes cover a large part of the voivodeship of Krosno, running along the border with Czechoslovakia and the Ukraine. The highest mountain here is the **Tarnica** (4,374 ft/1,346 metres). The alpine pastures, the *Połoniny*, are particularly worth exploring; they are interlaced with numerous hiking trails which, although easy in themselves, sometimes require considerable stamina due to their length.

More than half of this area is thickly wooded. Right in the middle of the mountains is the **Bieszczadzki Park Narodowy** – a natural park which is a haven for brown bears, herds of bison, lynxes and eagles. Tourists visiting by car can see this region best from the panoramic road, the *Pętla Bieszczadzka* (Bieszczady Loop), that winds through the most interesting parts of the foot-hills – through a landscape that is one of the most unusual in Europe.

A further attraction of Bieszczady is the **Jezioro Solińskie**, the reservoir of Solina. The dam was built in 1968 and the lake thus created, which is also called the "Sea of Bieszczady", covers an area of 8 sq. miles (21 sq. km). Excursion boats leave from its shores, where there are numerous tourist and holiday cen-tres providing accommodation and en-tertainment for the holiday-makers.

A large proportion of the population of Bieszczady only came here after World War II, as a result of the govern-ment's resettlement policies. Many of the original inhabitants of these moun-tains belong to two small ethnic groups, the *Łemkowie* and the *Bojkowie*, and are adherents of the Greek Catholic or Russian Orthodox faiths.

The little old Orthodox churches are thus also one of the typical characteris-tics of the area, although unfortunately many of them have been converted into Catholic churches. The best-known of these is to be found in **Komańcza**.

There are a number of other places in Bieszczady that are well worth a visit: Baligród, Cisna, Komańcza, Lesko, Ustrzyki Dolne, Ustrzyki Górne and Wetlina.

Beskid Sądecki: The next interesting mountain region, Beskid Sądecki, is bordered by two rivers, the **Poprad** and the **Dunajec**. It consists of two moun-tain ridges, the **Radziejowa** (4099 ft/ 1263 metres) and the **Jaworzyna Krynicka** (3,786 ft/1,165 metres). There are numerous hiking trails across the wooded heights, all of which are clas-sified as easy.

Beskid Sądecki is best known for its abundant mineral springs. In the valley of the Poprad, an interesting river which has its source in the Slovak part of the Tatra Mountains and which forces its way through rocks and woods on to the Polish side, are numerous mineral springs, producing water which is con-sidered highly beneficial to people suf-fering with stomach, kidney and rheu-matic problems.

The region of Beskid Sądecki is also very attractive on account of the lively folk culture that is still to be found here. Unfortunately, however, the number of mountain villages in which the *Łemkowie* still practise the old tradi-tions in their original form is diminish-ing fast. The foothills are the home of the ethnic group known as the *Lachowie sadeccy*.

The capital of this region is **Nowy Sącz**. It was founded in 1292 by the Czech king, Wacław II and developed into a regional centre during the reign of Kazimierz Wielki (1333–70). The original layout of the town has been preserved intact, and some of the build-ings date from the 15th and 16th cen-turies. There is a comfortable hotel, the **Beskid** and a few very adequate guest-houses for those wishing to spend a little longer here.

Nearby is the little town of **Stary Sącz**, which dates back to the 13th century and is linked historically with Kinga, a queen beatified by the Church, who founded a nunnery for the order of St Clare. As well as several interesting churches, Stary Sącz has over 200 old town residences still gracing its medi-eval centre. Further tourist attractions are excursions on board the Radziejowa train and the possibility of trips into the Poprad Valley. With its peaceful setting, salubrious climate and variety of cul-tural events, including classical concerts in the old churches and the annual Fes-tival of Old Music, the little town is a good place for an interesting and varied holiday.

The oldest spa in Beskidy is the little town of **Krynica**, 28 miles (45 km) from Nowy Sącz. Back in the 18th century springs with marked healing properties were discovered here, which are today used for bathing and drinking cures for stomach, intestinal, heart, kidney and respiratory complaints. Around the turn of the century Krynica became increas-ingly popular, especially as a retreat among artistic circles.

Preceding pages: Nidzica Castle; wintertime in the Tatra Mountains.

The most famous writers, painters and musicians of Poland came here to be cured of their illnesses, among them the world-famous Polish singer Jan Kiepura, who was a regular guest in the 1920s and '30s and a good advertisement for Krynica. It was here too, after World War II, that the famous naive artist Nikifor embarked on his career.

This town is a good starting point for excursions into the Jaworzyna Krynicka mountains. For visitors who like to get to the top of mountains the easy way, there is a cable car running up the **Góra Parkowa**. Those touring by car should explore the **Pętla Popradzka** (Poprad Loop), a road through wonderful scenery which runs from Krynica via the spas of **Muszyna**, **Żegiestów** and **Piwniczna** to **Stary Sącz**. Also worth visiting is the lime tree reserve **Obrożyska** near Muszyna.

Pieniny and the Nowy Targ area: The town of **Szczawnica** has an almost equally long tradition as a spa. Situated on the **River Dunajec**, between the Pieniny and Beskid Sądecki mountains,

this little place is considered particularly beneficial for people with respiratory complaints. In the second half of the 19th century a naturopathic sanatorium was founded here, an institution which today offers modern inhalation therapy.

Szczawnica has many different attractions, including interesting wooden buildings and mountain folk traditions. It is however particularly to be recommended as a starting point for excursions into the Pieniny Mountains, a unique range of mountains with a complex geological structure and singular climatic conditions. Almost the entire area belongs to the **Pieniński Park Narodowy** (Pieniny National Park).

The highest peak in the Pieniny mountains, **Wysoka** (3,843 ft/1,025 metres) is located in the southern part of the range and can easily be reached from Szczawnica. The path to the top goes past the **Wąwóz Homole** gorge, cut deep into the rock. The most popular summit in the area is however **Trzy Korony** (Three Crowns) (3,191 ft/982

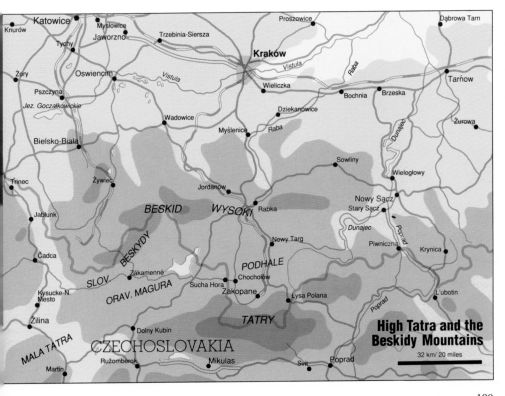

High Tatra and the Beskidy Mountains

32 km/ 20 miles

metres). The best place to set out from in order to get to the top of Trzy Korony is **Krościenko**, a picturesque village situated on the River Dunajec.

A trip on the River Dunajec: The raft rides on the Dunajec, which winds through the picturesque gorges of the Pieniny, are one of the biggest tourist attractions in Poland. The river, which can be dangerous at high water, flows swiftly between steep cliffs, with the fragile-looking raft shooting along on its surface. There is, however, no need for any anxiety since the trips are led by local mountain people, raftsmen who are experts at their task. They also wear the traditional costume of the region, which adds to the attraction of the ride. The excursion begins in **Stromowce Wyżnie**, lasts around two hours and is an unforgettable experience.

The region of Pieniny today belongs to Poland and Czechoslovakia. The border runs across the top of the mountains and along the Dunajec. In spite of the troublesome terrain, this region was traversed by trade caravans and military columns for centuries, and it was for this reason that the former rulers of the region had castles and fortresses built on top of the hills. Their ruins can still be seen, romantic memorials to a past age. Near the summit of Trzy Korony the remains of the old fortress **Zamek Pieninski** can be visited.

Further to the west are two castles dating from the 14th century, **Czorsztyn** and **Niedzica**, which stand facing one another on opposite sides of the Dunajec. They are built on the ruins of former pre-Christian fortresses and their many different owners over the centuries were usually rivals. Today Czorsztyn is a ruin and the castle of Niedzica is partly used as a museum.

It is still something of a mystery why the famous will of the last Inca, Tupac Amaru, is kept in Niedzica. Amaru's daughter Umina married the last owner of the castle and the will is said to have been unearthed at the castle by a descendant of the Inca, who then vanished under mysterious circumstances.

Today the beautiful Pieniny landscape **Cultivation in Gorce.**

WITKACY

One particular personality who is very closely linked with Zakopane is Stanisław Ignacy Witkiewicz-Witkacy (1885–1939), one of the most original exponents of Polish culture. He was a painter, art theoretician, philosopher, writer and dramaturg all in one person.

Although he was born in Warsaw, it was Zakopane that became the centre of Witkacy's life: his father, Stanisław Witkiewicz, a well-known painter, art critic, writer and creator of the original "Zakopane Style", which he applied both to architecture and the design of objects for every-day use, had already es-tablished himself here.

In 1890, at the age of only five, Witkacy made his debut as an artist in the weekly magazine *Przegląd Zakopiański*, and it was only a few years later that his pictures were exhibited in Zakopane for the first time. Brought up to be an artist by his father, from the time he was a child he enjoyed the society of the cultural elite who came to spend their holidays in Zakopane. It is a well-known fact that he had a relationship with the actress Irena Solska; this was described by Witkacy himself in his autobiographical novel *622 upadki Bunga*.

After the suicide of his fiancée he fled from Zakopane – going first to Australia, where he took part in a scientific expedition led by the ethnographer Bronisław Malinowski, and later to Russia, where he served as a soldier and survived World War I. From 1918 on he lived permanently in Zakopane, mostly staying in one of the guest-houses run by his mother. In 1933 he moved to Witkiewiczowka on Antalowka hill, a house built in Zakopane Style; it is now planned to use these premises to found a Witkacy Museum.

The opening of his artist's studio, which he called *Firma Portretowa von St I. Witkiewicz* (the Portrait Firm of St I. Witkiewicz), also dates from this period. Several hundred portraits were pro-duced here – most of which were commissioned, and many of which were artistic experiments car-ried out under the influence of psychiatric drugs and alcohol. Even when he was a young man his painting was never primarily realistic, but always contained visionary and utopian elements. His early self-portraits are impressive works of art revealing carefully chosen colour and psychologi-cal depth. The sharp lines of these paintings how-ever, already show signs of the tendency towards caricature which was to characterise his later por-traits, in which the faces were distorted and given grotesque demonical features. His *Composition with three female forms* depicted here (oil on canvas, 1917–20) is indicative of this develop-ment, but is also an example of the way in which Witkacy incorporated his fresh impressions of the colourful and exotic world of the Pacific and the horrors of the war he had just experienced.

Most of his pictures are exhibited in the muse-ums of Słupsk and War-saw, and in the Tatra Museum in Zakopane.

Witkacy wrote the ma-jority of his plays in the dramatic highland sur-roundings of the Tatra mountains. He founded the "Formistic Theatre" in 1925 and in addition he put on several productions in Morskie Oko, such as *Wariat i zakonnice* (The Madman and the Nuns), *W małym Dworku* (In the Little Manor), and *Nowe wyzwolenie* (New Libera-tion).

Witkacy was very ac-tive socially, and lost no opportunity of exchang-ing creative ideas with his large circle of acquaint-ances and fellow artists, but he was also involved in the academic world, working in the areas of philosophy and art theory (theory of pure form). Before World War II he was one of the organisers of the General Vacation University (*Powszechny Uniwersytet Wakacjny*) in Zakopane.

The Soviet army's invasion of Poland shocked and disappointed him to such an extent that he committed suicide. He was one of Zakopane's highly original characters, and there are numerous jokes and anecdotes relating to his eccentric be-haviour. Witkacy is commemorated in the old cemetery with a symbolic gravestone next to the grave of his mother.

The St I. Witkiewicz Theatre in Chramcowki Road was founded by young actors with the object of producing his plays, so that even today people can continue to profit from the life and work of this brilliant outsider.

is threatened by a dam, which is being built on the Dunajec in the vicinity of Czorsztyn in spite of a massive resistance campaign that has been kept up for over 20 years.

The **Gorce** and **Beskid Wyspowy** mountains seal off this region to the north. Tourists who visit these mountains are mainly experienced travellers who are not deterred by long distances and the lack of accommodation or good road and rail connections.

Between Gorce and the Tatra lies **Podhale** – an area which is of both ethnographical and historical interest. The largest town in Podhale is **Nowy Targ**, a settlement dating from the 13th century, which was for a long time the centre of the whole region. For a long time it was the seat of the royal administration and judiciary and it also became famous for its fairs, a tradition which continues to the present day. Every Thursday the market "in the city", as the people living in the mountains say, is the main attraction for both local inhabitants and visitors.

Among the points of interest in Nowy Targ are the little **Church of St Anna** in the town's cemetery, which dates from the 13th century and is said to have been founded by brigands from Podhale, and the **Church of St Katharina** situated in the town centre.

The sculpture of the Virgin Mary and Child in nearby **Ludźmierz** is a cult figure widely revered in the Podhale. Every year numerous Catholics from the Polish and Slovakian foothills come to Ludźmierz for the fair held on 15 August, the feast of the Assumption of the Virgin.

The village of **Dębno**, also in the vicinity of Nowy Targ, is well-known for its beautifully preserved larchwood church dating from the 15th century, and named after the Archangel Michael. The church was decorated by unknown artists with splendid paintings in the early Renaissance style. Similar paintings can be seen in the churches of **Harklowa** and **Grywald**; these, however, are not so well preserved.

Zakopane and the Tatra mountains: In the last century, from the 1870s onwards, this little village at the foot of the Tatras started to play an increasingly important part in the life of Poland, which in those days was divided between Prussia, Austria and Russia.

Following the example of the "discoverer" of Zakopane, the Warsaw doctor Tytus Chałubiński, an increasing number of Polish intellectuals came to settle here. Zakopane soon became both a cultural and a political centre, in fact the symbolic capital of Poland.

After World War I the little town in the Tatra mountains continued as the meeting point for prominent personalities from the Polish cultural scene. Many artists moved permanently to Zakopane, among them the well-known poet Jan Kasprowicz, the composer Karol Szymanowski, the Dutch pianist Egon Petri and the painter and dramaturge Stanisław Witkiewicz.

Zakopane still has a reputation as a town of artists, a place which draws creative people in search of a suitable environment in which to relax or work. The town has 30,000 inhabitants, a

Left: wooden church in Zakopane. **Below, above** the forests in Pleniny.

number that is swelled every year by over 2 million visitors, mainly people who flock here in the winter months to go skiing.

One of the unusual features of Zakopane is the regional culture of the mountain people, a living culture that is still part of everyday family life, and still very readily displayed to visitors. At church festivals the local people appear in their traditional costumes and in their homes they continue to speak their own dialect.

Every year in September Zakopane is the scene of the international **Festival of Highland Folklore**, which attracts large numbers of visitors. There is an important collection of local folk art in the Tatra Museum of Zakopane and **Kościeliska Road**, with its old highlanders' houses, is rather like an open-air museum of regional architecture in which people are still living.

The houses built by Stanisław Witkiewicz in the **Zakopane Style** are a synthesis of various types of folk art; the Zakopane Style represents an at-tempt to combine elements of local art and architecture with elements of Polish tradition as a whole. The most beautiful example is the Villa **Dom pod Jodłami** which was built in **Koziniec** in 1897 for the Pawlikowski family. Equally worth seeing is the chapel in **Jaszczurówka**, built in 1908. The old cemetery is a monument to all the many well-known personalities who were connected with Zakopane at various times in its past .

The cultural significance of the town is also underlined by the numerous museums dedicated to famous cultural personalities such as the composer Karol Szymanowski, mentioned above, or the literary figures Jan Kasprowicz and Kornel Makuszyński.

Zakopane is the gateway to one of the greatest of Poland's natural treasures, the beautiful Tatra mountain chain. These mountains, the highest between the Alps and the Caucasus, belong partly to Poland and partly to Czechoslovakia. The highest summit on the Polish side is the **Rysy** (8,121 ft/2,499 metres).

The Tatra is an enchanting area, with

An enduring mode of transport.

its alpine scenery and abundance of streams, waterfalls and lakes, of which the **Morskie Oko** (literally sea eye) is the largest. From Zakopane it can be reached by bus, followed by a short walk, in a total of around five hours.

The most beautiful spots are connected by an extensive network of hiking trails, which range in difficulty from simple walks to rock climbs. Mountain climbing in the Tatras is greatly facilitated by the professional support of the local mountain guides.

There is a volunteer rescue service which looks after hikers in case of accident. When walking here, however, it must not be forgotten that the whole of this mountain area is an extensive national park, the Tatra National Park, and there are special protective regulations. It is possible to hike in the Tatras in both the summer and the winter, but your safety will depend largely on how experienced you are.

Zakopane has excellent winter sports facilities for skiers of all grades of expertise, and is suitable both for alpine sports and cross-country skiing. A cable car runs up the most popular mountain, the **Kasprowy** (6,450 ft/1,985 metres), and in good snow conditions there are over 50 ski-lifts in operation in the Zakopane area.

In addition to those who come to tour the area or practise winter sports, many visitors also come to Zakopane for the cultural events, such as the excellent concerts in the Museum villa **Atma**. Numerous galleries, such as the authors' gallery belonging to the famous Polish artist Władysław Hasior, organise exhibitions of professional and naive art. The new **Witkacy Theatre** at 15, Chramcowki Road received enthusiastic reviews from the moment it opened and is very popular with visitors.

Zakopane once hosted the Winter Olympic Games, and is hence very well provided with tourist accommodation: there are a number of comfortable hotels, youth hostels and mountain huts and several hundred guesthouses.

Orawa and Babia Góra: North of Zakopane is the unique village of

Below, charcoal burner. Following pages: the "Redyk": a festival is held in Zakopane when the sheep are led down from mountain pastures.

Chocholów. The original old wooden houses lining the main street are some of the best examples of the beautiful carpentry that is characteristic of the Podhale region. Their timber is slotted together rather than fixed with any nails. From here the road leads to **Orawa**, which is the least known of all the foothill areas. From the gentle hills of the delightful countryside stretching between Poland and Slovakia there are wonderful views of the nearby Tatra and Beskid Wysoki mountains. Since public transport facilities are rather lacking, it is recommended to come here by car from Cracow, Katowice or Zakopane. Although this area has only a few points of interest, these are particularly worth seeing.

Foremost among these is the little holiday village of **Orawka**, which dates back 400 years. The exceptional wooden church of St John the Baptist, which is decorated with interesting paintings (including a *biblia pauperum*, an illustration of the Ten Commandments on the choir wall) was built 100 years later.

A little farther on from Orawka is the large village of **Zubrzyca Górna**, where many wooden buildings typical of this region have been preserved.

Something not to be missed is the **Orawski Park Etnograficzny** (Folklore Park of Orawa). This is an open-air museum which contains a complete farm that once belonged to a mayor, including all the various farm buildings and stalls, traditional tools and household objects. The oldest buildings date back to the 17th century.

To the northwest of Orawa the mountain of **Babia Góra** rises to a height of 5,606 ft (1,725 metres). A number of hiking trails of varying degrees of difficulty lead to the summit, and it is well worth the climb, at least in clear weather, for the unforgettable view it offers of the Tatra, the Beskids and wide expanses of the foothills and Silesia that will be your reward.

Reasonable accommodation and sustenance are offered to tired and hungry tourists by the Markowe Szczawiny restaurant and hostel situated not far from the summit.

ŚLĄSK/SILESIA

The first settlers that are known to have lived in Silesia belonged to a Germanic group, the Vandals. The name for this area was probably derived from that of one of their tribes, the *Silings*. After their withdrawal in the 6th century Slavic tribes pressed forward into the region, and in the 9th century it was combined with Bohemia.

After the founding of the arch-bishopric of Wrocław in the year 1000 Silesia was ruled by the Polish Piast dynasty. In the 12th century it was split up into two duchies: Lower Silesia, which was governed by Prince Bolesław, and Upper Silesia, which was governed by Prince Mieszko.

In the 13th century Silesia flourished both economically and culturally, as a result of the strictly centralist policies of its rulers. With the death of Bolesław III in 1348 the rule of the Piasts came to an end, and with it the political unity of the country, which was broken up into 17 small principalities. Silesia once again become the property of the Bohemian crown, which in return renounced its rights to Poland.

In 1526 Silesia came under the Habsburg ruler Ferdinand I and remained part of this empire for 200 years. During the Silesian wars of 1740–63 Frederick the Great took Lower Silesia and a large part of Upper Silesia, leaving only the southern region of Upper Silesia under the Habsburgs.

As a result of the Treaty of Versailles in 1919 a small part of Silesia went to Czechoslovakia, and the rest of the area was divided between Poland and the German Reich.

Following the peace conferences after World War II the whole of Silesia returned to Poland – after 600 years. The German population was displaced and the area was resettled by Poles from the former eastern areas of Poland.

There are now around 3.2 million people living in Silesia. While 98 percent of the population used to be German, now 98 percent is Polish.

UPPER SILESIA

Through the economic policies of Frederick the Great which encouraged the building of iron and steel works and mines, industrialisation in Silesia made rapid strides. By around the turn of the last century, it was competing with the industrial areas situated on the Rhine and the Ruhr.

On account of the heavy industry sited here, the conurbations between **Gliwice** and **Dąbrowa Górnicza** are among the most endangered environments in the world. The capital **Katowice** is made up of 70 former villages located in the southern highlands. The oldest, **Bogucice** and **Dab**, were founded in the 13th and 14th centuries. The urbanisation began in 1865, and for this reason there are many elements of historicism, Art Nouveau and modernism in the architecture of the town, as illustrated, for example, by the theatre or the old station. Most of the churches date from around the turn of the century and were built in the neo-romantic or neo-Gothic styles that were popular at the time.

One particularly good example of the architectural style that prevailed between the two world wars in the construction of churches is the basilica of the **Cathedral of Christ the King** by Xavery Dunikowski.

The **Voivodeship Council Building** is also representative of the architecture of this period. The **Silesian Museum** near the market includes an interesting section devoted to the works of Jan Matejko, Mojzesz Kisling, Aleksander Gierymski, Jerzy Nowosielski and other 19th-century Polish artists. The skyline of the city of Katowice is dominated by an enormous sports hall, popularly known as the "saucer"; close by is a memorial to the people's uprisings of 1919–21.

The main points of interest in the medieval town centre of **Gliwice**, one of the oldest towns in Upper Silesia, are the Gothic **All Saints Parish Church**, the neoclassical town hall, surrounded by town residences which have been restored true to the original, and the **Piast Palace** with its museum, which was restored in 1960.

The main attraction in the rather new town of **Chorzow** is a municipal park dating from the 1950s which has a very wide range of recreational facilities: a fairground, planetarium, observatory, rose garden, cable car and zoo. Further attractions in this park are the **Silesian Gateway** and a group of romantic-looking wooden buildings dating from the 19th century.

Będzin is situated on the border between Silesia and Małopolska or Little Poland. In the 14th century it occupied a key position in the defence system of the new Polish state. **Będzin Castle** was built at approximately the same time; today it houses a weapons museum. The museum that is accommodated in a **Baroque Palace** in the town centre is also well worth visiting.

In the industrial settlement of **Dąbrowa Górnicza**, east of Będzin, is the largest iron and steel works in Poland, the "Katowice", which began operating in 1976. The mining town of **Tarnowskie Góry** to the north developed as a result of the rich deposits of silver and lead in the area, and it was here, in 1788, that the first steam-driven engine in Europe was put into operation. Today the town is an important railway junction for the transportation of coal to the north.

The mining of precious metal ores stopped at the beginning of the 20th century. Since then the **Czarny Pstrąg** seam with its museum of ore mining has become a tourist attraction. In the **Bobrowiki** district of Tarnowskie Góry a 6,375-ft (1,700-metre) long path has been created at a depth of 150 ft (40 metres) in the old mines, where more can be learned about mining practices, and which includes a large silver chamber that is particularly worth seeing.

For centuries **Piekary Śląskie** has been a place of pilgrimage and the focal point of the Upper Silesian cult of the Virgin Mary. The final destination of the pilgrims who come here is the **Basilica** and the **Piekarski Devotional Church** situated on **Cerekwica Hill**.

Preceding pages: the Cistercian monastery in Krzeszów. Only a few masters the art of instrument making remain in Poland. Left, evening magic in the Jura Mountains.

North of the Silesian highlands is the region of **Rybnicki Okręg Węglowy**. Although **Jastrzębie Zdrój** has officially been a spa since 1861, it is also the location of a large modern coal mining centre. In 1980 mass strikes were held here which – together with the strikes in Gdańsk and Szczecin – led to the founding of Solidarity.

Between Katowice and Bielsko, next to an area of woodland, is **Pszczyna**, a medieval town which was the seat of the Hochberg family until 1945. The palace was then rebuilt as a museum, where visitors can now stroll through rooms decorated in Renaissance and neoclassical style. In the hall of mirrors chamber concerts are held at which music by the former court kapellmeister P. Telemann is played. The palace is surrounded by a romantic park dissected by the **River Pszczynka**. Nearby there is a bison reserve.

Jura Cracowska-Częstochowska: This attractive holiday region is situated next to the border between Upper Silesia and Małopolska, a rocky area running from Częstochowa to Cracow and characterised by caves, wild gorges, gentle valleys and mixed woodland with a wide variety of trees. The highest point is **Podzamcze Ogrodzienieckie**. In the Middle Ages this border area was defended by a series of imposing castles and fortresses, known as eagle's nests because of their inaccessibility. Ruins of these old castles can still be seen along the "**Eagle's nest route**", which starts with the **Wawel** in Cracow and finishes with **Jasnogorski Castle** in Częstochowa.

Częstochowa is a place of pilgrimage of special significance for all Polish Catholics. The destination of the pilgrims is the Black Madonna, a Byzantine icon. It is situated in the **Chapel of the Virgin Mary of Częstochowa** in the baroque monastery of Jasna Góra, which belongs to the Pauline order. The icon originated in Constantinople, but was brought to Silesia by the Pauline order under the leadership of Prince Władysław in 1382 and from then on remained in the care of the order. Chemical processes, of which people in

those days were ignorant, made the once white Madonna turn black. As a result miracles and visions were attributed to the painting and the **Virgin Mary Sanctuary** became a place of pilgrimage for people from all over the country. In the **Museum** in the old monastery printing works is a treasury containing precious votive offerings presented by the Polish kings in the 17th century.

Near **Olsztyn** on the eagle's nest route are the ruins of a castle built by Kazimierz (Casimir) the Great, which was destroyed by the Swedes in 1655. Not far from here, in **Złoty Potok**, is the palace of the Raczynski family and a manor where Zygmunt Krasiński (1821–59) wrote his romantic poems.

The little town of **Żarki** has a Renaissance church, also a 19th-century synagogue, which is today a cultural centre, and a Jewish cemetery. In **Mirowie** and **Bobolicy** further castle ruins testify to the eventful history of this region. The oldest building in Jura Cracowska-Częstochowska is the Romanesque **Church of St John the Baptist** in **Siewierz**. Close by are the ruins of **Ogrodzience Palace**, which are also worth a visit. The **Palace** was so sumptuously furnished by its owner, the wealthy merchant Boner, that it even rivalled the highly elaborate castle of Wawel. Further on in the direction of Cracow is **Olkusz**, which has the oldest zinc and lead mines in the area. Because these metals contain a high content of silver, Olkusz was for many years also called "Silver Town".

Adjoining Olkusz is **Pustynia Blędowska**, an area of around 12 sq. miles (30 sq. km) which with its unusual drifting dunes and extensive river sandbanks is in sharp contrast with the prevailing geographical features found in this region.

On the border with Wielkopolska, **Oświęcim**, where the Soła flows into the Vistula, was originally the site of a 12th-century castle, and in 1317 became the capital of an independent principality. Its recent history is of a much grimmer nature. During World War II, in the concentration camps of **Auschwitz** and **Birkenau** which were situated here,

The Basilica of Jasna Góra.

thousands of Jews, resistance fighters and prisoners of war met their deaths. The systematic mass murder that took place claimed victims from all the countries of Europe. On the sites of the former concentration camps there is a display of photos and film material from the camp archives: the camp of Birkenau has been left more or less as it was. At the end of the loading ramp where the people condemned to die were taken, is a memorial to all victims of fascism everywhere in the world.

Situated on the **River Skawa** in the **Auschwitz Hollow** is the town of **Zator**, which was ruled until 1513 by Silesian princes, and subsequently became part of the Republic. Points of interest are the old town walls, the Gothic **Parish Church of St George** and a **Palace** in the romantic style with numerous neo-Gothic features.

Wadowice, located between Bielsko-Biała and Cracow, is the birthplace of Karol Wojtyła, who later became Pope John Paul II: he lived here from 1920 until he left grammar school. The only remaining medieval building in the town is the **Presbytery of the Parish Church**. In the vicinity is **Kalwaria Zebrzy-dowska**, an important place of pilgrimage for southern Poland. Object of the pilgrimages is the **Basilica of Our Lady of the Angels**, perched on a wooded hill next to a Bernardine monastery. The Virgin Mary sanctuary was consecrated in the year 1887, and on this hill, which is the oldest calvary in Poland, there are annual performances of passion plays. Kalwaria Zebrzydowska is also one of the biggest centres of the Polish furniture industry.

The **West Beskid Mountains**, in the Polish part of the Carpathians, form the southern boundary of the Upper Silesian industrial area. Among the towns included in this area are **Beskidy Śląski**, **May**, **Żywiecki**, **Makowski** and **Wysoki**. The administrative centre of the region is **Bielsko-Biała**, a town mainly supported by the textile industry. The centre of the town was designed around the turn of the century by a Viennese architect.

A Silesian miner.

North of Bielksto-Biała is the second most popular ski resort in Poland after Zakopane. **Szczyrk** at the foot of **Klimczok** (4,496 ft/1,199 metres) possesses the only ski slope in Poland authorised by the International Ski Organisation. The road from Szczyrk to Wisla has panoramic views of the mountains towering above the **Salmopoliski** valley with its popular holiday resorts **Wisła** and **Ustroń**. Abundant chlorine, soda, bromide, iodine and iron springs have led to the establishment of numerous sanatoria in this district. A chairlift has been built on the slopes of **Czantoria**.

On the summit of this mountain are the sources of the **Czarna** and the **Biała Wiselka**, which meet in Czarne to become the largest river in Poland, the **Vistula**. On the banks of the **Olza** is the border town of **Cieszyn**, from 1282 to 1653 the capital of a principality run by a branch of the Silesian Piasts. The **Chapel of St Nicholas** is built in the form of a Roman rotunda, incorporated in a Gothic monastery belonging to the Benedictines and Dominicans. Around the market square are buildings dating from the Renaissance.

Further to the west, on either side of the gently flowing Odra are the fertile Silesian lowlands. In the south the landscape is a little hillier. The extraordinarily good climatic conditions are perfect for agriculture, and although there has been increasing air pollution during the last 20 years due to a Czech coking plant situated not far away, the area is still very popular with holiday-makers keen on outdoor pursuits.

Opole is the administrative and also the cultural centre of the region. Originally the site of a fort constructed by the *Opole tribe*, the town itself, situated on the right bank of the Odra, was founded in 1217. There are many reminders of its early history, including the massive **Tower of the Piast Castle**, small sections of the **defensive wall**, a **bastion** by the Little Market, the **Church of the Holy Cross**, the **Dominican Church of Our Lady of Sorrows**, and the St Anna Chapel, also called the **Piastowske**

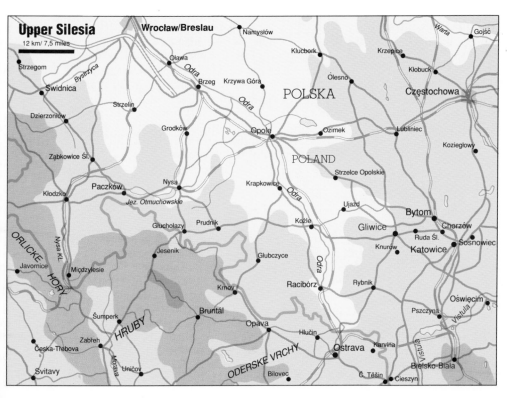

Chapel. In this chapel are several paintings and a number of Gothic tombs and epitaphs of particular interest. The town centre, situated on the banks of the **Młynówka Canal**, has been restored and has retained its Renaissance atmosphere. Every year in the third week of June the town is flooded with visitors who come here to enjoy the Festival of Polish Song.

On the island in the middle of the Odra and the north bank there is an interesting zoo and the road to Wrocław leads past a large open-air museum where reconstructed buildings such as windmills, smithies and silos from the 17th century are displayed.

High up above the river between Opole and Wrocław is **Brzeg**. This town on the Odra had its heyday in the 16th century when it was the capital of the principality. The **Renaissance palace** dates back to this time and is a particularly magnificent example of this architectural style: it is with some justification that it is frequently compared with the Wawel. The **Town Hall** is also from this period. **Brzeg** is today a centre of the food industry. To the north is **Grodków**, a town that has also preserved some evidence of its former glory in the form of two of the original four city gates and the **Parish Church of St Michelangelo**.

Nysa on the northwestern edge of Opolszczyzna was the capital of the episcopal principality of Wroclaw for more than 600 years and was at the height of its importance in the 16th and 17th centuries. During the invasion of the Red Army in March 1945, 80 per cent of the town was destroyed: of the original 28 bastions and four towers of the medieval defence system only two towers and a small fragment of wall now remain.

The Gothic **Church of St Jacob** in the town centre is a wonderful example of European church architecture. With its three naves, 19 chapels and three porches, this church is of monumental size, and the fact that it was built in the 13th century makes its dimensions even more impressive: it has a height of 285 ft (76 metres), a length of 258 ft (69 metres) and a width of 95 ft (25 metres). The **Church of St Peter and Paul** and the Jesuit monastery are from the baroque era.

After the war the town expanded economically as a result of the opening of a factory producing pick-up trucks. Its products were highly successful and much in demand in Common Market countries. In the western part of the town is a very popular recreational area with two artificial lakes offering opportunities for watersports.

Situated on one of these lakes is **Otmuchow**, a settlement dating from 1155 with an interesting church, the **Basilica of St Nicholas**. A few miles to the west, at the foot of the Gold Mountains, is **Paczków**, a town which is popularly known as the Polish Carcassonne, because of its well-preserved medieval city features and fortifications. Next to the town walls is the **Church of St John**, a massive Gothic church with three naves. On its west side is a finely carved portal.

Along the border are some picturesque little towns such as **Głuchołazy**, a spa and the birthplace of natural healing. Its dominant features are the **Baroque Church of St Lawrence** with its two towers, and the **Tower of the Lower Gate**. In the neighbouring town of **Prudnik** remains of the town walls with the Lower Gate and a cylindrical stone tower have been preserved.

To the north is **Biała**, a town which was formerly mainly inhabited by Jews. Today the only reminder of this aspect of the community's history is the Jewish cemetery.

Bordering the Upper Silesian industrial area are the **Góra Św. Anny** (St Anna Mountains) (1,515 ft/404 metres). The place of the same name situated on the **Chelmer Ridge** has been the centre of the St Anna cult since the 17th century. It boasts a **Basilica of St Anna**, 37 chapels and three devotional churches.

Not far from the monastery is a copy of the cave of the Virgin at Lourdes and a pilgrim house where the faithful stay. **Mount St Anna** was the site of fierce fighting between Polish rebels and the army in 1921.

The Black Madonna.

WROCŁAW

Wrocław is situated in the centre of the Silesian lowlands. The city's position on the road which linked Western Europe with Russia had a crucial influence on its development. Wrocław dates back to the 10th century when a settlement was established on the Ostrów Tumski. Later the Ślężanie built a castle here, and in the year 1000 the king of Poland founded the first diocese on Polish soil in Wrocław. Until 1526 the town was governed by the kings of Bohemia, and after this date came under the rule of the Habsburgs. In 1939 Breslau, as the Germans called it, numbered over a million inhabitants, and was one of the largest towns in the whole of the German Reich. During the war the town was badly damaged by bombs.

Once again, however, visitors can admire the unique interplay of architecture and landscape that makes **Ostrów Tumski** particularly attractive. Amongst the buildings in this complex, reconstructed after the war, are one of the most beautiful Gothic town halls in Europe, and the **Jesuit College**, which is today the university. The focal point is the **Cathedral of St John the Baptist** with its Renaissance stone portal, winged altar dating from 1522, alabaster pulpit and Chapel of Our Lady. The **Church of the Holy Cross** is a two-storeyed hall church, one of the few examples of its kind in Europe. It contains the tombs of the Wrocław bishops.

The **Town Hall** dates from the 13th century, but has undergone many alterations in the course of its history. Its south facade is decorated with artistic old carvings. Inside are rather bare, functional rooms but also two chambers which are splendidly decorated, the **Grand Hall** and the **Princes Hall**. Today the Town Hall houses the **City Historical Museum**.

In the main building of the university the **Aula Leopoldina** is also worth a visit: the walls are decorated with illusionistic paintings, the work of J.K. Handkes. Amongst the numerous other architectural attractions the facade of the Gothic **Church of St Mary Magdalene** in **ul.** Szewska is particularly outstanding with its beautiful Romanesque portal originating from the former Benedictine Abbey.

It is worth taking time in Wrocław to visit the great variety of museums the town has to offer. The **National Museum** has a large collection of medieval Silesian art and an exhibition of modern Polish art. Amongst the exhibits of earlier date is a Gothic sarcophagus from Ostrów Tumski with the following Latin inscription: "Prince Henryk IV passed away in the year 1290. After years of excellent government of Silesia, Cracow and Sandomierz".

Bas-reliefs on the side of the sarcophagus depict two eagles, representing the Polish crown and the principality of Silesia. The palace of the Spaetgen family at **33 ul. Kazimierza Wielkiego** is now the home of the **Ethnographic Museum**. Next door to it is the **Archaeological Museum**.

In the round building in **ul. Parkiniego** is the impressive **Panorama Racławicka**, a huge 360 degree painting of a battle, 390 ft (120 metres) in length and 48 ft (15 metres) in height. It was painted in 1894 by the artists W. Kossak and J. Styka on the 100th anniversary of the battle between the Polish army led by Kosciuszko and the Russian army. This picture hung in **Lwów** until 1939 and only came back to Poland from the Soviet Union in 1985.

Surrounding Wrocław: West of Wrocław is **Środa Śląska**, one of the oldest settlements on the trade route from Germany to Russia. Its old medieval town centre has been preserved in its original form. Particular points of interest are the oval marketplace, fragments of the town walls and the **Parish Church of St Andrew**, which has kept its late Gothic interior in spite of the repeated reconstructions which this building has undergone.

In **Prochowice** on the **River Kaczawa** is the ruin of a castle with its inner walls preserved more or less intact. Further north, at the point where the Kaczawa flows into the Oder, is **Lubiąż**, where there is a large baroque monastery, originally founded by monks of the Cistercian order. The oldest of the monastery churches, which dates back to the 13th century, is surrounded by chapels built at a later stage in the history of this complex. The main building has a length of 724 ft (223 metres) and the interior is decorated with numerous frescoes.

Since 1957 the area between **Legnica** and **Głogów** has been dominated by the copper industry, which has also resulted in a high level of atmospheric pollution. In the heart of this region is the former trading settlement of **Lubin**, a charming town with its Gothic architecture, fragments of town wall, fortified tower, church and ruined castle.

It is also the copper-processing industry that has led to the rapid economic expansion of **Legnica**. Both the importance and the problems of this town are probably partly due to the fact that it was the place where the largest garrison of the Red Army was stationed. Legnica was originally the capital of the Trezbovites, a Slavic tribe, then became a Polish diocese and finally, through its good situation on the Kaczawa, an important trading centre. Among the points of interest in this town are the early Gothic castle, which has a Renaissance portal by Johannes von Amberg. After the fire in 1835 it was rebuilt according to a design by Karl Friedrich Schinkel, the architect responsible for many of the neoclassical buildings in Berlin. Further important buildings are the **Parish Church of St Peter and St Paul**, a Gothic hall church with a Romanesque font, and the former presbytery of the baroque **Church of St John**, which contains the **Mausoleum of the Piasts**, the princes of Legnica-Brzesk.

Not far from Legnica is **Legnickie Pole**, which was the scene of the biggest battle in Europe in the Middle Ages, when, in the year 1241, an army composed of Polish, Bohemian and German knights fought against the Tartars. The mother of Henryk II the Godfearing, who led the Christian army and was killed on the battlefield, founded a parish church in honour of her son. And it

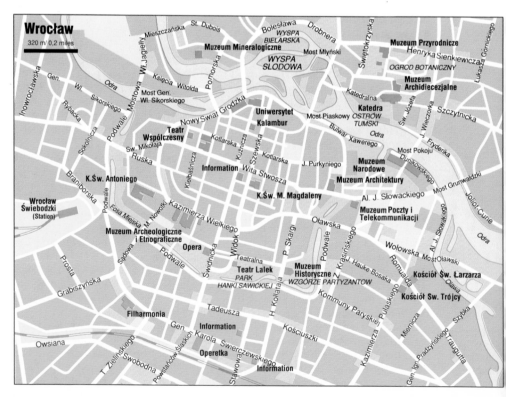

was in her memory, in turn, that the Bernadine Abbey with the **Church of St Hedwig** was founded in the 18th century. The vault of the baroque church is decorated with frescoes by the Bavarian master K.D. Assam.

In the town of **Chojnów** is a Renaissance palace, built during the reign of the Prussian King Friedrich III. It was later extended, and today its rooms have been put to good use as a museum. Also in Chojnów you will find impressive remains of medieval fortifications and a Gothic church.

From the 12th century onwards, the town of **Złotoryja** flourished as a result of the gold panning that was carried out here. After the vein of gold had been exhausted, the citizens of Złotoryja turned instead to the production of cloth. A number of medieval constructions are still standing: fragments of the original town walls including a smithy bastion, the Romanesque-Gothic **Parish Church of the Virgin Mary**, the **Church of St Hedwig** and the **Franciscan monastery** with its combination of Gothic and baroque architectural styles.

Jaworze was the capital of the principality for a short period during the 14th century, and its market square is still surrounded with imposing town residences. The **Regional Museum** is housed in the Franciscan monastery. The Protestant **Church of Peace** is also worth seeing: it has a wooden interior with galleries and interesting paintings dating from 1710. On the site of the former concentration camp **Rogoznica** are a mausoleum and an exhibition to remind us of the crimes once committed in this place.

Perched on top of a basalt hill is the town of **Strzegom**, one of the oldest settlements in Silesia. Even before Christ there was a castle here belonging to the Sorbs, which was later used as a fortress by the Poles. The medieval **Church of St Peter and St Paul** has elaborately carved portals and gable windows, and a manneristic interior. The **Church of St Barbara** was a Jewish synagogue until 1456.

Beyond the original town walls with the **Beak Bastion**, are numerous old quarries and mines which were once a profitable source of basalt and granite. In the old medieval town centre of **Bolków** on the **Nysa Szalona** you will find the oldest stone castle in Poland. Bolków's picturesque market square is situated on top of a hill, with ancient arcades and houses, the town hall and the **Parish Church of St Hedwig** clustering round it.

To the north is **Głogów**, a town with a long history which, in the 10th century, was one of the strongest citadels in Poland and the residence of the Piast princes. After 1745 the town was a key factor in Prussian military strategy. During the repeated battles that took place in 1945 it was almost completely destroyed. The baroque palace, the Gothic tower that was originally part of the fortifications, the late baroque church and the **Corpus Christi College** which was designed by the Italian architect J. Simonetti, have all been reconstructed.

A further place of interest in this area is **Brzeg Dolny** with its unusual park. At the centre of this park is a neoclassical palace dating from 1785, the work of the architect K.G. Langhans. At **Trzebnica** the Cistercian order founded the first convent on Polish soil, building on to a Romanesque basilica already in existence on this spot. The architecture of the convent today is all in the style of the 18th century. The basilica contains the elaborate early Gothic **Chapel of St Hedwig**. Surprisingly, the second largest cloister complex in Poland is today in use as a hospital.

Oleśnica, a town situated on a low hill, has a Renaissance palace which was once the residence of the Electors and an interesting church, the **Church of St John the Evangelist**. It was an important centre of the Polish Reformation in the 16th century. The old ducal fortifications of the town, including the **Breslau Gate**, have also been preserved and are suitably handsome.

Further to the south between the **Odra** and **Oława** is the former diocese of **Oława**, which later belonged to the palace of the Prince of Brzesk. Situated on the market square is a town hall designed by Schinkel and a baroque tower.

Strzelino marks the beginning of the foothills of the Sudeten Mountains; it is in these hills that most of Poland's granite is quarried. In Strzelino itself the **Church of St Gotthard**, a Romanesque rotunda dating from the 12th century, merits a visit. At nearby **Henrykówa** is a large Cistercian cloister, which includes the noteworthy **Monastery Church of St Mary**. Particular features of this monastery are the numerous paintings and the richly carved pews. In the abbey garden is the largest yew tree in Poland: the trunk is 39 ft (12 metres) in diameter.

The *Henrykówa Book*, the first manuscript in Polish, was written in the abbey in the 13th century.

Ziębice, where the River Oława has its source, has retained its old medieval town centre and defensive walls with their towers and bastions. The **Church of St George** has a very interesting interior reflecting a variety of styles from different epochs. The princes' palace was taken over in the 18th century by a Protestant community. Next to the former monastery is the **Church of St Peter and St Paul** which is in the rather unusual form of a Greek cross.

South of Wrocław, on the edge of the **Kotlina Kłodzka**, is the town of **Ząbkowice Śląskie**, which for centuries has been famous for its glass production. Worth looking at are the bastions and fortified towers, the Gothic **Church of St Anna** and the Dominican monastery. Ząbkowice Śląskie was the site of the first Renaissance palace in Poland, but this building, which had a courtyard with wide cloisters, unfortunately no longer exists.

In **Kamieniec Ząbkowicki** are a former **Cistercian Monastery** and the ruins of the neo-Gothic **Hohenzollern Palace**, built during the last century by K.F. Schinkel and situated on a hill in the midst of an English-style park.

A little further to the north in the direction of Wrocław is the **Góra Ślęża**. Two thousand years ago this mountain was the most important cult location of the Sorbs and from the 5th century onwards it was settled by West Slavs. In the museum in **Sobótka**, which is situated at the foot of the Góra Ślęża, cult objects and sculptures dating from the 3rd to the 1st centuries BC can be seen. Next to the **Church of St Anne** is a further prehistoric sculpture and a Romanesque lion figure.

This whole area has been designated a national park. It is criss-crossed by mountain streams which all flow into the Ślęża; this then joins the Odra northwest of Wrocław.

Adjoining the foothills of the Sudeten is the large basin through which the **Nysa Kłodzka, Bystrzyca, Ścinawka** and **Biała Ladecka** rivers flow. At the centre of this basin is **Kłodzko**, a town which was founded in 1223. Its oldest construction is the Gothic **Stone Bridge**, built in around 1390 and decorated with baroque reliefs. There is also a citadel bristling with towers and fortifications as well as three large monasteries belonging to the Franciscans, the Order of St John and the Jesuits.

The Franciscan **Church of the Virgin Mary** is richly decorated with interesting paintings and frescoes by the Prague master A. Scheffler. The special feature of the parish church with its two towers is a baroque altar designed by K. Tausch.

On the border between Silesia and Bohemia at the foot of a higher part of the Sudeten mountains in the valley of Nysa Klodzka is the beautiful little diocesan town of **Bardo**. Centre of the cult of the Virgin Mary of Bardo in the early Middle Ages, it became a popular spa in the 19th century. The single-nave baroque church contains a wood-carving as well as a Gothic sculpture of Our Lady of Sorrows.

A further attraction in this area is **Wambierzyce**, located at the foot of Góry Stołowe. On a hill in the centre of the town, pyramid-shaped steps lead up to a monumental basilica from the baroque epoch and a group of calvary chapels. Near the church is a delightful exhibition of mechanical nativity scenes.

The **Kłodzko** region is well-known

for its healing mineral springs. The first recorded mention of the healing powers of these springs was in the year 1272 and the first hydros and sanatoria were established in Polanica, Duszniki, Kudowa and Lądek in the 17th century. The composer Chopin stayed in **Duszniki**, a centre of paper production, on the journey through Poland that eventually led him into permanent exile in Paris. To mark the occasion the town holds an annual Piano Festival.

The oldest of the Sudeten spas, **Lądek**, was known for its mineral springs even before it was granted a town charter in 1282. The spa of Kudowa is on the Czechoslovakian border. Nearby is Czerma, which has an unusual baroque chapel: the floor is laid with some 3,000 human skulls.

In the **Bystrzyca** valley is **Świdnica**, a town which, right from its beginnings, was in competition with Wrocław for supremacy as a trading centre. The town enjoyed a reputation for excellent beer and high-quality linen products. Up until the end of the 14th century it had special town rights equivalent to those of a principality, and it subsequently became a citadel.

On the site of the former cemetery is the Protestant Church of Peace, a wooden building with richly decorated ceilings and galleries. In the old town hall on the market square is an exhibition of the history of trade in Swidnica.

The town of **Świebodzice** is worth seeing for the medieval features that have been preserved. Up until the 15th century the palace of **Książno** belonged to the Piasts of Świdnica, and after this to the Hochbergers. During the German occupation there were plans to convert this building into a fortress for Adolf Hitler and the necessary extensions were begun, with parts of the original building being completely destroyed in the process. Remains of the beautiful medieval stone tower and the Renaissance wing have, however, been preserved.

The Nobel prize winner Gerhard Hauptmann (1862–1946) stayed for some time in Książno. On the slope where the palace is situated is an Eng-

Kłodzko on the River Neisse.

lish Garden with exotic trees, which is still a very pleasant place for a stroll. Nearby are the buildings of a stud farm.

Points of interest in **Kamienna Góra** are the ruins of a large Renaissance palace, a row of baroque houses with arcades on the market square, and an exhibition on the subject of weaving in the town's museum.

In nearby **Chełmsko Śląskie** a street of centuries-old weavers' cottages has been preserved, among them the **House of the Twelve Apostles.**

The Cistercian Abbey of **Krzeszów** is one of the most outstanding examples of baroque architecture in Silesia. The former **Parish Church of St Joseph** in the immediate vicinity is well-known for its frescoes; they are the work of M. Willman, the man otherwise known as the Silesian Rembrandt.

The River Bobr and its tributaries, the Kamienna and the Lomnica, flow through the densely populated and heavily industrialised area of **Kotlina Jeleniogórska**. The former diocesan town of **Jelenia Góra** is the administrative and cultural centre of the region. From the Middle Ages onwards it was an important regional trading centre, and its economic development proceeded rapidly during the age of industrialisation. It was not long afterwards that tourism also became an important source of income, as the town is not lacking in interesting things to see.

Jelenia Góra still has its medieval town centre, together with impressive fortifications from this period. On the market square is an imposing **Town Hall**, surrounded by merchants' houses. The **Parish Church of St Erasmus and St Pancras** has a Renaissance tower with a later addition in baroque style. Inside, itts main altar is the work of two Norwegian sculptors, T. Weisfeld and J. Kretschmer.

Outside the medieval town walls stands the Protestant **Church of the Holy Cross** dating from 1718, which was designed by the Swedish architect M. Franz. The interior is decorated with frescoes painted by the Prague master A.F. Schaffler, assisted by the local artist J. F. Hoffmann.

There is also a museum with an exhibition of 17th- and 18th-century glass, ranging from everyday glassware to works of art.

The spa of **Cieplice** has today been incorporated into Jelenia Góra. It once belonged to the Order of St John, and the monks used the local mineral springs in the treatment of the sick.

The town has long had a reputation for excellent cut glass, as well as being a centre of the paper industry. Points of particular interest are the monastery with the **Church of St John the Baptist** and the palace dating from the end of the 18th century.

Located on the **River Kamienna** is **Piechowice**, well-known for its glass industry. **Kowary**, on the **River Łomnica** which runs along the country's border, was once an ore-mining centre. Today the main industry of the town is carpet weaving.

North of Jelenia Góra, in **Siedlecin**, is an interesting residential tower. It is constructed of stone and decorated inside with a series of unique medieval

The initials of a headless Frederick the Great in Srebrna Góra.

paintings, which have secular themes.

On a basalt hill not far from **Wleń** are the ruins of a medieval castle: from the tower there is an excellent view of the town and the mountains. Nearby is a **palace** which has now been converted into a sanatorium.

Lwówek Śląski on the River Bóbr, which originated in 1217, was the first town on Polish soil where the Magdeburg Laws were applied. Large sections of the medieval fortifications have been preserved, and there is a Gothic town hall which also has elements of Renaissance architecture and a late Gothic hall church with two towers, the **Church of the Assumption** .

The main mountain range, the **Karkonosze**, stretches for 22 miles (36 km) between **Przełęcz Szklarska** (2,976 ft/885 metres) in the west and **Przełęcz Kowarska** (2,362 ft/727 metres) in the east. The highest mountain is **Śnieżka**, (5,206 ft/1,602 metres), followed by **Szyszak** and **Średnica**. Only 28 percent of this range of mountains is on Polish territory, and the rest is in Czechoslo-

vakia. The thickly-wooded mountain slopes are severely endangered by atmospheric pollution, largely caused by power plants in Czechoslovakia and the eastern part of Germany.

Pines and mountain ash grow up to a level of 4,060 ft (1250 metres); after this the vegetation consists of dwarf pines and Carpathian birches. There are numerous deer, mouflons and owls.

The **Karkonosze National Park** has an area of 13½ acres (5.5 hectares) and is well provided with guesthouses for those wishing to explore it on foot. **Szlarska Poręba**, which is popular with tourists, is picturesquely situated on the shores of the Kamienna. Nearby, **Szrenice** has a chair lift for the skiers who come here in winter: from its summit there is a broad ski slope leading right to the bottom of the valley.

Karpacz is a good starting point for excursions into the highest areas of the Karkonosze.

In the Bierutowice district of Karpacz is the "**Wang**", a wooden church brought here from Norway in the 19th century.

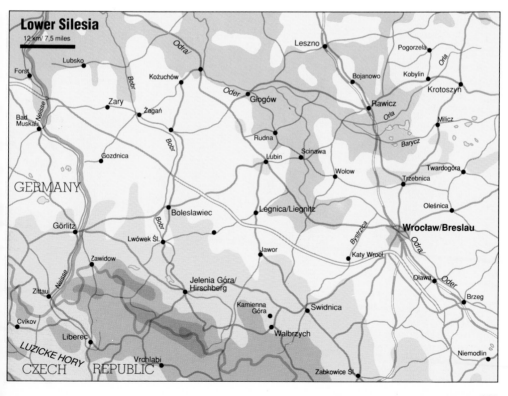

Lower Silesia

12 km/ 7,5 miles

Forst · Lubsko · Leszno · Pogorzela · Orla · Kobylin · Krotoszyn · Kożuchów · Bojanowo · Żary · Zagań · Oder · Głogów · Rawicz · Orla · Milicz · Bad Muskau · Neisse · Bóbr · Rudna · Ścinawa · Barycz · Gozdnica · Lubin · Wołów · Twardogóra · Trzebnica · GERMANY · Bolesławiec · Legnica/Liegnitz · Oleśnica · Görlitz · Bóbr · Wrocław/Breslau · Lwówek Śl. · Jawor · Bystrzyca · Katy Wrocł · Odra · Zawidów · Zittau · Neisse · Jelenia Góra/ Hirschberg · Oława · Oder · Brzeg · Cvikov · Kamienna Góra · Świdnica · Liberec · Wałbrzych · Niemodlin · LUŻICKE HORY · Vrchlabi · CZECH REPUBLIC · Ząbkowice Śl.

WIELKOPOLSKA/ GREATER POLAND

One of the largest provinces in Poland is situated in the west of the country along the central and lower stretches of the River Warta, which is the largest tributary of the Odra. It was here that the state of Poland came into being. Today Wielkopolska has a thriving economy and a highly developed agricultural system. Its neat towns and villages and hotels and guesthouses of a high standard make travel through this part of the country a pleasure.

In the 9th century the rulers of the Piast dynasty were able to combine the scattered territories of the Polan tribe into a single dominion, thus laying the foundation stone for a new sovereign state: Poland. Residences were established in centrally located castles, **Gniezno**, **Legnica** and **Poznań**, and the rule of the princes, at first limited to Wielkopolska, was soon extended to the adjacent territories.

In the year 1000 a diocese was founded in **Gniezno**, and the town became the first Polish metropolis of the Roman Catholic church. Until the beginning of the 19th century the country's kings were crowned in the cathedral of Gniezno. While first Cracow and then Warsaw took over Gniezo's role as the secular capital of the country, the city is still considered to be the spiritual centre of Poland.

In the ensuing centuries prosperity increased as trade in this part of the world began to flourish, aided considerably by the fact that numerous European trade routes from Western Europe to Russia and Lithuania and from the Balkans to Scandinavia passed through Wielkopolska.

In the 19th century Wielkopolska – like Silesia – was one of the areas annexed by Prussia. In towns and villages patriotic organisations were formed which resisted the "germanisation" policies of the occupying powers. Liberation from Prussian occupation was achieved as a result of the Wielkopolska Uprising of 1918–19.

POZNAŃ

The capital of Wielkopolska is situated on the River Warta and is a major junction for the road and railway network of the region. Over the years it has become an important industrial centre, the location of some of the country's major industrial combines, including the largest manufacturer of ships' engines in Europe, H. Cegielski.

Eight institutions of higher learning are carrying out intensive research in a wide variety of areas. The "Western Institute" is studying the relations of Poland with the western industrialised countries, with particular emphasis on the relationship between Poland and Germany. With its three well-known choirs (male voices with boy sopranos) and the annual H. Wieniawski International Violin Competition, Poznań is also a thriving cultural centre.

Poznań dates back to the 9th century, when a large fortified castle was built on an island in the Warta. This was soon expanded, and became one of the main castles of the Polish state. In 1253 Poznań was granted its city charter and became the capital of Wielkopolska.

Poznań's eventful history continued with considerable economic expansion as a result of the revival of European trade at the beginning of the Middle Ages, and the city began to establish a reputation as a trade fair centre. In the 19th century the city played a major part in the Polish independence movement and the struggles for liberation from the Nazis. After 1945 reconstruction proceeded rapidly and the population doubled by comparison with what it was at the beginning of the war.

By the end of the war more than half of the city had been destroyed. However, as in Warsaw and Gdańsk, it has now been rebuilt as it was before. The new buildings, on the other hand, especially the hotels, residential and office complexes near the main station, have more in common with the municipal architecture of the West.

With its numerous interesting sights,

including excellent museums, palaces and castles, and attractive countryside, such as the **Wielkopolski National Park**, within easy distance, Poznań is the number one tourist attraction amongst the towns of the region.

A tour of Poznań is best begun on the **Ostrów Tumski**, the peninsula between the River Warta and the River Cybina. The cathedral is the oldest "temple" of Christianity in Poland; it was originally built in 968, and there were numerous extensions, the last being in the 16th century. Reconstructed after World War II, its present form is that of a Gothic basilica with three naves and radiating chapels, with large baroque towers dominating the front facade. In the crypt the 10th century foundations are still visible, and there are also an original font and fragments of tombs of the first rulers of Poland. The Gothic main altar, dating from 1512 and originating from the "Silesian workshop" is indisputedly the church's most outstanding feature. In the Byzantine-style Golden Chapel are the tombs of the first kings, Mieszko I and Bolesław Chrobry.

Near the cathedral are two Gothic buildings, the **Church of the Holy Virgin** dating from the 15th century, which has been preserved entirely in its original form, and the house where the members of the cathedral choir were once accommodated, which dates from the beginning of the 14th century.

Also near the cathedral are the bishop's palace and ancient houses where the canons once lived.

The building housing the present **Lubranski Academy** in the southern part of Ostrów Tumski dates from 1518, and was once the location of the first university in Poznań. Its most attractive feature is its courtyard, which is surrounded by arcades. In the neighbouring house, the **Archdiocesan Museum** contains interesting collections of sacred art from the province of Wielkopolska.

The modern architecture of the seminary is in sharp contrast with the rest of the buildings in this old part of Poznań. Here priests receive training for their work abroad, including the spiritual care

Preceding pages: springtime; the early-Slavic settlement of Biskupin. **Left,** feeding the birds in Poznań's old city.

of Polish emigrants all over the world.

On the other side of the little River Cybina is the municipal district of **Srodka**, centred around the **Church of St Margaret**. Until the 18th century it was a separate town, and it has retained its own special atmosphere.

On the outskirts of Srodka is the Romanesque **Church of St John**, one of the first brick-built churches in Poland. Nearby is **Lake Maltańskie**, which was created by damming up the Cybina. From 1985 until 1990 one of the best rowing and canoe regatta courses in Europe was established on this lake, and the world canoe championships were held here in August 1990.

Just east of Lake Maltańskie is **Wielkopolska Zoo**, the largest and most beautiful zoo in Poland. The animals live in spacious compounds in conditions which closely resemble their natural habitat.

In 1253 a new town was founded in accordance with the Magdeburg Laws on the left bank of the Warta. Most of the medieval defensive wall which surrounded it was pulled down at the beginning of the 19th century. The centre of the town was the marketplace, which still goes by the name of **Old Market Square**. Most of the buildings of this medieval town, today's old town, were destroyed during World War II. They have been reconstructed and today form one of the most beautiful old town complexes in Poland.

The Market Square is dominated by a beautiful **Town Hall**, designed by the architect Jan Baptist Quadro. This building, with its Renaissance rooms and unique coffered ceiling, now contains the **City Historical Museum**.

There are several ancient churches in the old town, of which the **Parish Church** in **Gołębia Road** is especially interesting. Built about 1800 it has a particularly splendid interior with monumental pillars and altars. Amongst the various museums located in the old town is the **Musical Instruments Museum** (Stary Rynek 47), one of the best of its kind in Europe, with valuable instruments from Poland and all over

The marketplace in Poznań, one of the most beautiful architectural ensembles in the whole of Poland.

236

the world. The highlights of the museum are a collection of Polish stringed instruments from the 16th to the 20th century, the Chopin room and the assortment of folk instruments..

On **Przemyslaw Hill** are the remains of Poznań palace and a baroque church belonging to the Franciscan order.

The modern town centre west of the old town originated around the turn of the century. On **Plac Wolności** (Freedom Square) is the **Raczyński Library**, a neoclassical construction dating from 1829, which was built in imitation of the Louvre in Paris.

Close by is the **National Museum**, which has a splendid collection of Polish and international art – the best of its kind in Poland.

Also in this part of town is one of the oldest hotels in Europe, the "**Bazar**". Stylish and full of atmosphere, it is always a good place to take a break from sightseeing and enjoy a cup of coffee and a slice of cake.

On **Mickeiwicz Square** are two important monuments of particular interest, one to Adam Mickiewicz (1798–1855), who was one of Poland's greatest poets, and one in memory of the workers' uprising of 1956, known as Poznań June. A short distance from Mickiewicz Square there is an interesting mixture of buildings in a variety of styles dating from the beginning of the 20th century.

North of the centre are the remains of a large citadel which was almost completely destroyed in 1945. Today there is a park on this site and a cemetery for the Commonwealth soldiers who died during World Wars I and II.

In **Wilan Park**, in the Lazan district of Poznań, is one of the largest palm houses in Europe. It contains around 17,000 tropical plants.

Adjoining the outskirts of Poznań is a large region of park and woodland. In the middle of this, to the west, is an area of lakes. On **Lake Strzesynskie** is an open-air swimming pool, and there is also a motel and an international camp site here. **Lake Kierskie**, which has an area of 741 acres (300 hectares), is very

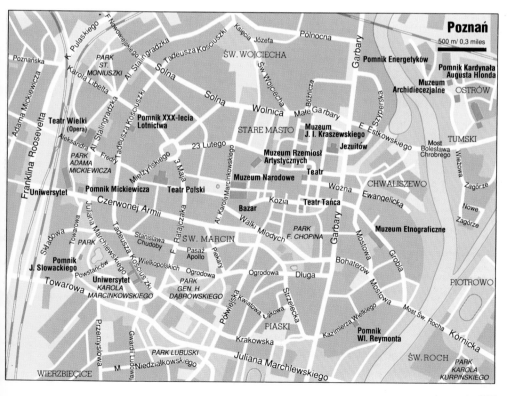

popular with sailing enthusiasts because of its ideal wind conditions.

Poznań Fair: An international fair has been held annually in Poznań since 1925. It is linked with the medieval tradition of the St John fairs which even in those days were a regular meeting point with a European flavour.

The first fair in modern form was organised in 1921, and in 1929 it was coupled for the first time in the history of the new republic with a representative general exhibition concentrating entirely on Poland. In 1947, on the occasion of the first fair after World War II, only 12 countries were represented, but in subsequent years interest in the fair increased massively, and the exhibition centre was greatly enlarged to cater for it: in 1990, on the occasion of the 62nd International Fair, 4,200 exhibitors from 38 countries were accommodated in 24 halls and 80 pavilions.

The main event held is the Industrial Fair in June, the scope and objectives of which are comparable with the Hannover Fair. What it cannot offer in quantity it makes up for by functioning as a bridge between Western markets and the markets of Central and Eastern Europe, and by providing attractive conditions in particular for small and medium-sized suppliers. Since Leipzig will now no longer be able to fulfil this function, the Poznań Fair is unique in this respect. In addition to the Industrial Fair, 10 specialised trade fairs are held every year, including the *Salmed*, a fair for medical equipment, the *Polagra* and the *Interart*.

Visitors and exhibitors who attend these fairs do not feel that they are stuck out in the middle of nowhere, since the convenient location of the exhibition centre right in the town and close to the main station makes it invitingly easy to sample the thriving business and cultural life of the town.

The Fair's administration is located at: Międzynarodowe Targi Poznańskie, ul. Glukowska 14, Poland – 60-734 Poznań (tel: 061/69 93 41; fax: 061/66 58 27; telex: 413251 targ pl).

The surroundings of Poznań: With the exception of Poznań, none of the towns

Young street vendors.

BUSINESS IN POLAND

In German, "Polish economy" is a derogatory expression, used to imply that something is a shambles. If there was ever any truth in this, it is certainly no longer appropriate today. This is in any case the view of around 2,000 western investors, who are now doing successful business in Poland after founding joint enterprises. The conditions for this are extremely favourable, since the relevant legal regulations impose few restrictions on those wishing to embark on business ventures in Poland.

The "Joint Venture Law" for newly founded limited companies provides, for example, a three-year tax exemption with the possibility of extending this for another three years. There are plenty of indications that a five-year period of tax exemption will soon become the general rule.

In addition, foreign investors have the freedom to do almost exactly what they want in their companies; they can operate together with a Polish partner, but they can also found a one-man company and bear all the risks on their own. As long as it is within the boundaries of the law, it is entirely up to the shareholders and the ingenuity of their lawyers to decide what they do and how they do it.

The formalities of founding a company are extremely simple, and, at the most, two months after the company contract has been signed the investor will receive the permission of the Investment Agency in Warsaw that is responsible for such matters. Up until now this has only been refused in about 3 percent of cases.

Under the present economic conditions, the possibilities are almost unlimited. Poland has a large and interesting market, which after over 40 years of communist rule and the mismanagement that this involved, is thirsting for modern goods and technology. The state companies are frequently on the verge of ruin and are thus particularly interested in becoming partners in joint enterprises. These firms usually have sufficient land, factories and warehouses and a well-trained workforce which is willing to work extremely hard. And all this with average monthly wages of £100 per employee per month. Although this figure is beginning to show signs of increasing, it will probably be several decades yet before the level of wages reaches those of England or America – if it ever does.

In addition to the state firms, there are also several thousand private firms waiting eagerly for a Western partner with sufficient capital to found a joint venture. Their hope is that this much sought-after partner will contribute not only money but also valuable technical and financial know-how.

A great deal of care is, of course, necessary in the selection of a business partner. In the country at present the atmosphere is rather like that of a gold rush, together with the accompanying mentality, and there are many bloodthirsty sharks out for a quick kill; in this large country between the Odra and the Bug it is no easy matter to track down the swindler who has vanished with the money.

In order to avoid a disaster the best policy is to avail oneself of the assistance of a reputable agency. One such agency is the BIG (Economic Information Bank) set up in Gdańsk by the trades union Solidarity, which has a register of several thousand firms from all parts of Poland who are interested in embarking on joint ventures.

This bank cannot, of course, guarantee success, and even Solidarity itself is not always able to make all its dreams come true. Thus one of the "economic marriages" it was most anxious to see take place, between the former Danzig Lenin shipyard and the sole heiress of the US Johnson concern, Barbara Piaseska-Johnson, who is of Polish origin, finally did not materialise in spite of mutual "declarations of love".

However, it does not have to be a merger of such spectacular proportions; a capital investment of just US$50,000 is all that is necessary for entrepreneurs to play a part in the business life of Poland.

All it takes are a little courage, a little money, and a little bit of pioneering spirit – and then off to the country of (almost) unlimited opportunities. There is not likely to be another chance like this in the present millennium. Remember the famous quote of Mikhail Gorbachev: "Life will punish those who come too late!"

of Wielkopolska are major business centres, and the region is almost exclusively dominated by agriculture.

Poznań itself is situated in the middle of an extensive region of forest. To the south, at a distance of approximately 10 miles (15 km) from the town centre, is the Wielkopolski National Park, which covers an area of 24,710 acres (10,000 hectares). It has the typical landscape of the Polish lowlands: deciduous woods with many different types of vegetation, moraines and lakes. The most beautiful part of the park is Lake Góreckie, which has the ruins of a romantic castle on one of its islands.

Twelve miles (20 km) to the south of Poznań are two places which are popular destinations for excursions. The main point of interest in the little town of **Kórnik** is the extensive park, situated on the edge of a lake. Particularly impressive is the variety of different kinds of trees to be found here, around 2,500 varieties in all, and there are also some very old trees. At the edge of the park is a palace dating from the 14th century, which was altered architecturally at a later date. Today it houses a museum with a collection of splendid furniture, paintings and military exhibits.

Rogalin, a village situated on the Warta, also has a beautiful park; this merges with an oak forest, which has the greatest number of old oak trees of any forest in Europe. Some of these trees are already 800 years old. The most famous are three oaks which bear the names of the legendary Slavic brothers *Lech*, *Czech* and *Rus*, the founders of Poland, Bohemia and Russia.

In the park is a palace built in the neoclassical style; its rooms are open to the public. A gallery exhibiting excellent Polish and Western European paintings and a collection of coaches are accommodated in pavilions next to the palace.

Twenty-one miles (35 km) northwest of Poznań is the small town of **Szamotuly**. Szamotuly is distinguished by two architectural monuments which should on no account be missed: one is a Gothic parish church with a magnificent interior, and the other is a palace

complex, also Gothic, where the original interior has been reconstructed.

East Wielkopolska: The **Szlak Piastowski**, a road which leaves Poznań in a northeasterly direction, goes past a number of places very closely connected with the early beginnings of the Polish state and thus over 1,000 years old. It is no coincidence, therefore, that this road is named after the first dynasty of Polish kings, the Piasts.

The first place of interest along this route is **Lake Lednica**. One of its islands contains the remains of early Romanesque buildings, once the residence of a prince. Massive earthworks are all that are left of a castle that was built here in the 11th century. At an earlier date the island was connected to the shore by bridges, the total length of which was 2,240 ft (700 metres).

Some idea of what life used to be like in this region can be obtained from the open-air museum on the shores of the lake. Fifty buildings primarily made of wood – the windmills are the most spectacular – provide modern visitors with a vivid picture of everyday life in the Middle Ages.

A little further on, the road approaches a town that has been built on hills: **Gniezno**, the very first capital of Poland. One of its most interesting features is **Gniezno Cathedral**, the seat of the Polish archbishops since the year 1000. Today it is the most monumental Gothic "temple" in all Poland.

Amongst the particular features of the splendid interior are the tomb of the first Polish martyr, St Wojciech (Adalbert), numerous archbishops' tombs and the ornate portals and grilles of 14 chapels. In the church archives and the treasury of the cathedral are numerous collections of ancient books and works of art, the oldest of which date back to the 10th century. Some of these collections are on display to the general public.

Not far from Gniezno are three attractive lakes. On the shores of one of them, **Lake Jelonek**, is a museum, built in the 1980s, covering the history of Poland during the reign of the Piast dynasty. North of Gniezno is **Biskupin**. In the

Still time for a smile after a day of mucking out.

1930s, archaeologists excavated an original Slavic settlement on the peninsula of Biskupin Lake and in the well-preserved wooden buildings which date back 2,500 years found artefacts from the Luzycka art period (Bronze Age). The site has now been declared an archaeological reserve. Part of the settlement has been reconstructed and provides visitors with a unique picture of the way people lived in prehistoric times.

Not far from Biskupin, in **Wenecja**, is a delightful narrow gauge railway museum, and in the summer visitors can even go for short rides in a steam train.

Continuing along the Piast road from Gniezno we come to the towns of **Trzemeszno, Mogilno, Strzelno, Kruszwica** and **Inowrocław**. In **Trzemeszno** is a church that dates back to the 10th century but which today is characterised by the imposing structure and large domes typical of the baroque epoch.

In the vicinity of Trzemeszno there are several lakes, most of which have a rather unusual, elongated shape. This is the result of glacier channels created during the Ice-Age.

Mogilno is the site of one of the first Benedictine monasteries in Poland, which originated in the 11th century. A church in Romanesque style was built at the same time, and although it was later repeatedly rebuilt it has still kept many of its original Romanesque elements, in particular the unique crypts. Further points of interest along the Piast road are described in the **Pomorze Zachodnie**/West Pomerania chapter.

One of the country's major roads, the International Expressway no. 30, leads out of Poznań in the direction of Warsaw. It remains an expressway until Wrzesnia, and then becomes a motorway until it reaches Konin. This part of Wielkopolska is a flat, exclusively agricultural area and there is very little woodland.

Thirty miles (50 km) from Poznań is **Września**. This town contains mementos the way in which the Polish inhabitants heroically struggled against "germanisation" during the occupation of this part of Poland by Prussia.

When the school children went on strike to demand religious education in Polish in 1901, this set off a chain of protests throughout Wielkopolska, and the vigorous campaign of the Poles for their rights attracted attention in all the countries of Europe. The school which started the protests is now a museum. The classrooms in which the protest was fomented have been recreated.

The little town of **Miloslaw**, 10 miles (16 km) south of Wrzesna, is famous for the battles that took place here during the revolution in 1848. Its 18th-century church and neoclassical palace, both in the attractive setting of a large park, are well worth a visit. In the neighbouring village of **Winna Góra**, next to the chapel, is the grave of the Polish general Jan Dąbrowski, a national hero from the epoch of the Napoleonic Wars.

In the village of **Lad** on the Warta an extensive monastery was built by the Cistercians in the high Middle Ages. This was rebuilt in the baroque style and is now one of the most beautiful examples of architecture from this epoch in the whole of Poland. The monumental style of the church architecture, the splendid interiors and the wall paintings are particularly impressive.

Konin on the Warta is an industrial centre, with all the problems this entails. Due to the large deposits of brown coal, enormous electric power plants and factories (including an aluminium works) have been concentrated here. Since 1960 the town has increased sevenfold. However, in spite of all the modern infrastructure, interesting elements of Konin's early medieval past, such as the stone column dating from 1151, have been preserved. The column is to be found next to the Gothic church in the old town, a building which dates back to the 15th century. In the palace situated in the **Gosyawice** district of Konin is the Regional Museum, which includes a collection of paraffin lamps – it must not be forgotten that this is a mining town.

In the vicinity is an open-air museum as well as a Gothic church dating from 1444. North of Konin are countryside areas popular with holiday-makers. In

Slesin there is a triumphal arch, erected in 1811 in honour of Napoleon. It is the only monument of its kind in Poland.

On the Warta there are two interesting little towns: Koło and Uniejów. The special feature of **Koło** is an architectural rarity: a Gothic church with an Art Nouveau interior. **Uniejów**'s main attraction is a Gothic castle, which tourists can experience from a different angle: it has been extended and converted into a comfortable hotel.

With its 110,000 inhabitants, **Kalisz** is the second largest town in Wielkopolska, after the capital Poznań. It is situated on the **River Prosna**, a tributary of the Warta. The town is particularly proud of its registry of births, marriages and deaths, the oldest in Poland: it was mentioned 1,800 years ago in the work of the Roman traveller Ptolemaeus. Today Kalisz is one of the most important centres of the Polish textile industry.

The old town of Kalisz has a number of interesting buildings: the **Church of St Nicholas** dating from the 13th/15th centuries with its splendid interior, the late baroque **Collegiate Church of St Joseph**, the neoclassical building accommodating the voivodeship offices and the church and monastery of the Franciscan order, originating from the 13th century and rebuilt during the baroque era.

On the banks of the Prosna, situated at the edge of a beautiful and spacious park, is a neoclassical theatre. In the museum which covers the Kalisz region, archaeological, historical and ethnographical collections provide further information about the area. **Asnyka Road** in a newer part of Kalisz, has two modern churches which have only recently been built and are interesting for their avant-garde architectural design.

The three places of interest that are particularly worth visiting on the road from Kalisz to Poznań are Gołuchow, Żerkow and Ćmielów.

In **Gołuchow** is a magnificent Renaissance Palace, in the attractive setting of an extensive park. Its rooms are also worth visiting for their interesting col-

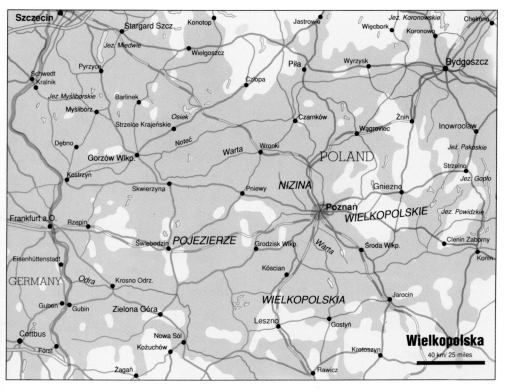

lections of paintings, period furniture and precious vases. Adjoining the museum park is a woodland area.

In the woods at Gołuchow is an erratic, a huge boulder left over from the last Ice Age, which has a diameter of 71 ft (22 metres) and a height of 12 ft (3.5 metres).

Picturesquely located between moraines on the edge of the Warta valley are Żerków and Smielow. The special feature of the quiet little town of **Żerków** is its baroque church.

The famous Polish poet Adam Mickiewicz stayed on a number of occasions in the village of **Śmielów**, a fact which has made it famous all over Poland. Certain events which took place in Śmielów and its surroundings, feature in Mickiewicz's well-known work *Pan Tadeusz*, which is one of the most important poetic works in the Polish language. In the village is a museum dedicated to the poet; it concentrates solely on the romantic epoch and is appropriately accommodated in a neoclassical palace dating from 1800.

The southern border of Wielkopolska is formed by the **Ostrzeszowskie** Hills. In **Autonien**, a village on the busy road from Poznań to Silesia, is an old park full of oak trees with a wooden palace that is worth a visit. It was built at the beginning of the 19th century and its designer was the well-known Berlin architect Karl Friedrich Schinkel. Today a convalescent home and a very pleasant café are accommodated within its walls.

South Wielkopolska: South Wielkopolska is a rich agricultural area and has the highest concentration of farms of any region in Poland. It is, however, equally rich in architectural monuments and places of historical interest.

Leszno, which dates back to the Middle Ages, today has around 60,000 inhabitants. One particularly well-known citizen of this town was the leading Czech pedagogue Jan Amos Komensky. On the market square is an impressive baroque **Town Hall**, a work by the Italian architect Pompeo Ferrari. The splendid parish church was also one of **"Old Faithful"**.

244

his creations. In **Strzyżewice**, which is a suburb of Leszno, you'll find an airfield for gliders; the world gliding championships have been held here on two occasions.

Situated on the road from Poznań to Leszno is **Kościan**, a small town which has a Gothic parish church. The surrounding villages such as **Turmi**, **Racoca** and **Popów Stary** all have imposing houses, originally built for the aristocracy, that are well worth visiting. In the ground of one neoclassical palace in Racoca there is one of the largest stud farms in Europe.

On a hill in neighbouring **Lubin** is a Benedictine church built in the Romanesque style. At a later stage in its history its architecture was enriched with Gothic and baroque elements.

Probably one of the most beautiful churches in Poland is the **Church of the Philippians** on the **Holy Mount of Gostyń**. It is a copy of the Santa Maria della Salute church in Venice and is particularly striking with its massive dome. A special feature of the interior is a picture of the Madonna dating from 1540 which has a realistic view of the the town in the background and is the earliest example of its kind in Polish art. The Gothic church with its Renaissance interior and the neoclassical palace of **Pawłowice**, a village east of Leszno, are also worth a visit.

On the road from Leszno to Wrocław is the little town of **Rydzyna**, which has kept many of its 18th-century features: the market square and its surroundings, and a most impressive magnate's residence. The palace – which is surrounded by a country park – has been converted into a luxury hotel.

In the vicinity of **Przemet**, a village northwest of Leszno, is a delightful area of lakes that should not be missed. There are numerous convalescent homes in this area, the largest of which is situated in **Boszków**, by **Lake Dominicki** with its crystal-clear waters. It is possible for tourists to stay in some of these homes.

West Wielkopolska: On the road from Poznań to **Zielona Góra** is the town of **Grodzisk**. It is known for the strong beer it produces, which is brewed from wheat and malt. The excellent flavour of Grodzisk beer is due to the local springs; their special quality was discovered back in the 14th century. Many monuments to the town's glorious past are to be found on its squares, and there is also a Renaissance church.

On the market square of nearby **Rakoniewice** are four old houses complete with arcades. The former Protestant church now functions as a fire brigade museum.

The town of **Wolsztyn** on the River Obra is attractive to many tourists, who are drawn by the possibility of living in royal style in the neoclassical palace that is now a hotel. And anyone who is a water sports enthusiast will be spoiled for choice with the many lakes in the area, all of which are connected by the Obra or artificial canals; the facilities are particularly ideal for canoeists.

On the western border of historic Wielkopolska is the little town of **Międzyrzecz**. Perched on a small hill above the Obra is a carefully restored Gothic castle. In the house within the courtyard walls there is a museum with historical and ethnological exhibits. Also worth seeing is the Gothic parish church, which has a beautiful star vault and a modern interior.

Six miles (10 km) south of Międzyrzecz is the village of **Gościków**, which is surrounded by old trees. Its special feature is a former Cistercian monastery which was built in the 13th century, with baroque architectural elements added at a later stage.

North of Międzyrzecz, in the hilly area close by the lakes, is **Rokitno**, location of a baroque church with a picture of the Virgin Mary which is the destination of numerous pilgrimages.

To the west and southwest of Międzyrzecz are fortifications used in World War II, the largest of their kind built in Europe at the time. Construction was begun in 1934 and the repeated offensives of the Red Army resulted in their constant extension, the final additions being completed in 1944.

The whole complex consists of 55 individual defence points, with walls of a thickness of up to 8 ft (2.5 metres). The fortifications are connected by a network of underground tunnels with a total length of 30 miles (50 km), through which it was possible to drive vehicles the size of a train. Part of the underground area was also taken up by armaments factories. In January 1945 the fortifications were captured by Soviet tank units and large sections of the complex were blown up.

Today many groups of tourists come to see the remains of these fortifications. This is, however, a rather adventurous undertaking, and is only advised for those not afraid of the risks involved. The underground labyrinth is an easy place in which to get lost and the wells located in it are additional traps for the unwary, especially children.

The best place to go down into the underground system is at **Kalawa**, a village 5 miles (8 km) south of Międzyrzecz. Some of the corridors are the day-time hide-out of huge flocks of bats. In addition there are 10 different kinds of bat that come here to hibernate in the winter, so that this section of the underground system has also been declared a nature reserve.

Northwest of Poznań on the lower reaches of the Warta are the **Międzychódzko-Sierakówskie Lakes**, which is the most beautiful scenic area in Wielkopolska. Among its attractions are over 100 lakes, moraines, woods, hiking trails and recreational facilities, and it is thus an area very popular with holiday-makers. In the Renaissance church of the town of Sieraków itself the main altar has a painting from the Rubens workshop that should on no account be missed. A further attraction of Sieraków is the state stud-farm, concentrating on the special breed of horses that comes from Wielkopolska. It also organises riding holidays.

The lakes which are near to towns also have facilities for holiday-makers, the largest such centre being situated on **Lake Jaroszewskie**. Lake Lutomskie with its steep banks and the impressive beech wood close by form part of a nature reserve: this is located 2 miles (3 km) from Sieraków and can be reached by following the "**Black Path**".

Międzychód, situated between the River Warta and Lake Kuchennie, still has its original old town centre. Particularly attractive are the gabled houses.

On **Lake Mierzyńskie**, which is surrounded by woods, the large holiday centre is a very pleasant place to stay. Between the Warta and the Noteć is one of the largest forested areas in the country, the **Notecka Forest**. In the autumn mushroom gatherers from all over the country flock to this hilly area with its dense covering of pines.

North Wielkopolska: North Wielkopolska is a hilly, primarily wooded region which has numerous lakes. One of its beauty spots is the **Noteć Valley**.

With three factories all producing porcelain, **Chodzież** is one of the main centres of this industry in Poland. The town is picturesquely situated between three lakes and is surrounded by moraines. On the **River Gwda**, a tributary of the Noteć, is the town of **Piła**, which was founded in the 15th century. This is the present-day capital of North Wielkopolska.

The elegant Hotel Rodio is recommended as a base from which to visit the many different points of interest in this part of Wielkopolska and Pomerania. The town of Piła itself was badly damaged during World War II and none of its historic buildings have remained.

North of Piła, and over the border in Pomerania, are the remains of the Pomeranian Wall built in World War II, crossing an area of forests and lakes. They are described in greater detail in the article on West Pomerania.

One of the main attractions of **Czarnków** is its scenically beautiful location on the edge of the hills and the Noteć Valley. It also possesses a Gothic church.

Ziemia Lubuska: In the western part of Wielkopolska is Ziemia Lubuska, a region stretching to the country's border along the Odra and the Nysa-Tuzycka. It is thickly wooded and has many rivers and lakes. The capital, **Zielona Góra**, is a town of considerable size, and is charmingly situated close to the Oder valley at the foot of a chain of hills. In the past this was a wine-growing area.

The original form of the town has been retained, and there are numerous interesting old buildings such as the **Town Hall** and the **Church of St Mary**.

The **Church of St Jadwiga** is worth seeing for the Gothic elements of its architecture. In the **Ziemia Lubuska Regional Museum** is an exhibition on wine growing and production.

Four miles (7 km) south of the town centre, in **Ochla**, is an ethnological park in which examples of regional architecture have been preserved. In the palace at **Swidnica**, a village on the road to Żary, the archaeological museum has some interesting exhibits.

In the southern part of **Ziemia Lubuska**, which once belonged to Lower Silesia, there are many interesting towns. In **Kożuchów** large sections of the medieval town walls have been preserved. One particularly imposing piece of architecture is the 13th-century church, which has a baroque interior.

Żagań, situated on the River Bóbr, has preserved its original medieval town structure. Particularly outstanding is the

A safe refuge.

Augustinian Church with its variety of architecture. Other old buildings which have been preserved include two monasteries, a seminary and a granary. The seminary has now been turned into a hotel. In one of the monasteries is a library which dates from 1732 and was used by the famous astronomer Kepler; the other monastery belongs to the Franciscans, and dates back to the 13th century, but was rebuilt in the 18th century. Żagań's most splendid architectural monument is the **Italian Palace**, picturesquely situated in a park on the banks of the Bobr.

The town of **Żary** was founded in 1260. Once famous for its cloth and linen, Żary is today an important centre of the Polish clothing industry. A late Gothic hall church, the palace and carefully restored town residences have remained from its days as a thriving medieval urban centre.

Lagów is in a particularly beautiful location between high moraines and two lakes. Its most outstanding architectural monument is a palace built in the 15th century for the Order of St John, with a high tower which commands a wonderful view of the surrounding area. The palace now accommodates a hotel and a restaurant. Lagów is still guarded by its medieval protective wall with the two gates leading into the town. The nearby lakes are well provided with facilities for holiday-makers.

The landmark of the nearby town of **Jemiołów** is a 974 ft (320-metre) high mast belonging to a television transmitter. On the Warta, on the border between Ziemia Lubuska, Wielkopolska and Pomerania, is **Gorzów Wielkopolski**, which was granted a town charter as long ago as 1257. Special points of interest are the Gothic church dating from the 14th–15th centuries and the granary with its special shaft construction.

South of Gorzów, surrounded by woods and lakes, is the popular holiday resort of **Lubniewice**. East of this is **Strzelce Krajeńskie**. Its medieval protective walls have been preserved almost completely intact, and are built entirely of erratic blocks.

POMORZE/ POMERANIA

The region of Pomerania is located between the Odra and Vistula rivers. It is bordered on its northern edge by a 124-mile (200-km) coastline which stretches along the Baltic Sea. Running along its southern edge are the glacial valleys of the Warta and Noteć rivers.

Even as early as the founding of the state of Poland, this area occupied a special position; today, due to their historical and ethnographic diversities, a differentiation is made between Gdańsk-Pomerania/East Pomerania and West Pomerania.

Displacement, flight and resettlement have marred the fate of the population of this region – and this not only in recent times. Wends, Swedes and Danes left their marks here just as surely as the Germans and Poles did.

West Pomerania: This region, which occupies the countryside between the Odra and Leba rivers, has experienced an extremely turbulent history. It was first settled by pre-Slav groups. In the 10th and 11th centuries the Polish kings battled fiercely with the **Wielecki Alliance** for the right to rule the area. In the 12th century the Germans were forced to relinquish to the Polish king, Bolesław Krzywousty, their territorial claims; however, together with the Danes, they were able to re-establish their sovereignty at a later date. Starting in the 15th century, West Pomerania once again became closely tied to Poland before being annexed first by Sweden in the 17th century and then by Prussia in the 18th century. It was not until the signing of the treaty of German unification that the area became once again, under international law, a part of Poland.

The landscape of West Pomerania is generally characterised by its numerous hills and lakes. Near **Bytów** the hills reach an elevation of almost 820 ft (250 metres). The largest lakes can be found around **Myślibórz**, **Pojezierze Drawskie** and **Bytów**. The region's capital city of **Szczecin** lies on the western border of Poland. Stargard Szczeciński,

Kołobrzeg, Szczecinek, Koszalin and Słupsk are among the other large cities found here.

A whole series of popular resorts line the coast; the most well-known among these are the towns of Miedzyzdroje, Pobierowo, Kołobrzeg, Mielno, Ustka and Łeba. Pojezierze Drawskie and Pojezirze Bytowskie, located relatively close to the coastline, also merit a visit. Aside from a few Gothic churches, castle ruins and palaces, this region has almost no architecturally important sights; however, the serene and romantic landscape found here make it an enchanting area and a popular destination for those seeking rest and relaxation.

Szczecin: The capital of West Pomerania is located 40 miles (65 km) inland from the Baltic Sea, between the Odra River and Lake Dąbie. It is an important junction for traffic on the waters as well as the land. The city, with its five institutions of higher education, is a centre for learning and culture. The Szczecin harbour is one of the Baltic Sea's most important and the adjoining town of Swinoujscie enjoys a reputation as an extremely lively outer port.

Szczecin's history dates back to the days when it was a Slavic settlement in the 11th century. In 1237 the city was granted its charter. In the years between the 13th and 18th centuries its harbour developed into an important commercial trading centre for fish and grain. Starting in 1720 the city came under Prussian rule.

The old town in the western part of Szczecin awaits the visitor with several interesting sights, one of which is the Gothic **Church of St Jacob**. Unfortunately, only a few of the original contents of this church are still remaining.

In the **Museum** in the Gothic **Town Hall**, exhibits provide visitors with interesting information about the history of the city. The outside of the building is also noteworthy for its unusual ceramic decorations. Just a few steps away is the **Loitz Family House** with its two lofts. Here one also finds the former city scale. An especially beautiful example of West Pomeranian church architecture is found

254

in the **Church of St John** situated on the banks of the Odra. The nearby **Renaissance Palace** of the Pomeranian royal family, originally built in the 16th-17th century, was reconstructed after the war. Its five wings and two inner courtyards make this building an impressive one. The palace houses a museum, the royal family's crypts and a theatre.

The belfry offers a magnificent panoramic view of the city and the harbour. At the foot of the palace the remains of a medieval fortress, the **Bastion of Seven Coats**, can be seen. Here, too, is the **Church of St Peter and Paul** with its splendid ceramic decorations.

One should not miss the opportunity to visit the baroque **Assembly Palace** which is located in the **Street of the Polish Soldiers**. This building houses the national museum with its fascinating collection of sculptures, paintings and handcrafted items. The nearby **Haften Gate** at Zwyciestwa Square and the **Brama** *Hołdu Pruskiego* represent the remains of the wall which formerly surrounded the city. These remnants

date from the early 18th century. An impressive eclectic complex of buildings constructed at the beginning of the 20th century is found on the steep banks of the Odra. It is called **Wały Chrobrego** and is home to the city offices and national museum.

Turning to the north, the harbour soon comes into view. From here one can embark on a sightseeing tour of the harbour by boat or a journey by ship to Świnoujście. The streets and squares of the northern sections of this city are laid out in a star-shaped pattern, all ending at **Grundwaldzki Square**. This neighbourhood, with its houses dating from the 19th and early 20th century, is especially interesting.

A bit further to the north is **Jasne Błonia** with its towering monument which was constructed in honour of the dramatic political events of 1979. Here, too, is the **Kasprowicz Park** which directly adjoins the woods of the Wrkzansker Heath. The spacious **Cemetery Park**, with its large variety of trees and weathered old gravestones,

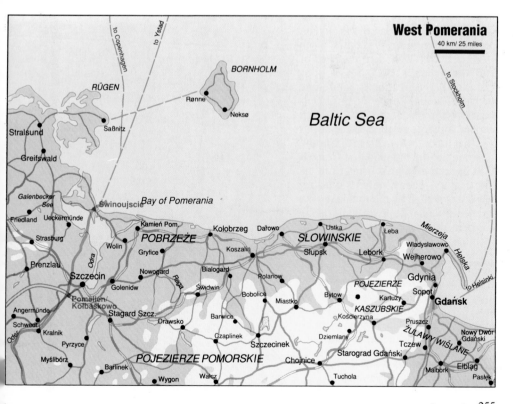

provides a lovely place for visitors to relax in natural surroundings.

The neighbourhoods of **Zdroje and Dąbie**, both of which were independent villages in former times, are located to the south. Zdroje borders directly on the **Bukowa Heath**. Wooded moraine hills surround the green waters of the area's appropriately named **Emerald Lake**.

South and east of Szczecin: About 16 miles (25 km) to the east, on the Ina, is **Stargard Szczciński**. This city, with its numerous Gothic structures, attracts a large number of visitors. The triple-nave **Church of the Holy Virgin Mary**, built in the 15th century, has a charming inner balcony as well as several other architectural refinements. The town hall, rebuilt after the war, has a beautiful roof and front construction. The structure is surrounded by some commonplace townhouses which house the regional museum.

An almost perfectly preserved brick wall dating from the 13th–14th century encloses the old part of the city. It has three gates, one of which is the **Hafentor** on the Ina.

An **International Cemetery** is located in the northern part of the city, on the **Ulica Reymonta**. This burial place was constructed to honour the dead of both world wars.

In a southerly direction, a picturesque road leads alongside the Odra. Travelling along this road, one passes through numerous places steeped in memories of earlier times. In the village of **Chona**, for example, the monumental **Church of St John the Baptist** dates from the 15th century. Today, only its ruins remain, surrounded by the remnants of a defensive wall. The town hall, dating from the same era, is also worthy of attention.

The village of **Trzcinski Zdrój**, lying on a picturesque lake, likewise awaits visitors with a number of interesting sights; among these are a church and town hall dating from the 15th century as well as 14th–15th century fortress walls with gates which are still intact.

Further along on the route to the south are towns which are more well known for their roles in recent Polish history.

Here, for example, one can see the forts along the Odra which were erected by Polish and Russian soldiers in April of 1945 shortly before the capture of Berlin. Several monuments to the Polish battles for freedom along the Odra River are found around the small city of **Cedynia**. **Moryn** has the character of a resort town, nestled on a lake between two hills.

The small city of **Myślibórz**, located in an area of numerous lakes, is surrounded by the fragments of a medieval wall. The structure of the 13th/14th-century parish church is fascinating. The walls are built of loose stones piled on top of one another – a typical method of construction for early Gothic churches in this region of Pomerania. Myślibórz's majestic town hall dates from the baroque era.

Taking time for a pause in **Pyrzyce** is definitely to be recommended as this town offers an unusually large number of interesting sights. Among these are the well-preserved town wall and the **Church of Mauritius**, built of blocks

The coast is rimmed by primeval forest.

of granite. Both structures date from the 13th century.

To the east, on the lower part of the **Drawa**, is the **Drawska heath** with its expansive wooded areas. The landscape here presents the perfect setting for those interested in outdoor pursuits like hiking and cycling.

The **Drawa** is also ideal for extensive kajak trips. The stretch between **Czaplinek** and **Krzyż** is especially suitable for this pastime.

Pas Pojezierzy: The landscape of West Pomerania is dominated by its many lakes, most of which are surrounded by lovely wooded hills. The **Pojezierze Drawskie** (Drawa Lake District), including the towns of Drawsko Pomorskie, Połczyn Zdrój and Szczecinek, is the most scenic region of its kind. There are about 200 lakes in this area. The largest and most beautiful of these is **Lake Drawsko** on whose shores is located **Czaplinek**, a popular town for tourists. To the north, the **Road of 1,000 Curves** leads through the picturesque **Valley of the Five Lakes** to

Połczyn Zdroj, a city famous as far back as the 14th century for the healing powers of its waters. This attractive and popular resort lies nestled between high moraine hills.

The Pomeranian Wall (**Wał Pomorski**) stretches from **Szczecinek** through Wałcz and Tuczno to Krzyz. It was built of ferroconcrete by the Germans in the 1930s as part of an ambitious system of fortifications. It was not until 1945 that Polish soldiers managed to break through this massive wall.

Monuments and military museums in **Podgaj** near Jastrowie, in **Wałcz** and in **Mirosławiec** serve as memorials to the battles fought here.

The clearest picture of how the wall once looked can be gained by visiting the remnants found near Wałcz. This city, on the shores of two lakes, has a chillingly large military cemetery where victims of World War II are buried. It is also the site of the training camp for the Polish olympic team.

In the charming town of **Tuczno** visitors can spend the night in a castle

The Pomeranian Lake District.

hotel with modern decor. The huge remains of the Pomeranian Wall, blown up by Polish soldiers, can be seen in the neighbouring village of **Strzaliny**.

The **Pojezierze Bytówskie**, couched among high wooded moraine hills, begins east of the Drawski lakes. The village of **Biały Bór**, at the edge of the lake country, organises a "holiday in the saddle" program for visitors. In **Bytów** tourists can storm an impressive crusade-era castle housing a museum. Afterwards, visitors may even want to rest their weary heads in one of the castle's hotel rooms. In both these villages one finds many traces of Kashubian folk culture. More about this can be gleaned from the chapter about East Pomerania.

Along the Baltic Sea coast: The islands of **Wolin** and **Uznam** are located in the northwest of Poland, between the Gulf of Szczecin and the Baltic Sea. A portion of Uznam belongs to Germany. **Świnoujście** is a typical port city where mass-produced goods are dispatched. Ferries to Hamburg, Copenhagen and Ystad can be boarded here. The city has a fishing harbour as well as fish-processing plants.

The western part of Świnoujście, with its long sandy beaches, caters to tourism. There are vacation cottages to let and, during the summer, many cultural events take place, one of which is the **Arts Festival for Academic Youth**.

A portion of Wolin has been turned into a large national park, the **Woliński Park Narodowy**. The park serves to protect the unique beauties of the island – the unusual geological formations, the steep banks and the overhanging cliffs. Eagles and other protected species can be seen in the woods. At the edge of the park is the holiday resort of **Miedzyzdroje**. The town of **Wolin**, located in the south of the island, flowered economically in the 9th and 10th centuries. This was the central location, as early as the pre-Christian epoch, for the **Trinity of the Gods** cult.

Kamień Pomorski, a city which joined the Hanseatic League in the 14th century, is located 6 miles (10 km) from the sea at Kaminski-Haff. The Romanesque-Gothic cathedral lends an impressive medieval atmosphere to this town. The lovely tones of the church organ are especially enjoyable during the city's annual summer festival of organ music.

Other noteworthy sights in Kamień Pomorski are the **Church of the Holy Virgin Mary** built in the 18th century, the 14th-century **Church of St Nicholas** which houses the regional museum, the fragments of the wall of defiance and the late-Gothic town hall. Sailing boats can be hired at the harbour, giving visitors the opportunity to explore the area by sea.

The opposite shores of the mainland are lined with a number of holiday villages. The Baltic Sea villages of **Dziwnów**, **Dziwnówek**, **Mrzezyno**, and **Dźwirzyno** enjoy a reputation throughout Poland as first-class areas for recreation and sport.

Large portions of the coastal region have suffered from severe erosion. Despite efforts to protect the coastline, much land has been swallowed by the sea. This is especially evident in **Trzesacz** where the ruins of a Gothic church, constructed in the 14th century 1.2 miles (2 km) from the coast, have been licked by the waves since 1901.

Trzebiatów lies on the Rega. It was founded in the 13th century and has managed to preserve its medieval character. The special attractions of this city are the Gothic **Church of the Holy Virgin Mary** with its towering steeple, typical in West Pomerania, and the late-Gothic city gate.

From Trzebiatów, a narrow-gauge railway carries passengers to the other coastal towns.

Kołobrzeg, located at the mouth of the Parseta, is a port city as well as a holiday resort. The city history began in the year 1000 when King Bolesław Chrobry established a bishop's see here. The city was 90 percent destroyed in World War II but has since been totally rebuilt. Notice the **Church of the Holy Virgin Mary**. Its monumental interior is decorated with pieces from the 14th–17th century. Those who make the effort of climbing to the top of the brick steeple are rewarded with a magnificent panorama of Kołobrzeg and the surrounding area. Similarly, one should not miss seeing the fragments of the medieval city wall with its bastions and earth fortifications dating from the 17th and early 19th centuries. The military museum contains weapons and other pieces salvaged in 1945.

A lighthouse on the beach of Kołobrzeg warns passing ships of danger, and a monument serves to remind the community of their allegiance to the sea. Holiday cottages are scattered throughout the park which stretches along the beach. These are mainly occupied by those who come here to improve their health by means of the natural mineral water and mud baths. Lying behind the dunes to the east of Kołobrzeg are yet more holiday settlements .

Below, fishing boats at low tide. Following pages: the quaint provincial town of Słupsk.

Nearby, between the sea, lakes and flooded meadows, is a piece of land whose unique and bizarre beauty is said to work magical charms on visitors to the area. For this reason, the villages of **Ustronie Morskie**, **Sarbinowo** and **Mielno** receive steady streams of them.

Koszalin, a medium-sized industrial city, is the source of supplies for the resorts along the coast. In the city centre one can visit the 14th/15th-century **Cathedral** – modern decor inside – as well as the regional museum with its collection of artifacts from the surrounding area.

The sleepy fishing village of **Darłowo** is located near the mouth of the **Wieprza**. It was granted its charter in 1270. The resort of **Darłówek** lies directly on the sea. The Pomeranian prince Eryk I, former ruler of Denmark, Sweden and Norway, once lived in the castle here. The streets, alleys and squares of the central part of the town have retained their medieval character; the medieval city fortifications, as well as one of the city gates, have also been preserved. The sarcophagi of the Pomeranian royalty are found in the chapel of the Gothic parish church and a baroque town hall decorates the central square.

The recently restored **Castle** of the Pomeranian sovereigns, built in the 14th century, is an absolute jewel of a

structure; today a museum is housed within its walls.

Slawno, located just 12 miles (20 km) from Darłowo, has several monuments which are well worth visiting. The remains of the medieval city wall, as well as the immense Gothic **Parish Church**, are among the more interesting sites in this town.

Jarosławiec is one of Poland's most beautiful resorts. This is due partially to its proximity to **Lake Wicko**. Old romantic fishermen's homes and half-timbered houses inhabited by peasants surround this lake.

At the mouth of the **Słupia** is the small port of **Ustka**, a very popular holiday resort village. The harbour was first built to serve **Słupsk**, a new, postwar town which is located 12 miles (20 km) away. This city, which has a population of 110,000 is the largest in the coastal region. From the lengthy list of noteworthy sights here, a few are especially worth mentioning: the Gothic **Parish Church** dating from the 14th century and the **Castle of** the Pomeranian sovereigns; the **Church of St Jacek**, with its royal burial tombs, is found on the castle grounds, as is a late-Gothic mill in which there is now an ethnological museum. The castle itself, built by Boguslav X, contains a **Museum for Central Pomerania** and an art museum dedicated to the works of Witkacy. It also houses a hotel.

The most famous of the European wandering dunes run along the eastern portion of the West Pomeranian coastline between **Rowy** and **Łeba**. A huge park, containing the large lakes of **Łebsko** and **Gardno** as well as the **Łeba Harbour**, has been created here. These wandering dunes push eastward about 26 ft (8 metres) annually, swallowing large areas of woods and sometimes even villages in the process.

Kluki is the site of Kashubian half-timbered houses. The coastal village of **Łeba** is an attractive holiday destination with a busy fishing port. A bit to the west, in the **Rabka National Park**, one still finds remnants of V-2 rocket launching pads abandoned after the end of World War II.

GDAŃSK AND EAST POMERANIA

The history of East Pomerania begins with its annexation by Poland in the 10th century. In the years thereafter, the area's fate was mainly influenced by the rivalries played out between the Germans and the Poles. These all began when Prince **Konrad Mozowiecki** decided to try to bring East Pomerania under his rule with the assistance of the German Order of Knighthood. However, these political ambitions were not very carefully thought out.

The Order was quick to respond to the appeal for assistance. However, once on the scene, it quickly became apparent that they would use their position as a means of strengthening the German presence in East Pomerania. The princes of East Pomerania and Greater Poland resisted this presence bitterly for many years thereafter so that the knights were unable to fully bring East Pomerania under their control until the year 1309. As a compromise, they agreed in the **Truce of Toruń** (1466) to recognise Polish sovereignty over the so-called king's Prussia.

The harbour city of Gdańsk, just as the town of Toruń, was an important trading centre and played a special role within the economy of East Pomerania. Even today this area around the mouth of the Vistula River is closely tied, both economically and culturally, to East Pomerania. The three cities of Gdańsk, Sopot and Gdynia are crowded so closely together here that they are known as the "**Tri-city**".

The history of Gdańsk is inseparable from the history of East Pomerania. Founded in the 10th century as a fortification, it came under the rule of the German Order of Knighthood in 1308. It was not until 1466 that the Polish sovereign was able to overthrow the knights and re-establish his rule. From this time on, the city blossomed and developed into one of Europe's largest harbour cities.

After the second division of Poland, the region fell to the Prussians. Only in

1919, with the Treaty of Versailles, did Gdańsk gain the status of a free city. Although the city lay in ashes in 1945, it was rebuilt after the war and today it follows its historic form.

Rising phoenix: Since the end of World War II, the city has once again been under Polish rule. It was not until 1975 that the last rubble of the war was cleared away. Despite the enormous destruction and Poland's extremely tenuous economic situation after 1945, there was never a question as to whether the country's most important port should be reconstructed – the only question was how it should be done. There were suggestions that a totally new and modern city should be built on the site but the concept which finally won through was for an historically accurate reconstruction, especially for Gdańsk's old town, which had been completely levelled during the bombing.

Reconstruction presented a huge challenge for architects and planners. Although a portion of the original building materials, for instance from church walls, towers, gates and steps, could be retrieved from beneath the rubble, they were mainly incomplete.

The first problem was to determine exactly what still remained. Pieces lay scattered everywhere, hardly any of the buildings were adequately documented and a large portion of the archives had been destroyed in the war. Often there were only photographs from which to work. In the **Mariacka ulica**, for example, the planners had only one single stairway on which to orient themselves. From this localised point, they had to recreate, out of a field of ruins, the structures along this street. This was a monumental task.

The realistic decision to ensure construction of adequate living space for the population meant, to a certain extent, the sacrifice of historical accuracy. Thus, some of the too-narrow alleys were not rebuilt; the living complexes which had formerly been crowded into small spaces were now spread out and broken up by green areas and service centres. Although the width of the houses and their interior architecture were also consciously changed for reasons of space, in the city centre, particularly around the **Long Market**, the house facades and traditional form of the brick roofs were painstakingly restored in their original forms.

Some new structures were, however, included in this historic ensemble. One example is the post office; its facade contains a variety of elements, representing the progression of the city's architecture over the years.

Work began in 1946 with the repair of still-existing structures to prevent their further decay, and was, for the most part, completed in 1960. The new silhouette of Gdańsk today, despite all the painful losses, is one of a prosperous commercial city and port, proud of its tradition. Gdańsk is a bustling metropolis, with almost half a million residents. It has become a focal point for events of wide-ranging historical significance. The development of Solidarity has inevitably put its stamp on the recent history of the city.

To follow the tracks of history, the

Preceding pages: the castle in Malbork on the Nogat; traditional stooks. **Left**, a pretty girl in Gdańsk. **Right**, the mighty town hall.

WHY GDAŃSK BECAME THE CRADLE OF "SOLIDARITY"

Lech Wałesa, who rose to become president of the country, is a son of Gdańsk. Here he pays tribute to the city that nurtured Solidarity, the catalyst in Poland's liberation from Soviet-style communisim.

This city's role in 20th-century history has been dramatic. On 1 September 1939, when the Germans used the dispute concerning Gdańsk as a pretence for an attack on Poland, many short-sighted western Europeans cried, "We don't want to lay down our lives for Gdańsk ."

Forty years later Gdańsk once again came into the public spotlight. This time it was the breeding ground for the independent labour union Solidarity. And once again there were many nervous neighbours who saw only danger in the breeze of freedom blowing from the Polish coast.

Fearing a Soviet intervention and the resulting political instability in Europe, these anxious people warned us to keep quiet; they stifled our hopes. Solidarity – and the international solidarity for the Gdańsk labourers – proved stronger this time.

Visitors to our city easily find their way to the monument in the form of three crosses at the Gdańsk shipyard. Striking workers were murdered here in December 1970 in a hail of fire from the military. They sacrificed their lives for more than Gdańsk – even at a time when nobody could foresee what far-reaching effects their struggle would have on the future of all of Europe. Their resistance and deaths were experiences from which we learned various lessons; they enabled us to carry out a successful battle without bloodshed 10 years later.

We ask ourselves why this Polish city should be the one where it was possible to organise the fight against communism so successfully. Why was it here rather than anywhere else that courageous and inventive activists found enough broad support among workers, intellectuals and artists to found Solidarity?

One answer can surely be found in the history of this city and the valuable standards it has passed on to its children. Gdańsk produces the type of citizen who looks steadfastly toward the future, who courageously takes the initiative and pushes towards his goal using reason and moderation. The citizens, merchants, dock workers and craftsmen, ingenious but also principled, led to this city's greatness as early as the 16th century.

Being open to the world, through the harbour and membership in the Hanseatic League, is also part of Gdańsk tradition – the spirit of freedom and independence could not be stifled here. Direct contact with visitors from all over the world has kept us open to new ideas and able to resist the pressures of indoctrination.

This especially applies to the workers of Gdańsk who always felt themselves cheated out of the just rewards of their good and honest labour. Many new residents moved into the city following the end of the war but they did not destroy the existing communal structure within Gdańsk. On the contrary, it was exactly this creative mix of cultures, ideas and experiences which laid the essential groundwork for new and pioneering solutions to Poland's problems.

The development of Solidarity is the best example of this. The resounding slogan of the year 1980 was "good bread for good work". Of course the call for freedom was within everyone's heart all over Poland, but it was also clear to each and every one of us that such a cry at that time could have led to a Soviet intervention.

And yet, 10 years later, we have attained our goal – in a revolution without force and without bloodshed, a revolution which overthrew the communist regime and set an example for democratic freedom initiatives throughout central Europe.

Toward the close of the war, when the battles over Gdańsk had already ended, the victorious Soviet army destroyed much that represented the culture, tradition and history of the city. The desire to rid the area of any remnants of the Nazi rule can not alone be the excuse for these drastic actions.

Could it have been that the Soviet leaders already then anticipated that the impulse signalling the beginning of the end for communist rule would originate from freedom-loving Gdańsk?

best place to start is in the city centre which lies on the **Motlawa** and **Radunia** canals. Here one finds the **Old Town**, the "old main city" and the old suburb. The architecture here is mainly Gothic and Renaissance.

The most magnificent houses are found along the **ul. Długa**. The kings once paraded into town on this street. The **Dominican Market** has been held here annually since 1972, a market whose tradition dates back to the 13th century.

The ul. Długa can be reached through the **Golden Gate**, constructed in the 17th century. Directly beside this is **St George's Court**. From under the gate's arch one has a view along the entire length of the street. The thin tower of the **Town Hall**, dating from the 14th–15th century, towers overhead. In its lavishly-decorated interior one finds Gdańsk's city museum.

Another symbol of the city of Gdańsk, the **Neptune Fountain**, with its original 16th-century wrought-iron border, stands in front of the quarter's most impressive building, the **Artus Court**. This Renaissance structure was once the seat of the wealthy Gdańsk merchants guild.

The ul. Długa ends at the **Długi Targ** (Long Market). The square is lent a special atmosphere by the patrician houses which line its edges. The most remarkable among these is the **Złota Kamienica** (Golden House), built in the 17th century and covered with gold-plated low reliefs.

At the end of the Long Market is the **Zielona Brama** (Green Gate). It leads down to the wharfs of the Motlawa, the site of the city's harbour for several centuries in former times.

Today, one looks out from here on to an island containing many old ware-houses. When reconstruction is finished, it is planned to make this the new commercial and cultural centre of Gdańsk. Along the wharfs are many quaint little jewellery shops. Most of these sell amber, the gold of the Baltic Sea. Here, too, many art galleries have opened their doors. A huge wooden crane which dates from the 15th century towers over the

river. The **Żuraw**, known as Crane Gate, was accurately restored after the last war. Directly next door is the restaurant Pod Żurawien from whose terrace diners can appreciate a beautiful panorama of the canal. From here one can also watch the excursion boats as they pass by the Westerplatte peninsula on their way to Sopot or the Hel peninsula.

Parallel to the Long Market is the **ul. Mariacka** (Mariacka Street), one of the city's most atmospheric streets. Pedestrians strolling here can still experience a taste of the romantic, old-fashioned aura of this once affluent port.

This street, as mentioned above, was reconstructed after being destroyed during the war. Its old splendour was so convincingly restored that it was used in the filming of Thomas Mann's novel *Buddenbrooks*. Although the book was actually set in the Hanseatic city of Lübeck, the film-makers were unable to find any area of comparable architectural value in that city.

The **Church of the Holy Virgin Mary** is located at the end of Mary Street. It

took over 159 years, from 1343 to 1502, to complete construction of this church which is the sixth largest in the world.

South of the "main city" is the former **Old Suburb**. The **Św. Trójcy** (Church of the Holy Trinity), built at the beginning of the 16th century and visible from afar, towers over this district. Many art treasures are housed in the area. The **Museum Narodowe** (National Museum) is located in a former monastery and proudly displays the famous painting by Hans Memling, *The Last Judgement*. The museum also contains a collection of Polish paintings and design objects including the renowned Gdańsk furniture.

At the mouth of the dead Vistula, about 3 miles (5 km) from the centre, is the peninsula **Westerplatte**. It gained fame in September, 1939 when 180 Polish soldiers, under the leadership of Major **Henryk Sucharski**, stood their ground against the superior German attackers. It was the shots directed against these courageous defenders of liberty, fired from the *Schleswig*

Holstein, a German tank cruiser, which started World War II.

Oliwa is probably the most beautiful of the suburbs. It is located north of Gdańsk's old town. Here one finds a large Cistercian monastery, whose cathedral dates from the first half of the 13th century. Interestingly, however, the four-part basilica is also composed of Renaissance, baroque and rococo elements. Many renowned musicians have performed concerts on the monastery's famous **Organ of Oliwa**, built in the years 1763–88.

The modern assembly hall "Oliwia" is located along the road from Oliwa to Sopot. This hall hosted the first and second regional conferences of Solidarity, meetings which were important milestones along the country's road to democracy.

Sopot and Gdynia: The former village of **Sopot** once belonged to the fiefdom of the Cistercians of Oliwa. The patricians of Gdańsk made it into a spa and at the beginning of the 19th century Sopot became a first-class health and bathing

The historic "Mariengasse".

resort. It is easy to understand why these former citizens selected this area for their holiday retreat. The lovely wide sandy beaches of Sopot provide the ideal backdrop for long strolls, accompanied by tame sea gulls and swans. A special attraction is the pier which juts 1,693 ft (516 metres) into the sea. Be sure to visit the fabulous **Grand Hotel**, a charming reminder of an earlier era, located just beside this pier. You may even feel inclined to check into one of the hotel's lovely old-fashioned rooms for a few nights. Completely renovated in 1990, the hotel offers the luxurious charm of a classic hotel with a beach-side terrace, tea dances, stylish dining and Poland's most elegant casino. There is no swimming pool, but a splendid tennis club is located just 660 ft (200 metres) away.

This town, with its many houses built in turn-of-the-century style and its tree-lined streets, stylish cafés and pubs, is one of the most attractive in the region and it attracts its fair share of visitors. For those interested in entertainment, the Sopot Opera has, among other events,

an annual **International Song Festival**. Horse fans can enjoy a visit to the well-equipped race track.

Gdynia lies 6 miles (9 km) west of Sopot and is Poland's second largest port. The former village began its evolution into a modern city with a commercial and military port when the Polish administration assumed control in 1920. It is too industrial to be of much interest to most tourists, but it does have an excellent oceanographic museum and naval museum. The museum ship *Błyskawica* is tied up at the **Nabrzeże Pomorskie** wharf. The ships of the naval academy, including the splendid sailing school ship named *Dar Młodzieży*, are anchored not far away.

The Gulf of Gdańsk: The narrow peninsula of **Półwysep Helski**, washed by wind and waves, lies to the north. It is 21 miles (34 km) long. The water is still clean and clear, making swimming a pleasure. Those who want to remain for a while in this region will find that the many small villages here offer a wide array of inexpensive hotels, private

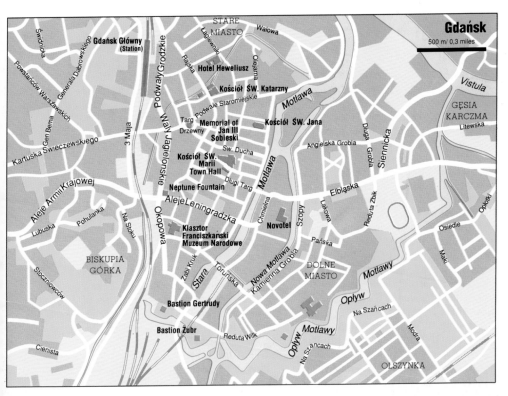

rooms and camp sites. These towns are: **Jastrzębia Góra**, the romantic fishing port of **Władysławowo**, **Chałupy**, **Kuźnica**, **Jastarania**, **Jurata** and, on the outer tip of the peninsula, the old fishing village of **Hel** whose turbulent history is recorded in the fishing museum.

At the entrance to the peninsula is the commercial colony of **Puck** which developed out of a Slavic settlement. During the reign of **Władysław IV**, Puck was the home port of the Polish war fleet.

To the southwest of Puck is **Wejherowo** with its historically-protected Franciscan monastery dating from the year 1650. Equally interesting here is a group of 26 baroque chapels, known as the **Kalwaria Wejherowska**, built during the years 1649–55 on the hillsides around the town.

Pojezierze Kaszubskie/Kashubian Lake District: Southwest of the "tri-city" is a particularly charming landscape with exceptional recreational value. The highest point of this hilly region is the **Wieżyca** which reaches 1,080 ft (329 metres). This is also the source of the rivers **Radunia**, **Wierzyca**, **Wda**, **Słupia** and **Łeba**, all of which flow into the Baltic Sea. The largest lake is **Wdzydze**.

On its shores, near **Wdzydze Kiszewskie**, is a Kashubian open-air museum with 52 acres (21 hectares). This museum, with its historic structures from the region, provides an ideal opportunity for visitors to learn more about Kashubian culture and tradition.

Kartuzy, surrounded by lakes and woods, is the capital of Kashubia. The monastery of the Order of the **Carthusians**, with its church dating from the 14th century, presents an unusual picture – the roof is shaped in the form of a casket. In its interior, which stems from the 15th century, the influences of the settlers who lived in the area at that time can be recognised. The **Kashubian Museum**, with its fascinating exhibits of Kashubian culture, provides a good insight into how life was formerly lived in this region.

A bit further to the northwest is the 1,000-year-old city of **Kościerzyna**, the present centre of Kashubian culture. The smaller towns of this area are also charming, for example **Chielmo**, a village which borders on three lakes – **Białe**, **Kodno** and **Rekowskie**. Chielmo is well-known for its factory which produces Kashubian ceramics. The factory has been in the hands of one family, the Netzels, for several generations.

The town of **Zukowo** is famous as a traditional centre for the lovely Kashubian embroidery. The church and monastery of the Order of Norbertines, built in the early 13th century, are also noteworthy.

The **Kashubian National Park** was founded in 1983 in the central part of this lake country. One of Poland's largest forested areas, the **Bory Tucholskie** (Tuchola heath), lies to the south, where the **Wda** and **Brda** rivers converge. The especially narrow "finger lakes" here characterise the area's landscape, as do the innumerable artificial lakes, such as **Lake Kornowski** near **Kornow**. Watersports enthusiasts flock to the Brda and Wda rivers to enjoy their wide variety of activities.

The nature preserve **Cisy im. L. Wyczółkowskiego** near Wierzlas and the archaeological-biological preserve of "**Kręgi Kamienne**" (stone circles) are especially interesting for all those with a fascination for nature. The latter is located in **Odry**, north of Czersk, in a solitary and heavily-wooded area.

At the western tip of the heath is **Tuchola**, the area's tourist centre. The town's medieval panorama as well as the remnants of its fortified walls draw numerous visitors annually. **Koronowo**, with its uniquely beautiful landscape on the banks of the Brda, lies at the southern end of the Tuchola Heath.

The **Pojerzierze Starogardzkie** (Starogard Lake District), with its diversified landscape, borders directly on the Kashubian Lake District. **Tczew** was founded at its edge, on the shores of the Vistula river. The Polish naval academy was formerly located here. Its building has, since 1988, been the home of the **Vistula Museum**.

Further to the south, on the Wierzyca, the town of **Pelplin** is worth a visit. It has a large monastery from the Cistercian Order. The triple-nave **Church of the Holy Virgin Mary** is the site of Europe's second largest Renaissance altar. Here, too, is a precious medieval manuscript of the **Gutenberg Bible** as well as pictures by Herman Han and Bartłomej Strobel. Still more sacred objects and medieval manuscripts are housed in the Diocesan Museum.

Gniew is located at the junction of the Wierzyca and Vistula rivers. The town formerly belonged to the Cistercians before falling to the German Order of Knighthood. The well-preserved churches and walls here, dating from the 16th century, are archaeologically notable, as is the complex of houses with open balconies, unique in Pomerania. On a nearby hilltop one finds a wonderful Gothic castle whose square-shaped form is reinforced with turrets at each corner. The inner courtyard surrounds the baroque residence of Sobieski.

South of Gniew, likewise on the Vistula, is **Nowe**. Here the Polish furniture industry has its centre. An imposing medieval fortress containing a castle chapel and other churches, rises above the river.

The **Wysoczyzna Świecka** (the highlands of Świecka) stretch to the south of the Starogard lake region. The urban focal point is **Swiecie**. This town was the headquarters for the commander of the German Order of Knighthood from 1309–1466. The ruins of the former moated castle of the Teutonic Knights as well as a Gothic church can be found at the fork of the Wda and Vistula.

On the right bank of the Vistula: Poland's most northerly recreational area is located to the east of the mouth of the Vistula. Some of the individual holiday resorts here are separated from the sea by a narrow strip of dunes and woods; others lie directly on the coastal beach belt of **Mierzeja Wiślana**. Here one finds the villages of **Mikoszewo**, **Jantar** and **Stegna**, among others. The nearby town of **Stutthof** gained notoriety as the site of a concentration camp.

Krynica Morska is in the middle of this peninsula, and not far from the Soviet border, on the Vistula delta, is the peaceful community of **Frombork**. This town has an important fishing port. The famous astronomer Nicholas Copernicus lived here from 1512–52, during which time he wrote his renowned work *De revolutionibus orbium coelestium*.

Frombork's most impressive structure is the Gothic cathedral, with its mighty defensive walls, built in the 14th century. Copernicus lived and worked in a tower similar to the one seen here, in the northwestern portion of the fortress. The nearby museum provides interesting exhibits illustrating the life of this genial scientist.

The **Wzniesienie Elbląskie** hills lie to the south. The highest elevation of this late-moraine landscape, the **Góra Milejewka Hill**, rises above this lovely landscape which is covered with beech and oak forests. The capital of this voivodeship, **Elbląg**, is the focal point of the region, being a centre for industry, commerce, culture and tourism. Its history dates back to the 9th century; in

Bay of Gdansk

32 km/ 20 miles

the 16th and 17th centuries it developed into a flourishing port.

Despite catastrophic destruction in World War II, the city still has several noteworthy structures. At the **Market Gate** one sees the remains of the former city wall, dating from 1319. Especially interesting, too, is the Dominican **Church of the Holy Virgin Mary** from the 13th–14th century which now houses an art gallery. The Gothic **Church of St Mikołaj**, with its 312-ft (95-metre) tower and Gothic and Renaissance fixtures, should also not be missed.

A nature reserve, the **Bażantarnia**, is located in the southern part of the city. And just below Elbląg one finds **Jezioro Druzno**. This lake, which is slowly being filled in by all kinds of vegetation, has been declared a bird sanctuary and thus provides a protected area for about 150 species of waterfowl, such as herons and swans.

The town of **Malbork** lies on the **Nogat** river to the southwest of Elbląg. This town is most famous as the location of the mighty Teutonic Knights castle. This castle was once the seat of the Grand Master of the Order (*see facing page*).

Further to the south, on the right bank of the Vistula, is **Kwidzyń**. Here one still finds remnants of the structures of an old castle complex: the triple-nave church with its two-storey presbytery and tower, both dating from the 14th century, is directly connected with one wing of the castle. The castle complex is quadrangular and contains a museum.

The landscape of **Pojezierze Chełmińskie** stretches along the Vistula, Osa and Drwęca. At the northwestern edge is the historical capital of **Chełmno**, the seat of the bishop's mission for the Christianisation of the population since 1215. The city was governed under a modified system of Magdeburg law and was architecturally laid out accordingly. Successive Polish and Prussian city planners followed this example.

The medieval city walls surround about 200 structures which have been preserved as monuments. The most impressive is the 16th-century Renaissance

The church of St Nicholas in Elbląg.

MALBORK CASTLE

Palaces and castles are a part of Poland's history and heritage – testimony to its power during the later Middle Ages and the post-Renaissance period. Cracrow and Warsaw both have royal castles, while the towns and the countryside contain large fortified dwellings and palaces that once belonged to Polish magnates.

On the eve of Poland's dissolution in 1939, private residences with 100 indoor servants still existed. But no castle in Poland is more potently symbolic than the massive fortress at Malbork, formerly belonging to the Teutonic Knights.

Work began on the castle at Marienburg (as Malbork is known in German) in 1274. It was to be the finest, most impressive, most awe-inspiring of all the Knights' fortifications which, on a lesser scale, were already dominating much of the Vistula's route downstream from the coast. Within two years the land around the new edifice was a municipality in its own right – a status conferred by the Order.

Construction continued apace. In 1309 the Grand Master moved his headquarters from Venice. During the 14th century the first construction, or Upper Castle, was joined by a Middle and finally by a Lower Castle.

Granaries were built along the river and an outer ring of defence walls was erected. Finally, a splendid palace was built for the Grand Master between the Upper and Middle Castles.

The meaning of all this was not lost on the Poles. The monastic-military Order – which had been invited into the country by Prince Konrad of Mazovis following the Crusades, to use against a troublesome pagan tribe – was now – 150 years later – the territorial master of much of the north.

Here the Vistula hinterland was a gloriously rich and fertile area for all the principal bounty of medieval trade. Wood, hides, amber, furs, cloth, horses and, above all, grain, were increasingly becoming the property of the occupying Order, based on their new martial edifice at Malbork.

"The very sight of Malbork Castle was enough to strike terror into the heart of every Pole," wrote Nobel prizewinner Henryk Sienkiewicz in his novel *The Teutonic Knights*, "for this fortress, with its upper, middle and lower castles, was something that was absolutely incomparable with any other in the world. In sheer immensity it surpassed anything the Polish knights had seen in their lives. The buildings seemed to grow out of each other, forming a sort of mountain rising from the surrounding lowlands."

But Poles are not easily frightened by the formidable, and by the start of the 15th century the first climax in German-Polish relations was fast approaching and inevitable. It was to be the battle of Grunwald in 1410, the largest set-piece battle of the Middle Ages. It was to end in the total military defeat of the Order, mainly by the action of Polish cavalry. They also scattered and annihilated a company of English archers recruited, largely by false propaganda, by the German side. This was happening five years before Agincourt.

After many decades of peace, the Poles were unwilling to fight. But the Order, which had ambitions in Lithuania, tried to drive a wedge between Poles and Lithuanians. Failing in their political scheming, the Teutonic Order declared war on Poland in 1409.

Matters came to a head in July 1410. The Poles, fearing a long war of attrition, organised a massive hunting expedition to obtain meat. Then, on 15 July 1410, the army of the Order under their Grand-Master Ulrich von Jungingen, fought a combined force of Poles, Lithuanians and Tartars commanded by King Władysław Jagiełło. In one day the battle was over. The Grand Master and the flower of his army were dead. Malbork itself did not fall until 1466, but the power that it represented had been brought down at Grunwald. After 1466 Malbork became a Polish royal residence.

Today the Castle, after much destruction during the partitions and in World War II, is a beautifully restored museum that takes hours to tour properly. It houses a valuable collection of amber and is a monument to matters medieval, military, monarchial and monastic. Yet there is something more. This castle seems to exude, an almost forgotten concept, something which belongs to a vanished age: the age of chivalry.

town hall with its high Polish-style attic as well as the Gothic parish church.

About 19 miles (30 km) to the north of Chełmno is **Grudziądz**. Its medieval structure has remained unchanged. Of special interest are the Gothic parish church, several baroque Jesuit churches and an impressive group of warehouse buildings along the Vistula which are all joined together through a complex system of protective walls.

Near Grudziądz is **Radzyń Chełminski**, famous for its 13th-century **Teutonic Knights castle**, an architectural masterpiece of that age. The **Church of St Anna**, built at the beginning of the 14th century in a colourful variety of architectural styles, and containing altar pictures by B. Strobel, is also worth a visit.

About 4 miles (6 km) to the east is Rywald **Szlachecki**. A 15th-century sculpture of the Virgin Mary in the Capuchin monastery here makes this village a destination for pilgrimages.

At the southern edge of Pojezierza Chełminskie, along both sides of the Vistula, is **Toruń**, the largest city of the region. Its present population numbers 200,000. Founded in the 13th century as a commercial centre, this city was, for a long time, a member of the Hanseatic League. In the 17th century it became a centre for the Protestant movement and later for the Polish nationalism movement in Pomerania.

Today Toruń is an important educational and cultural centre: the **Nikolai Copernicus University** is one of Poland's best.

For those with a liking for stage productions, this city makes an interesting stopover as it is the site of annual theatre and puppet theatre festivals, drawing crowds from the entire northern region. If all this is not enough to entice visitors to make this town one of their destinations, it should be added that Toruń is one of the most beautiful cities in Poland.

This beauty is partially due to the medieval core of the city on the right bank of the Vistula. The focal point of the old town **Market Place** is the 14th-century **Town Hall** with its Dutch Ren-

aissance-style second storey which was added at a later date. The structure was changed again during the baroque period. Worth noting, too, are several of the residences located at the marketplace. The most interesting of these is the house **Pod Gwiazdą** which was built in the year 1697.

The churches of the city are also very impressive. These include the 13th-century **Church of the Holy Virgin Mary,** with its elegant Gothic chancel and late 14th-century polychromy, and the early 14th-century Cistercian **Church of St Jacob**. Additionally, the **Church of St John the Baptist** housing paintings by B. Strobel from 1640 as well as Poland's second largest bell, known as **Tuba Dei**, fascinates visitors.

The medieval **fortress**, located above the ancient crossing on the Vistula, is well preserved. It has a famous leaning tower. Another former castle of the Teutonic Knights, dating from the 13th–14th century, is found between the old and modern city.

For those interested in scientific his-

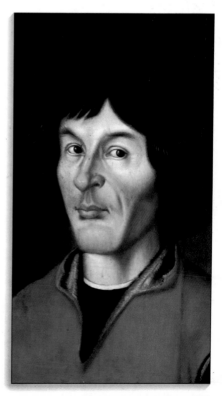

Left, the castle of the Teutonic Knights in Kwidzyń. **Right**, Nicholas Copernicus.

tory, a collection of documents and astronomical instruments dating from Copernicus's epoch is housed in the **Copernicus House** where the astronomer was born in 1473.

Travelling about 22 miles (35 km) to the east of Toruń, one reaches the town of **Gołub-Dobrzyń**, located between the lake districts of Chełminskie and Dobrzyńskie and the Drwęca. A half-Gothic and half-Renaissance castle is perched at the top of the steep banks. In recent years, this castle has been the site of international jousting tournaments and balls celebrating the carnival season. These take place under the patronage of the so-called "**White Lady**" (Anna Wazona).

Brodnica, gateway to the lovely **Brodnicki Park Krajobrazowy**, is located at the upper end of the river. Remnants of the medieval town's fortress, with its Masurian tower and the **Chełmińska Gate**, still remain. The ruins of a Teutonic Knights castle with an 279-ft (85-metre) high tower can be seen on the banks of the Drwęca.

A bit further along is **Kurzętnik**, whose city walls guard a castle dating from about 1330. Nearby is **Nowe Miasto Lubawskie** which also has remnants of medieval architecture. The Drwęca River forms a border to the lake district and is a popular destination for water sports enthusiasts. Due to its large numbers of trout and salmon, the river is an environmentally-protected area.

Bydgoszcz and surroundings: South of the tri-city, on the banks of the Brda and Vistula, is **Bydgoszcz**, the capital of this voivodeship. It has a population of 350,000. Founded by Casimir the Great in 1346, the city experienced its zenith in the 15th–16th century. It was the site of banks, warehouses, royal breweries and salt storage areas serving all of Pomerania. Goods were transported on the Vistula from here to Gdańsk. The city was destroyed during the wars with Sweden but blossomed once again under Prussian rule, albeit paying the high price of almost thorough "germanisation" during this time.

Bydgoszcz does not have many

Fishing in winter.

monuments, but the few it does boast are worth mentioning. The late-Gothic **Hall Church** (a hall church is one with several naves of the same height) houses a painting of the Virgin Mary with the rose. The **Main Library**, built in the second half of the 18th century, is also noteworthy with its large and valuable collection of old volumes. Additionally, the warehouses on the Brda and the **Church of Clarissa** as well as the **City Museum** merit a stop. The museum, named after **L. Wyczółkowski**, contains one of the largest collections of paintings by this artist.

At the outbreak of war in 1939 the Nazis met with fierce resistance from the town and mass executions were carried out once it was defeated.

The **Pojezierze Krajeńskie** stretches to the west of Bydgoszcz. Deep gorges cutting through the moraine hills make this an attractive landscape for tourists. **Sępolnie Krajeńskie** and **Więcbork** are also especially charming areas. The few existing structures from earlier eras date mainly from the 16th or 17th centuries.

There are churches in mixed Gothic and Renaissance style in **Kamienie Krajeńskie**, **Runowo Krajeńskie** and in **Waldów**, as well as late-Gothic churches in **Sadkowy** and **Wawelnio**.

North of here is **Chojnice**, a city which thrives on industry and tourism. Many examples of Gothic and baroque architecture are found here.

Kujawy: This region lies between the **Noteć**, the Vistula and Lake Gopło. Kujawy went down in recorded history relatively early. At the beginning of the 10th century it was under Polish domain and played an important role in the beginnings of the Polish state. It was always one of Poland's wealthiest provinces. From the 15th century until the first division of Poland, Kujawy was composed of two voivodeships whose urban centres were Inowrocław and Brześć Kujawski.

The health resort of **Inowrocław** is today the capital of West Kujawy. Its most interesting buildings are the triple-nave Romanesque **Church of the Holy Virgin Mary** of carved stone and the

Gothic-baroque **Church of St Nicholas**. To the northwest, on the large Lake Gopło, is the town of **Kruszwica**. Remnants of the 14th-century castle can still be seen here as well as the **Mysia Wieża** (Mice Tower) and an extraordinarily richly decorated Romanesque stone building in the form of a basilica. There is an interesting legend associated with this town. According to the story, Kruszwica was the centre of the legendary empire which was ruled by **Prince Popiel**. The king was supposedly eaten by a pack of mice, a misfortune which gave the above-mentioned tower its name.

A wide variety of water fowl enjoys the refuge of the **Nadgoplański Park Tysiąclecia**, with its countless lakes. The shores are used by the birds as nesting places and the entire region is environmentally protected.

Nearby is **Strzelno**, a village whose monastery makes it worth a stopover. The monastery's church is a combination of the early-Romanesque circular **Church of St Prokop** (about 1160) and the architecturally fascinating **Church of the Holy Trinity** (1133–1216). It contains unique flat-relief pillars and stylish tympana, making this a paradise for those with an interest in the history of architecture.

Przejezierze is nestled in the Miradzker woods on Lake Ostrowskie. This peaceful village is a mecca for visitors seeking rest and relaxation. A few miles to the west is the centre of the Polish linen industry, **Pakość**. The interesting sights in this village are the cloister complex dating from the 17th century and a calvary.

Radziejów, built on sand, is located to the east of Inowrocław. The city was founded in 1252 and the first Polish Piarist Collegium was located here from 1720–1890. The Gothic-style **Cloister** (1330–31) was founded by King Łokietek.

Travelling further to the east, one reaches **Płowce**. This area was the site of an immense battle between the army of King Łokietek and the Teutonic Knights on 27 September, 1331. On this occasion the knights came off worst.

Many monuments are found here which commemorate this historic event, for example a stone monument from the year 1961, the large cross and the knights' cemetery.

Not far from Włocławek, on a flat hill, is Brześć Kujawski. The town hall, built in 1824 in classical style according to plans drawn up by H. Marconi, and the impressive late-Gothic hall church are noteworthy.

In the eastern part of Kujawy, on the left bank of the Vistula, is the former bishop's see of **Włocławek**. Today this city has become an industrial centre with a population of 120,000. Its most interesting structure is the brick **Church of the Assumption**, built in 1411. In later years, further additions were made to the church in baroque style. Many small chapels surround the main church. The **Chapel of the Virgin** contains late-Gothic works by **Piotr from Bnin** and **Wit Stwosz** dating from the year 1493. The presbytery is flooded with a soft light which shines through a lovely window crafted by the Art Nouveau artist **Józef Mehoffer**.

One should also be sure to save time for a visit to the Gothic **Church of St Vitalis** (1330) with its famous 1493 triptych depicting the coronation of the Holy Virgin Mary. The 14th-century **Church of St John** dominates the old market place.

The vast park of **Gostyninko-Włocwławski**, with its 98,800 acres (40,000 hectares), stretches between the cities of Włocławek and Płock. It was opened in 1979. To the south of this park is **Kowal**, proudly known as the birthplace of the famous King Casimir the Great. North of Włocławek, between the Vistula, Drwęca and Skrwa rivers, the Dobrzyński lakes are scattered throughout the landscape, imparting special beauty to this region.

Dobrzyń nad Wisla, a former fortress on the border to Masovia, is located on the artificial lake of Włocławek.

The well-known silent film star Apolonia Chałupiec was born in Lipno which is about 14 miles (23 km) to the north. She gained fame under the stage name **Pola Negri** (1896–1987).

Storks live an undisturbed existence in Pomerania.

THE MASURIAN LAKE DISTRICT

The Masurian Lake District is located in the northeastern part of Poland. It includes three regions with extremely differing histories: **Warmia**, **Mazury** and **Suwalszczyzna**.

Warmia got its name from the old Prussian tribe known as the Warms which inhabited the region far back in history. Mazury, on the other hand, is a part of the former East Prussia. It was settled in the 14th century by Polish immigrants, though the name Mazury first came into use at a later date. Suwalszczyzna is in the east of Poland. The Jazowingowie tribe, relatives of the original Prussians, lived here until the German Order of Knighthood took over the area.

The conquest of the region by the German Order of Knighthood took place during the years between 1233 and 1283, resulting in widespread death and destruction among the original inhabitants. The population which remained was thereafter assimilated by the immigrants and soon lost its identity as an independent people.

The government under the German Order of Knighthood was well organised and dynamic. The Order protected itself by means of strongly fortified castles and found themselves in an ideal position to make further far-ranging conquests. It was not until the year 1410, in one of the largest European battles of medieval times, that history took a turn for the better for Poland and Lithuania. The fighting took place near the village of **Grunwald**, which still goes by its German name.

This battle, one of the most bitter of the Middle Ages, resulted in a portion of the region once again coming under Polish sovereignty. The remainder became a non-sovereign duchy. When Poland was divided, Prussia took over power here. Suwalszczyzna was returned to Poland after World War I and Warmia and Mazury after World War II. This area, with its varied and turbulent history, was under Swedish rule during three different periods, twice under that of the Tartars and for a lengthy period of time under Russian sovereignty. Each of these ruling powers inevitably left its imprint, but the marks left by the Germans are the most evident. This is in spite of the completion of a programme of "re-polonisation", as the Germans call it.

The landscape is made up of thousands of lakes, majestic hills and extensive wooded areas; most of the villages housing the sparse population of the area are located in clearings. These were formed by the last Ice-Age and have given Mazury the reputation as the "land of 1,000 lakes". **Śniardwy** and **Mamry**, located here, are Poland's two largest inland lakes.

Lovely primeval fir and pine forests blanket **Puszcza Augustowska and Puszcza Piska**. This wilderness offers a paradise for a wide variety of wildlife such as deer, wild boar, moose, bison, mountain-cocks, black storks and eagles. In the rushes along the banks of the lakes, swans, cranes, herons, crested divers and ducks find safe nesting places.

Attentive sea gulls accompany ships and boats as they ply the rivers and lakes. The waters are positively teeming with eels, pike and salmon trout. It can be counted as a great blessing that almost this entire region is environmentally protected by the state. The **Wigry National Park**, the **Suwalski and Mazurski** parks and the 80 nature preserves here provide nature with a welcome bit of breathing space.

Olsztyn, lying on the Łyna, is the largest city in this region. There was a castle here as long ago as 1334 and in 1353 the settlement was granted its charter. In 1454 its people, in unison with other northern towns, rose up against the Teutonic Knights and declared their allegiance to the Polish king. Prior to that time, it lay mainly within the protective walls of the castle but from then on the settlement expanded rapidly. The castle still survives and today functions as a museum documenting the history and culture of Warmia and Mazury. Its exhibits include

Preceding pages: a rural estate in Łabędnik near Bartenstein; having fun during the potato harvest. **Below**, the castle of the Teutonic knights in Olsztyn.

archaeological finds recovered from ancient burial sites in the area. From 1516–21 the genial astronomer Nicholas Copernicus served as the castellan here on behalf of his uncle, the bishop of Warmia. He lived in the south-west wing. Fragments of an astronomical chart drawn by him can be seen on the inside wall of the courtyard. In 1973, in honour of Copernicus' 500th birthday, a planetarium was opened in Olszytn, followed a few years later by the opening of an observatory.

After the first partition in 1772 Olszytn, like the rest of Warmia, fell under Prussian rule. Much of the development that grew up outside the old walled town therefore has a strong Germanic character. The headquarters of the Association of Poles in Germany, formed in the 1920s, was based here.

Several idyllic lakes embellish the nearby landscape. The largest, **Ukiśl**, is the site of a magnificent bathing beach. Those who would rather be on the lake than in it can hire a boat to propel themselves around or tour the waters on an excursion boat. The lakes of **Skanda** and **Kortowskie** also offer charming bathing areas.

The ruins of the Wolf's Lair, Adolf Hitler's former headquarters in **Gierłoż** near **Kętrzyń**, serve as a chilling reminder of the former Nazi occupation. During the years 1940–42, 80 buildings were constructed here, among them seven massive bunkers with walls measuring up to 26 ft (8 metres) thick. The whole thing was mined with explosives which a single plunger was to activate in case of imminent defeat. The complex was so vast that it was highly visible even in the forest and to disguise it it was covered by artificial greenery suspended on wires. For two years, with only short interruptions, Hitler occupied this compound, directing much of his war strategy from here, particularly that on the eastern front. It was here, too, on 20 July 1944, that Colonel **Claus von Stauffenberg** made his courageous, though unsuccessful, assassination attempt on Hitler. On the day the bomb exploded in Hitler's bunker the Führer

Following pages: evening time at Śniardwy Lake.

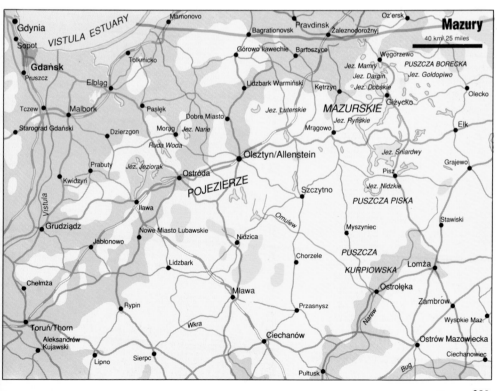

had adjourned elsewhere because it was too warm.

The headquarters were described by a General Alfred Jodl at the Nuremberg Trials as "a mixture of cloister and concentration camp. Very little news from the outer walls penetrated into this holy of holies."

Boat excursions: Almost the entire lake country surrounding the towns of **Augustów**, **Ostróda** and **Iława**, as well as the large Masurian lakes, are interconnected by means of a network of canals. The towns themselves are less interesting than the lakes they serve – although Augustow was founded by King Zygmunt in 1561. Excursion boats travel these lovely routes throughout the main tourist season. The most enchanting voyage is the five-part journey through the largest lakes. Normal passenger service operates between **Giżycko** and **Węgorzewo** (16 miles/25 km), Gizycko and **Mikołajki** (25 miles/40 km), Mikołajki and **Ruciane-Nida** (12 miles/20 km) and from Mikołajki to **Pisz** (16 miles/25 km). Additionally, excursions on the lakes can be booked in the towns of Giżycko, Mikołajki and Ruciane-Nida. Mikołajki, once an insignificant village, is now a favourite holiday destination among Poles.

Surely the most attractive portion of this canal network is found between Mikołajki and Ruciane-Nida, where the woods of Puszcza Piska line almost the entire route. The romantic sluiceway in **Guzianki** equalises the difference in water levels between the lakes of **Bełdany** and **Guzianka**.

The overland canal between Ostróda and **Elbląg** is fascinating from a technical standpoint. In addition to negotiating the two sluiceways on this 50 mile (80 km) long waterway, boats travelling this waterway must also pass through five slides. The boats are placed on trolleys and hauled up long slopes by means of water-powered machines. This is the only remaining system of this kind in the world which is still in use today. It makes for one of the most dramatic ways of entering the Masurian Lake District, an option, alas, only open to those arriving by boat.

INSIGHT GUIDES
Travel Tips

FOR THOSE
WITH MORE THAN
A PASSING INTEREST
IN TIME...

Before you put your name down for a Patek Philippe watch *fig. 1*, there are a few basic things you might like to know, without knowing exactly whom to ask. In addressing such issues as accuracy, reliability and value for money, we would like to demonstrate why the watch we will make for you will be quite unlike any other watch currently produced.

"Punctuality", Louis XVIII was fond of saying, "is the politeness of kings."

We believe that in the matter of punctuality, we can rise to the occasion by making you a mechanical timepiece that will keep its rendezvous with the Gregorian calendar at the end of every century, omitting the leap-years in 2100, 2200 and 2300 and recording them in 2000 and 2400 *fig. 2*. Nevertheless, such a watch does need the occasional adjustment. Every 3333 years and 122 days you should remember to set it forward one day to the true time of the celestial clock. We suspect, however, that you are simply content to observe the politeness of kings. Be assured, therefore, that when you order your watch, we will be exploring for you the physical—if not the metaphysical—limits of precision.

Does everything have to depend on how much?

Consider, if you will, the motives of collectors who set record prices at auction to acquire a Patek Philippe. They may be paying for rarity, for looks or for micromechanical ingenuity. But we believe that behind each $500,000-plus

bid is the conviction that a Patek Philippe, even if 50 years old or older, can be expected to work perfectly for future generations.
In case your ambitions to own a Patek Philippe are somewhat discouraged by the scale of the sacrifice involved, may we hasten to point out that the watch we will make for you today will certainly be a technical improvement on the Pateks bought at auction? In keeping with our tradition of inventing new mechanical solutions for greater reliability and better time-keeping, we will bring to your watch innovations *fig. 3* inconceivable to our watchmakers who created the supreme wristwatches of 50 years ago *fig. 4*. At the same time, we will of course do our utmost to avoid placing undue strain on your financial resources.

Can it really be mine?

May we turn your thoughts to the day you take delivery of your watch? Sealed within its case is your watchmaker's tribute to the mysterious process of time. He has decorated each wheel with a chamfer carved into its hub and polished into a shining circle. Delicate ribbing flows over the plates and bridges of gold and rare alloys. Millimetric surfaces are bevelled and burnished to exactitudes measured in microns. Rubies are transformed into jewels that triumph over friction. And after many months—or even years—of work, your watchmaker stamps a small badge into the mainbridge of your watch. The Geneva Seal—the highest possible attestation of fine watchmaking *fig. 5*.

Looks that speak of inner grace *fig. 6*.

When you order your watch, you will no doubt like its outward appearance to reflect the harmony and elegance of the movement within. You may therefore find it helpful to know that we are uniquely able to cater for any special decorative needs you might like to express. For example, our engravers will delight in conjuring a subtle play of light and shadow on the gold case-back of one of our rare pocket-watches *fig. 7*. If you bring us your favourite picture, our enamellers will reproduce it in a brilliant miniature of hair-breadth detail *fig. 8*. The perfect execution of a double hobnail pattern on the bezel of a wristwatch is the pride of our casemakers and the satisfaction of our designers, while our chainsmiths will weave for you a rich brocade in gold *figs. 9 & 10*. May we also recommend the artistry of our goldsmiths and the experience of our lapidaries in the selection and setting of the finest gemstones? *figs. 11 & 12*.

How to enjoy your watch before you own it.

As you will appreciate, the very nature of our watches imposes a limit on the number we can make available. (The four Calibre 89 time-pieces we are now making will take up to nine years to complete). We cannot therefore promise instant gratification, but while you look forward to the day on which you take delivery of your Patek Philippe *fig. 13*, you will have the pleasure of reflecting that time is a universal and everlasting commodity, freely available to be enjoyed by all.

Should you require information on any particular Patek Philippe watch, or even on watchmaking in general, we would be delighted to reply to your letter of enquiry. And if you send

fig. 1: The classic face of Patek Philippe.

fig. 4: Complicated wristwatches circa 1930 (left) and 1990. The golden age of watchmaking will always be with us.

fig. 6: Your pleasure in owning a Patek Philippe is the purpose of those who made it for you.

fig. 9: Harmony of design is executed in a work of simplicity and perfection in a lady's Calatrava wristwatch.

fig. 2: One of the 33 complications of the Calibre 89 astronomical clock-watch is a satellite wheel that completes one revolution every 400 years.

fig. 5: The Geneva Seal is awarded only to watches which achieve the standards of horological purity laid down in the laws of Geneva. These rules define the supreme quality of watchmaking.

fig. 7: Arabesques come to life on a gold case-back.

fig. 10: The chainsmith's hands impart strength and delicacy to a tracery of gold.

fig. 11: Circles in gold: symbols of perfection in the making.

fig. 3: Recognized as the most advanced mechanical regulating device to date, Patek Philippe's Gyromax balance wheel demonstrates the equivalence of simplicity and precision.

fig. 8: An artist working six hours a day takes about four months to complete a miniature in enamel on the case of a pocket-watch.

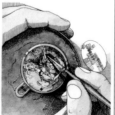

fig. 12: The test of a master lapidary is his ability to express the splendour of precious gemstones.

PATEK PHILIPPE
GENEVE
fig. 13: The discreet sign of those who value their time.

your card marked "book catalogue" we shall post you a catalogue of our publications. Patek Philippe, 41 rue du Rhône, 1204 Geneva, Switzerland, Tel. +41 22/310 03 66.

So, you're getting away from it all.

Just make sure you can get back.

AT&T Access Numbers
Dial the number of the country you're in to reach AT&T.

*AUSTRIA†††	022-903-011	*GREECE	00-800-1311	NORWAY	800-190-11
*BELGIUM	0800-100-10	*HUNGARY	00◇-800-01111	POLAND¹◆³	0◇010-480-0111
BULGARIA	00-1800-0010	*ICELAND	999-001	PORTUGAL¹	05017-1-288
CANADA	1-800-575-2222	IRELAND	1-800-550-000	ROMANIA	01-800-4288
CROATIA¹◆	99-38-0011	ISRAEL	177-100-2727	*RUSSIA¹ (MOSCOW)	155-5042
*CYPRUS	080-90010	*ITALY	172-1011	SLOVAKIA	00-420-00101
CZECH REPUBLIC	00-420-00101	KENYA¹	0800-10	SOUTH AFRICA	0-800-99-0123
*DENMARK	8001-0010	*LIECHTENSTEIN	155-00-11	SPAIN•	900-99-00-11
*EGYPT¹ (CAIRO)	510-0200	LITHUANIA◆	8◇196	*SWEDEN	020-795-611
*FINLAND	9800-100-10	LUXEMBOURG	0-800-0111	*SWITZERLAND	155-00-11
FRANCE	19◇-0011	F.Y.R. MACEDONIA	99-800-4288	*TURKEY	00-800-12277
*GAMBIA	00111	*MALTA	0800-890-110	UK	0500-89-0011
GERMANY	0130-0010	*NETHERLANDS	06-022-9111	UKRAINE¹	8◇100-11

Countries in bold face permit country-to-country calling in addition to calls to the U.S. **World Connect℠** prices consist of **USADirect**® rates plus an additional charge based on the country you are calling. Collect calling available to the U.S. only. *Public phones require deposit of coin or phone card. ◇ Await second dial tone. ¹May not be available from every phone. †††Public phones require local coin payment through the call duration. ◆ Not available from public phones. • Calling available to most European countries. ¹Dial "02" first, outside Cairo. ³Dial 010-480-0111 from major Warsaw hotels. ©1994 AT&T.

Here's a travel tip that will make it easy to call back to the States. Dial the access number for the country you're in to get English-speaking AT&T operators or voice prompts. Minimize hotel telephone surcharges too.

If all the countries you're visiting aren't listed above, call **1 800 241-5555** for a free wallet card with all AT&T access numbers. Easy international calling from AT&T. **TrueWorld Connections.**

AT&T

TRAVEL TIPS

GETTING ACQUAINTED

THE PLACE

The Republic of Poland is located in central Europe at a latitude between 54°50'N and 49°00'N, and at a longitude between 14°07'E and 24°08'E.

The border with Germany in the west follows the Odra, Poland's second largest river, and the Nysa Luzycka River for a total of 285 miles (460 km). The Czech Republic and Slovakia make up its southern border while Lithuania, Byelorussia and Ukraine form the border to the east. Poland's northern border made up with Russia and the Baltic Sea is over 325 miles (524 km) long.

Warsaw, the capital, is sited on the largest river, the Vistula, which flows northwards from the mountains to the Baltic. The country's major ports are Gdańsk, Gdynia, and Szczecin.

TIME ZONES

Poland is one hour ahead of Greenwich Mean Time. When it is noon in Warsaw it is 6am in New York and 8pm in Tokyo. Daylight saving time is in effect from May through to October when one hour is added.

SIZE

Poland extends 430 miles (690 km) from east to west and 400 miles (650 km) from north to south. The total land area encompasses 120,720 sq. miles (312,680 sq. km).

TOPOGRAPHY

Poland has a varied topography. To the north, the Baltic Sea coastline is composed of sandy beaches backed by dunes, steep slopes and cliffs. Picturesque lowland plains dotted with lakes, forests, rivers and canals make up the typical moraine landscape of the Northern Pomeranian and Masurian Lakelands. Lake Śniardwy, the largest lake in this area, measures 109,700 hectares (271,075 acres).

The central-Polish lowlands between the Odra and Bug rivers are cultivated extensively for agricultural use. The Sudeten and Carpathian Mountains stretch along Poland's southern boarders. The Sudeten belong to the oldest mountain massifs in Europe, the highest peak is Mount Śnieżka (5,255 ft/1,602 metres). The Carpathians are younger. The Tatra Range makes up their central part and is Alpine in character. The range contains Poland's highest peak, Mount Rysy, which is 8,200 ft (2,499 metres).

NATIONAL PARKS & NATURE RESERVES

Poland has 19 national parks, 90 landscape parks, and about 1,000 reserves. The **Białowieski National Park** (5 Park Pałacowy, 17-230 Białowieża. Tel: Hajnówka 12306) is the oldest forest park in the country, which has a breeding centre for European bison, *tarpan* (Polish horse), stag, roe deer and wild boar.

Słowiński National Park has moving sand dunes and unique desert landscape which includes a 328 ft (100 metre) wide beach. The nearby tourist centre has two camping grounds. There is a Slovine open-air museum in the village of Kluki. (Bohaterów Warszawy Ulica, 76-214 Smołdzino. Tel: Słupsk 116339/204).

Babiogórski National Park (34-223 Zawoja. Tel: Zawoja 110) contains the highest portions of the Western Bieszczady Mountains, including Mount Tarnica.

The largest national park in Poland, **Kampinoski National Park**, covers the ancient Vistula River Valley (49 Krasińskiego Ulica, 05-080 Izabelin, tel: Warsaw 342514/7226001).

For further details of national parks and nature reserves contact: the **National Board of the Polish National Parks**, 52/54 Wawelska Ulica, 02-067 Warsaw. Tel: 251493.

CLIMATE

Due to the country's lengthy coastline, the climate in Poland varies between oceanic and continental. Therefore, weather conditions are subject to dramatic change. Winter lasts about three months (December–February), but can be so severe that in many northern regions temperatures drop to minus 22°F (-30°C). Snow remains in the mountains until Easter. The summer months from June to August are generally hot with temperatures often climbing beyond 86°F (30°C). The traditional "Golden Polish Autumn" is usually sunny and dry.

THE PEOPLE

The total population of 38 million comprises German, Ukrainian, White Russian, Jewish, Greek and Russian minority groups. Sixty percent of all Poles live in large cities. Warsaw, the largest city, has a population of more than 1,700,000.

As a group, Polish emigrants are especially well represented in the former USSR (approximately 1,140,000), France (800,000), the USA (7 million), Canada (500,000) and in Brazil (45,000).

A Wise Man Never Thinks How Far He's Come. He Thinks How Far He Can Still Travel.

REMY **XO** BECAUSE LIFE IS WHAT YOU MAKE IT

Swatch. The others just watch.

seahorse/fall winter 94-95

shockproof
splashproof
priceproof
boreproof
swiss made

swatch
SCUBA 200

Ninety-five percent of the population is Roman Catholic. Throughout the entire country there are more than 12,500 churches. The remaining 5 percent are composed of about 500,000 members of the Orthodox faith; 75,000 believers of the Augsburg Confession; 38,500 Polish Catholics; 24,000 Old Catholics; 6,000 Methodists; 6,000 Baptists; 5,000 Jews; 4,500 Protestants (Calvinists); 1,700 Muslims and 830 Buddhists.

THE ECONOMY

Since 1990 Poland has been through a dramatic economic evolution. In the light of the handicaps that have plagued this progress the transformation can be seen as phenomenal.

There has been a rapid improvement in the business environment and the momentum for change is gathering pace. Many state enterprises are being privatised and this is creating the need for foreign business partners to invest in Polish companies.

Poland's geographical position allows the easy importation of raw materials and access to markets to the east and west. It is the largest market in central Europe with 25 percent of the population under the age of 15. The adult workforce is well-educated, and there is a tradition of trading with the east where they are, in many cases, the preferred business partner.

When the zloty was made freely convertible to residents inflation spiralled and, although high interest rates brought this under control, inflation has remained a problem. Foreign debt is also a headache and the reduction in markets in the east has not yet been offset by increased trade with west Europe.

GOVERNMENT

Poland is a parliamentary republic and the national legislature is bicameral. The Sejm (parliament) has 460 seats and the Senate has 100 members. Poland has universal direct suffrage over the age of 18. The national government is formed by the Council of Ministers headed by a prime minister. The head of state is the president.

The country is divided into 49 viovodeships, including the three city viovodeships of Łódź, Cracow and Warsaw.

PLANNING THE TRIP

WHAT TO BRING

What clothing you take on your trip depends on the time of year and where you plan to visit. In general, during the climate during the summer months is similar to that of the UK with less humidity. The winter, however, is cold with lots of snow in the mountains and temperatures falling below 0°C (-32°F).

ELECTRICAL ADAPTERS

Poland uses 220v, 50 cycles. Sockets are continental-type 2-pin round, so take an adapter with you.

FILM

Film and video cassettes are generally available in hotels. However, it is wise to bring your own film supplies with you. Customs regulations specify that each visitor can bring in 10 rolls of film or film tape. If you're looking for special materials, or want to have a faulty camera repaired, you'll need to track down an expert.

Photographing certain areas and edifices judged by authorities to be strategically important, e.g. railway stations, bridges, harbours, police buildings and military facilities, is prohibited.

MAPS

Note that several words are frequently abbreviated on Polish maps. Aleja (abbreviated as Al) means avenue, Ulica (abbreviated as ul and not capitalised in Polish) means street, Plac means square, and Rynek is Old Town Square. In addresses, house numbers usually follow the name of the street.

ENTRY REGULATIONS

PASSPORTS & VISAS

British visitors can stay in Poland for six months without a visa. Passport holders from most European countries, the USA and the Commonwealth can stay for up to 90 days without a visa; visitors from Bulgaria, Estonia, Macedonia, Mongolia and Romania can remain for up to 30 days without a visa while travellers from Hong Kong are allowed two weeks.

Visas remain valid for six months from the date of issue.

Visa extensions can be obtained from the Voivodship Offices of the **Ministry of Internal Affairs**, Foreign Visitors Department, 11 Floor, 47a/49 Wspólna Ulica, Warsaw. Children included on their parents passports are not charged any fees for visas.

Transit visas are valid for 48 hours. The visa of the destination country is a prerequisite to receiving a transit visa. Passport and visa regulations can change quite quickly so it's wise to check with the Polish consular mission in your country of domicile before setting off.

OTHER ENTRY REGULATIONS

Visitors to Poland are obliged to register their stay within 48 hours after crossing the border. Registration is performed by the hotel or camping site reception desk.

ANIMAL QUARANTINE

There is no quarantine in Poland. Tourists are allowed to bring in cats and dogs which have been inoculated against rabies at least 3 weeks before entering the country. Official proof of vaccination must be available upon request.

CUSTOMS

The following articles may be imported duty free:
Alcohol: 0.25 litre of spirits or white vodka, or 0.5 litre of vodka; up to 0.75 litres of wine and up to 1 litre of beer.
Tobacco products: up to 250 cigarettes or 50 cigars or 250g of pipe tobacco.
Food: up to 200g of coffee; up to 2kg of meat, fish and poultry products and 1kg of milk products.
Personal effects exempt from duty include cameras, musical instruments, typewriters, portable self-powered electronic goods, jewellery and most sporting equipment. For more details contact a Polish consular office.
Two sporting or hunting guns, one hand gun or one mace gun together with 100 rounds of ammunition for each weapon may be bought into the country if they are accompanied by permits issued by a Polish consular office.

HEALTH

Before travelling it may be a good idea to stock-up on elementary medicines. No inoculations are deemed necessary but make sure you have up-to-date tetanus boosters. You may want to visit a travel clinic before departure to establish if there have been any flash outbreaks of tyhoid or meningitis.

CURRENCY

The Polish zloty is convertible and there is no set limit on the amount of foreign legal tender that can be brought into Poland if it is declared in writing.

In 1995 the National Bank of Poland announced that some old bank notes (50, 100, 200, 500, 1,000, 2,000, 5,000, 10,000, 20,000, 50,000, 100,000, 500,000, 1,000,000 and 2,000,000) would be replaced by new notes that remove the last four zeros from larger notes. For example, exchange rates will change in the following fashion:

$$£1 = 30,0000 \text{ zl (old)}$$
$$£1 = 3.6 \text{ zl (new)}$$

Old style bank notes will remain in circulation at the same time as new notes for some time yet. Check exchange rates with your travel agent or bank before departure.

CASH, TRAVELLER'S CHEQUES, CREDIT CARDS

American Express, Visa, Eurocard, MasterCard, Diners' Club and JCB credit cards are accepted in all major hotels, restaurants, cafes, well-established shops, art galleries and car rental agencies. Cash can only be obtained against VISA cards in banks. Travellers' cheques are accepted all over Poland. Loss or theft of credit cards can be reported to PolCard in Warsaw, tel: 274513, 273040 and 274513. American Express cardholder, tel: 6353061/264460.

PUBLIC HOLIDAYS

Fixed Days
January 1, New Year's Day
May 1, Labour Day
May 3, the anniversary of the Constitution
August 15, Feast of the Assumption
November 1, All Saint's Day
November 11, National Independence Day
December 25, Christmas Day
December 26, St Stephen's Day

Movable dates
Easter Holidays (Sunday, Monday) and Corpus Christi.

GETTING THERE

BY AIR

Poland has regular connections to almost all the capital cities of Europe. Okęcie Airport, 6 miles (10 km) from the centre of Warsaw, is the hub of LOT Polish National Airlines worldwide service. There are daily flights from and to London, New York, Chicago and Montreal.

All LOT international flights are on wide-bodied B767s. Some flights are seasonal, the flight time

American Express offers Travelers Cheques built for two.

Cheques *for Two*ᴿᴹ from American Express are the Travelers Cheques that allow either of you to use them because both of you have signed them. And only one of you needs to be present to purchase them.

Cheques *for Two* are accepted anywhere regular American Express Travelers Cheques are, which is just about everywhere. So stop by your bank, AAA* or any American Express Travel Service Office and ask for Cheques *for Two*.

INSIGHT GUIDES

COLORSET NUMBERS

from the UK to Poland is approximately 2½ hours.

International flights can land at the following city airports: Cracow, Gdańsk, Katowice, Poznań, Rzeszów, Szczecin, and Warsaw.

For flight information at Warsaw International Airport contact: arrivals, tel: 469628; departures, tel: 469670; reservation and sale of tickets for international flights, tel: 469645.

LOT Polish Airlines Offices Abroad:

Amsterdam, Overtoom 60, 1054 HK, Amsterdam. Tel: (020) 6169266, fax: (020) 6169666.

Berlin, Budapester Strabe 18. Tel: (030) 2611505/06, fax: 2650806.

Chicago, 333 North Michigan Avenue, Suite 916. Tel: (312) 2363388/5501.

London, 313 Regent Street. Tel: (0171) 5805037, fax: (0171) 3230774.

Los Angeles, 6100 Wilshire Blvd., Suite 1450. Tel: (213) 9345151, fax: (213) 9345262.

Montreal, 2000 Peel Street. Tel: (514) 8442674/75, toll free for Canada 1-(800)-361-1017, fax: (514) 8447339.

New York: 500 Fifth Avenue, Suite 408. Tel: (212) 8691074, toll free (800) 223 0593.

Paris, 18 rue Luis-le-Grand, 75002 Paris. Tel: (1) 47420560, fax: 331 40170297.

LOT Polish Airlines Offices in Poland

Cracow, 15 Basztowa Ulica. Tel: 225076
Gdańsk, 2/4 Wały Jagiellońskie Ulica. Tel: 311161, fax: 312621.
Poznań, 69 Św. Marcin Ulica. Tel: 522847, fax: 525880.
Warsaw, 65/79 Aleje Jerozolimskie. Tel: 952953.

Foreign Airline Companies in Warsaw

Air Canada, 99a Marszałkowska Ulica (Metrolpol Hotel apt. 601). Tel: 6253537/584, 294001 ext. 601.
Air France, 21 Krucza Ulica. Tel: 6281281.
American Airlines, 20 Aleje Ujazdowskie. Tel: 6253002/0560, fax: 6253146.
British Airways, 49 Krucza Ulica. Tel: 6289431/3991
Delta Airlines, 11 Królewska Ulica, (Victoria Hotel). Tel: 260257, 279200.
KLM, 1 Plac Konstytucji. Tel: 6217041, 6284786, 6504444.
Lufthansa, 11 Królewska Ulica. Tel: 6302555, 275436.

BY TRAIN

There are regular daily services from London's Liverpool Street Station via the Hook of Holland and Victoria Station (via Ostend). On Saturdays (in season) charter couchettes are available on the train from Liverpool Street. Journey time from England is about 31 hours.

EuroCity trains connect Warsaw with Berlin.

Passengers who use this connection have links with Köln, Wiesbaden, Karlsruhe, Hamburg, Frankfurt and München.

All fast and express trains run on international links. Trains have 1st and 2nd class carriages, berths, sleepers and restaurant cars. Almost all international trains arrive at Warsaw Central Station, which is located at the city centre.

For train information in Warsaw contact: international, tel: 204512, 259942; domestic, tel: 2000361/69 and to make a seat reservation, tel: 365055.

BY SEA

A weekly service is operated by the *M/S Inowroclaw*, a freighter carrying passengers departing from either Tilbury on a Monday or Middlesbrough on a Tuesday and arriving in Gdynia on Fridays. The journey time is approximately 4 days. Contact: Gdynia America Shipping Lines (London) Ltd, Passenger Department, 238 City Road, London EC1V 2QL. Tel: 0171 2513389, fax: 0171 2503625.

BY COACH

Regular weekly services are run most of the year in luxury, air-conditioned coaches with bar and toilet facilities. The Poland Express goes either from London via Amsterdam to Poznań and Warsaw; or from London or Manchester/Birmingham to Wroclaw, Katowice and Cracow. The journey time is around 30 hours, with fare reductions for students, senior citizens and children.

BY CAR

Car registration documents, driving licence and Green Card are required. There is no limit on buying petrol and no restrictions on travelling within Poland. Petrol costs around £0.30 a litre in local currency. From the Hook of Holland or Ostend, the driving time to the Polish border is about 20 hours.

The Polish Motoring Association (PZM) can provide information about travelling around Poland and maps.

USEFUL TELEPHONE NUMBERS

997	Police
998	Fire Brigade
999	Ambulance
981	Roadside Assistance (PZM)
900	Long-distance Operator
901	International Operator
905	Telegrams
908	International Directory Enquiries
919	Radio Taxi
962	Speaking Clock
930	International Area Dialling Codes

Consulate LA (310)442-8500 Ext. 16   FAX (310)442-8515

USEFUL ADDRESSES

Polish National Tourist Centres Abroad
Germany: Polnisches Informationszentrum für Touristik, Waidmarkt 24, 50676 Köln. Tel: 230545, fax: 210465.
Netherlands: Pool Informatiebureau voor Toerisme, Leidsestraat 64, Amsterdam 1017 D. Tel: 6253570, fax: 6230929.
Sweden: Polska Statens Turistbyra, Kungsgatan 66, Box 449, S-10128 Stockholm. Tel: 216075, 218145, fax: 210465.
USA: Polish National Tourist Office, 333 North Michigan Avenue, Suite 224, Chicago, IL 60601. Tel: ~~236 9013~~, fax: (312) 2361125, telex: 282181. Polish National Tourist Office, 275 Madison Avenue, Suite 1711, New York, NY 10016. Tel: (212)3389412, fax: 3389283.

International Cultural Centres
The American Center. 13/15 Senatorska Ulica. Tel: 267015.
Austrian Institute of Culture. 8 Prózna Ulica. Tel: 209620.
British Council. 59 Jerozolimskie Avenue. Tel: 6287401-03.
Gothe Institute. 1 Defilad Square, Palace of Culture and Science. Tel: 200211 ext. 2209.
French Institute. 38 Senatorska Ulica. Tel: 277640.
Italian Institue of Cuture, 11 Foksal Ulica. Tel: 266288.
Russian Culture and Information Centre, 10 Foksal Ulica. Tel: 277621.
The Institute of Polish for Foreigners, 26 Nowy Świat Ulica. Tel: 263108.

UK TOUR OPERATORS

Polorbis Travel Ltd, 82 Mortimer Street, London W1N 7DE. Tel: 0171 6362217 or 637 4971, fax: 0171 436 6558.
Fregata Travel Ltd, 100 Dean Street, London W1V 6AQ. Tel: 0171 734 5101.
New Millennium Holidays and Travel Ltd, 20 High Street, Solihull, West Midlands B91 3TB. Tel: 0121 711 2232, fax: 0121 7113652.

US TOUR OPERATORS

Happy Holidays Travel, 5324 W. Lawrence Avenue, Chicago, IL 60630. Tel: (312) 282 1188.
American Travel Abroad Ltd, 250 West 57th Street, New York, NY 10107. Tel: (212) 586 5230, fax: (212) 581 7925. Or 4801 W. Peterson Ave, Chicago, IL 60646. Tel: (312) 725 9500, fax: (312) 725 8089.

SPECIAL TOUR OPERATORS

Polorbis, the tour operating and travel agency arm of Orbis, the state travel office, produces a varied and imaginative brochure. There is a Warsaw Opera Weekend, Activity Holidays and Health Spas; and a Tribute Tour taking in ghettos, castles, and the Pope's birthplace.

Sports-Tourist offers sporting events, sailing, canoeing and horseback riding in its programme.

In addition to all this, the **Polish Association for Tourism and Culture (PTTK)** organises hiking, rally, canoeing, sailing and motorcycling tours, as well as excursions on foot, on skis and in the mountains. Hiking and tour guides are available upon request. Contact: PTTK, 36 Swieokrzyska Ulica, 00-116 Warsaw, tel: 022/6208241.

Almatur, the travel agency run by the Polish Student Association, arranges reasonably priced individual or group tours for students including educational and cultural programmes, international student lodgings along the coast, on lakes and in the mountains. They also organise tours for film, fishing and horse-riding buffs. Contact: Almatur-Polish Co. Ltd. Travel and Tourism Office, 15 Kopernika Ulica, 00-359 Warsaw, tel: 263507, fax: 263507.

PRACTICAL TIPS

EMERGENCIES

SECURITY & CRIME

Theft is common in frequently visited areas. It's wise to leave valuables and jewellery in your hotel safe. It's also a good idea to park your car at guarded car parks. If in spite of all precautions something is stolen, report the theft at once to the hotel reception or police. The emergency police number is 997.

MEDICAL SERVICES

Visitors can get medical attention in any city clinic. Treatments and hospital stays must be paid for in foreign currency. Medications prescribed by Polish doctors may be paid for in zlotys. Make sure you take out adequate medical insurance to cover all eventualities before you arrive.

Chemists are open during normal business hours. In case of an emergency the addresses of the closest chemists on night duty is posted.

To be on the safe side, it's best to bring a supply of any special medications you need or think you might need with you on your trip.

INSIGHT *pocket* GUIDES

North America	Corsica	Middle East and Africa
Atlanta	Costa Blanca	Istanbul
Boston	Costa Brava	Kenya
British Coumbia	Cote d'Azur	Maldives
Florida	Crete	Morocco
Florida Keys	Denmark	Seychelles
Hawaii	Florence	Tunisia
Miami	Gran Canaria	Turkish Coast
Montreal	Hungary	**Asia/Pacific**
New York City	Ibiza	Bali
North California	Ireland	Bali Birdwalks
Quebec	Lisbon	Bangkok
San Francisco	Loire Valley	Beijing
South California	London	Bhutan
Toronto	Madrid	Canton
Latin America and The Caribbean	Mallorca	Chiang Mai
	Malta	Fiji
Bahamas	Marbella	Hong Kong
Baja	Milan	Jakarta
Belize	Moscow	Kathmandu,
Bermuda	Munich	Bikes & Hikes
Jamaica	Oslo/Bergen	Kuala Lumpur
Mexico City	Paris	Macau
Puerto Rico	Prague	Malacca
US Virgin Islands	Provence	Nepal
Yucatan Peninsula	Rhodes	New Delhi
Europe	Rome	New Zealand
Aegean Islands	Sardinia	Penang
Algarve	Scotland	Phuket
Alsace	Seville	Sabah
Athens	Sicily	Sikkim
Barcelona	Southeast England	Singapore
Bavaria	St Petersburg	Sri Lanka
Berlin	Tenerife	Sydney
Brittany	Tuscany	Thailand
Brussels	Venice	Tibet
Budapest	Vienna	Yogyakarta

United States: Houghton Mifflin Company, Boston MA 02108
Tel: (800) 2253362 Fax: (800) 4589501

Canada: Thomas Allen & Son, 390 Steelcase Road East
Markham, Ontario L3R 1G2
Tel: (416) 4759126 Fax: (416) 4756747

Great Britain: GeoCenter UK, Hampshire RG22 4BJ
Tel: (256) 817987 Fax: (256) 817988

Worldwide: Höfer Communications Singapore 2262
Tel: (65) 8612755 Fax: (65) 8616438

" I was first drawn to the Insight Guides by the excellent "Nepal" volume. I can think of no book which so effectively captures the essence of a country. Out of these pages leaped the Nepal I know – the captivating charm of a people and their culture. I've since discovered and enjoyed the entire Insight Guide Series. Each volume deals with a country or city in the same sensitive depth, which is nowhere more evident than in the superb photography. "

Sir Edmund Hillary

Don't be overcharged for overseas calls.

Save up to 70% on calls back to the U.S. with WorldPhone.®*

While traveling abroad, the last thing you need to worry about is being overcharged for international phone calls. Plan ahead and look into WorldPhone – the easy and affordable way for you to call the U.S. and country to country from a growing list of international locations.

Just dial 1-800-955-0925 to receive your free, handy, wallet-size WorldPhone Access Guide – your guide to saving as much as 70% on phone calls home.

When calling internationally, your WorldPhone Access Guide will allow you to:
- Avoid hotel surcharges and currency confusion
- Choose from four convenient billing options
- Talk with operators who speak your language
- Call from more than 90 countries
- Just dial and save – regardless of your long distance carrier back home

WorldPhone is easy. And there's nothing to join. So avoid overcharges when you're traveling overseas. Call for your free WorldPhone Access Guide today – before you travel.

Call 1-800-955-0925.

THE TOP 25 WORLDPHONE COUNTRY CODES.		
COUNTRY	**WORLDPHONE TOLL-FREE ACCESS #**	
Australia (CC)♦		
To call using OPTUS ■	008-5511-11	
To call using TELSTRA ■	1-800-881-100	
Belgium (CC)♦	0800-10012	
China (CC)	108-12	
(Available from most major cities)		
For a Mandarin-speaking Operator	108-17	
Dominican Republic	1-800-751-6624	
El Salvador♦	195	
France (CC)♦	19▼-00-19	
Germany (CC)	0130-0012	
(Limited availability in eastern Germany.)		
Greece (CC)♦	00-800-1211	
Guatemala♦	189	
Haiti (CC)+	001-800-444-1234	
Hong Kong (CC)	800-1121	
India (CC)	000-127	
(Available from most major cities)		
Israel (CC)	177-150-2727	
Italy (CC)♦	172-1022	
Japan♦		
To call to the U.S. using KDD ■	0039-121	
To call to the U.S. using IDC ■	0066-55-121	

COUNTRY	**WORLDPHONE TOLL-FREE ACCESS #**
Japan (cont'd.)	
To call anywhere other than the U.S.	0055
Korea (CC)	
To call using KT ■	009-14
To call using DACOM ■	0039-12
Phone Booths+	Red button 03, then press*
Military Bases	550-2255
Mexico ▲	95-800-674-7000
Netherlands (CC)♦	06-022-91-22
Panama	108
Military Bases	2810-108
Philippines (CC)♦	
To call using PLDT ■	105-14
To call PHILCOM ■	1026-12
For a Tagalog-speaking Operator	108-15
Saudi Arabia (CC)+	1-800-11
Singapore	8000-112-112
Spain (CC)	900-99-0014
Switzerland (CC)♦	155-0222
United Kingdom (CC)	
To call using BT ■	0800-89-0222
To call using MERCURY ■	0500-89-0222

(CC) Country-to-country calling available. May not be available to/from all international locations. Certain restrictions apply.
+ Limited availability.
▼ Wait for second dial tone.
▲ Rate depends on call origin in Mexico.
■ International communications carrier.
♦ Public phones may require deposit of coin or phone card for dial tone.

* Savings are based on typical hotel charges for calls back to the U.S. Your savings may vary depending upon originating country and hotel, time of day and length of call. All rates effective 7/94.

WORLDPHONE℠ From MCI

Let it take you around the world.

Emergency numbers. Tel: 999
For information about health services in Warsaw:
Tel: 262761, 268300
Medical Services in Warsaw (private consulting rooms and clinics). Tel: 278962.
Warsaw Medical Centre, 65/79 Aleje Jerozolimskie (Hotel Marriott). Tel: 6210646, 6305115.

WEIGHTS & MEASURES

Poland uses the metric system. For quick and easy conversion, remember that 1 inch is roughly 2.5 cm, a metre is roughly one yard, 4 oz is just over 100 grammes and a kilogramme is just over 2 lbs. As one kilometre is about five-eighths of a mile, so 40 km is 25 miles.

BUSINESS HOURS

Most businesses are open weekdays from 8am–7pm and close on Sundays.

Banks are usually open Monday–Friday mornings and in until 5 pm; the same hours apply to bureaux de change offices.

Post offices outside of large towns open from 8am to 8pm. They are open 24 hours in big cities.

TIPPING

It is usual to leave about 10 percent of a bill as a tip in a restaurant, barber shop and for taxi driver.

RELIGIOUS SERVICES

A large majority of the Polish population is Roman Catholic, and Poles attend church regularly.

Services in English can be found at the following places of worship:
Warsaw International Church. Christian Theological Academy, 21 Miodowa Ulica. Protestant, Sunday worship at 11am (in the summer 10am).
Mokotwska Christian Fellowship. 6 Zbawiciela Square. New Testament. Sunday 6pm.
Roman Catholic Service For Catholics Abroad. Caritas, 14 Radna Ulica. Sunday 11am.

Other services:
Basilica of St John the Baptist. 6 Kanonia Ulica (Old Town). Holy mass at 11am.
Augsburg Evangelical Church of the Holy Trinity. 6 Kreytowa Ulica. Confession at 10.15am on Sunday, service and holy communion at 10.30am.
Reform Evangelical Church. 74 Al. Solidarności. Sunday service at 10am.
Warsaw Eastern Orthodox Church. 52 Al. Solidarności. Sunday service at 10am.
Nożyków Synagogue. 6 Twarda Ulica. Saturday service at 10am.
Warsaw Mosque. 103 Wiertnicza Ulica. Friday prayer at 1pm (summer) and at 12 noon (winter).

MEDIA

NEWSPAPERS & MAGAZINES

There is a weekly German/English newspaper that corresponds to the Polish *Zycie Warszawy*. Three English-language newspapers, the *Gazeta International*, *The Warsaw Voice* and *Warsaw News,* are also published weekly and contain up-to-date reports concerning Poland and Europe. The youth magazine *Radar* is available in different languages.

International magazines and newspapers are available at hotel kiosks, the International Book and Press Clubs and in many bookshops.

RADIO

It is possible to pick up foreign transmissions such as the French programme *Fun Radio* in Cracow or RFI in Warsaw. During the summer you can tune in daily to news bulletins broadcast by Polish Radio's Channel 1 in German, English and French.

A short-wave radio is indispensable for those who really want to stay in touch. The frequencies which give the best reception of the BBC or the *Voice of America* tend to be in the lower wavebands (13 and 19 meters) during the day and higher ones (31 and 42 metres) at night.

Radio Frequencies
BBC World Service: Metres 17.01, 19.91, 31.88, 48.54. In some areas the BBC can be picked up on medium wave.
Voice of America: Metres 25.06, 31.02, 49.67, 50.04.

TELEVISION

There are two Polish television stations and depending upon the region you're in, access to foreign programmes. For example in Warsaw you can pick up Channel 1 from Moscow, in Cracow RAI/Italy, or in the west, programmes originating in Germany. All the more expensive hotels offer satellite television programmes.

POSTAL SERVICES & TELECOMS

Stamps are available wherever postcards are sold. Green letter boxes are for mail destined locally, red ones for foreign correspondence. Parcels, registered mail, special delivery mail and air mail may be sent from post offices. Envelopes, postcards, telecards, and pay phone tokens (A tokens for local calls and C tokens for longer or trunk calls) are also available.

Telecard machines have been introduced in Poland. Cards can be bought at the larger post offices, airports and railway stations and at some large hotels in Warsaw. They are sold in 50 and 100 units.

In Warsaw, information about post and courier services is available by calling: 204551.

Major cities and tourist centres have automatic telephone connections. Operator assisted calls may be ordered. A brochure containing a list of dialling codes is available at post offices. The Main Post Office in Warsaw is at 31/33 Świętokrzyska Ulica.

Polish area dialling codes
Bielsko-Biała: 0-85
Gdańsk: 0-58
Katowice: 0-32 or 0-3
Cracow: 0-12
Lubin: 0-81
Łodż: 0-42
Poznań: 0-61
Wrocław: 0-71

International dialling codes
Germany: 0049
Austria: 0043
Switzerland: 0041
Great Britain: 0044
USA: 001
Australia: 0061

TELEX, FAX AND OTHER SERVICES

In most large hotels and main post offices you can both send and receive a telex or fax. In addition to this, the best hotels offer an office service which includes access to computers and printers. A friendly request for further information at the hotel reception will put you on the right track.

TOURIST INFORMATION SERVICES

Polish National Information Centres in Poland
Bielsko-Biała, 2 Piastowska Ulica, 1 Warszawska Ulica, 43-300 Bielsko-Biała. Tel: 25844, fax: 22406, telex: 035499.
Chełm, 20 Lubelska Ulica, 22-100 Chełm. Tel: 53667, fax: 54185.
Cracow, 8 Pawia Ulica, 31-154 Cracow. Tel: 226091, fax: 220471.
Częstochowa, 65 Aleja NMP, Częstochowa 42-200. Tel: 241360, telex: 037686.
Gdańsk, 27 Heweliusza Ulica, Gdańsk 80-861. Tel: 314355/316637, telex 0512733.
Katowice, 11 Młyńska Ulica, Katowice 40-098. Tel: 539787/566, telex: 03112207.
Kielce, 12 Piotrkowska Ulica, Kielce 25-510. Tel: 48666.
Lubin, Ulica Krakowskie Prezmieście 78, Lubin 20-400. Tel: 24412/25339, telex: 0643229.
Nowy Sącz, 46a Jagiellońska Ulica, Nowy Sącz 30-300. Tel: 23724, telex: 0322663.
Płock, 38 Aleja Jachowicza, Płock 09-400. Tel: 629497.
Poznań, Stary Rynek 59, Poznań 61-772. Tel: 526156, telex: 0414601.
Siedlce, 40 Piłsudskiego Ulica, Siedlce 08-110. Tel: 22374.

Toruń, 1 Rynek Staromiejski (Town Hall), Toruń 87-100. Tel: 10931, fax: 10930, telex: 0552150.
Warsaw, 1/13 Plac Zamkowy, Warsaw 00-297. Tel: 6351881.

EMBASSIES

Australia: 3/5 Estońska Ulica, 03 903 Warsaw. Tel: 6176081/5, fax: 617756.
Austria: 34 Gagarina Ulica, 00-748 Warsaw. Tel: 410081/4, fax: 410085.
Belgium: 34 Senatorska Ulica, 00-950 Warsaw. Tel: 270233/5, fax: 6355711.
Canada: 1/5 Matejki Ulica, 00-481 Warsaw. Tel: 29805, fax: 296457.
Denmark: 19 Rakowiecka Ulica, 02-517 Warsaw. Tel: 482600, fax: 487580.

Consulate and visa section:
France: 1 Piękna Ulica, 00-477 Warsaw. Tel: 6288402/9, fax: 6252031.
Germany: 30 Dabrowiecka Ulica, 03-932 Warsaw. Tel: 6173011, fax: 294803.
Great Britain: Al. Rox 1, 00-556 Warsaw. Tel: 6281001/5, fax: 6252031.
Italy: 6 Dabrowskiego Pl., 00-055 Warsaw. Tel: 263471/3, fax: 278507.
Japan: 7 Grażyny Ulica, 00-548 Warsaw. Tel: 498781, fax: 481412.
Norway: 2a Fryderyka Chopina Ulica, 00-559 Warsaw. Tel: 214231/3, fax: 6280938.
Russia: 49 Belwederska Ulica, 00-761 Warsaw. Tel: 6213453/5575, fax: 6253016.
Switzerland: Al. Ujazdowskie 27, 00-540 Warsaw. Tel: 280481, 280482.
Spain: 1b/flat 10/12/14 Starościęska Ulica, 02-516 Warsaw. Tel: 499926, fax: 491297.
Sweden: 3 Bagatela Ulica, 00-585 Warsaw. Tel: 493351/3, fax: 4952243.
USA: 29/31 Al. Ujazdowskie, 00-540 Warsaw. Tel: 6283041, fax: 6289326.

GETTING AROUND

PUBLIC TRANSPORT

ON ARRIVAL

The Airportcity Bus Service in Warsaw runs from the airport to major hotels in downtown Warsaw. Tickets are available from the ORBIS desk at the airport, the LOT desk at the Marriott Hotel or from the driver.

BY TRAIN

Warsaw Central has good connections to all parts of the country, with well-equipped sleepers on over-night routes – for example, to Zakopane, the ski town in the Tatra mountains.

It is necessary to have a reservation on express and some fast trains. There are comfortable, non-stop express trains complete with dining cars running between Warsaw and Gdańsk/Gydnia, Poznań and Cracow. Travelling by railway in Poland – even taking into account the most recent price increases – is still quite reasonable. Tickets are available at train stations, at ORBIS or at travel agencies. For further information regarding transfers and connections, enquire directly at the railway station.

You may want to consider purchasing a POLRAIL Pass, valid for all Polish National Railways (PKP). This nontransferable pass is issued in the bearer's name for 8, 15, 21 day or 1 month periods, allows unlimited mileage within the specified time and can be use to reserve a sleeping or couchette place.

InterCity trains (which stop only at their final destination) and EuroCity trains, have 1st and 2nd class 6-person compartments. Left luggage rooms are open 24 hours a day at all major railway stations.

BY COACH

Tickets for the various public transport systems can be bought at kiosks. Remember to cancel your ticket every time you transfer. Combination railway and bus tickets are also available. The PKS National Bus Company buses run normal and express lines (on long-distance routes).

Tickets may be purchased at selected Orbis offices and travel agencies, bus drivers or from the Central Booking Office, 74 Żurawia Ulica, 01-680 Warsaw. Tel: 6300625/669, fax: 299 742.

BY BUS

Buses run on normal, shuttle and express lines. Night-time buses also run in major cities. Tickets may be purchased at newsstands, some shops and sometimes from bus drivers. In some towns ten-fare tickets are available. In Warsaw one-day and one-week passes and be bought from the booking offices of the Municipal Transportation Company (MZK), 37 Senatorska Ulica, tel: 273747.

BY TAXI

A vacant taxi can be recognised by its lighted sign. The best place to hail one is in front of a hotel, railway station or department store. It is also possible to call and order one directly (in Warsaw, tel: 919).

Between 10pm and 6am the standard fare is raised by 50 percent. Make sure when you get a taxi with a meter which indicates only one base unit. This will then be multiplied by a number on an authorised list to give you the total fare upon reaching your destination.

BY AIR

LOT maintain regular and seasonal connections with the major Polish cities. Children under the age of 2 who do not occupy a separate seat receive a 90 percent discount, children under 12 are eligible for a 50 percent discount.

Cracow Airport, tel: 116700
Katowice Airport, tel: 815042
Rzeszów Airport, tel: 32721
Warsaw Domestic Airport: information, tel: 469770; tickets, tel: 217021; international reservations, tel: 287580; domestic reservations, tel: 281009.

PRIVATE TRANSPORT

BY CAR

The road network in Poland is 136,702 miles (220,000km) long, making even the more remote tourist attractions relatively easy to reach. Roads have internationally recognised signs and you should drive on the right-hand side of the road. At night and in the evening it may be difficult to spot pedestrians on country roads, so watch out. Most main thoroughfares are usually kept in good condition, but side roads with their potholes and other deficiencies are a different story altogether. Wearing a seat belt is mandatory outside towns.

Speed limits:
– 60kph (37mph) built-up areas
– 90kph (54mph) car and motorbikes outside built-up areas and for tourists coaches and motorbikes on highways and expressways
– 70 kph (43mph) for cars and motorbikes with

trailers outside built-up areas, and for cars with trailers on highways and expressways
– 110 kph (68mph) for car on highways and expressways. On highways the minimum speed is 40 kph (24mph).

From November 1 till March 1 all drivers should have their side lights switched on from sunrise to sunset.

Fuel Stations

Most petrol stations in Poland belong to the CPN chain, but there are more and more privately owned stations open from 6am to 8pm or 10pm. There are 24-hour stations on international routes and in some big cities.

Lead-free petrol is available. 10 litres (2 gallons) of petrol can be imported into Poland or taken out on a fuel tank.

Breakdown Services

The Polish Motoring Association (PZM), tel: 981 or any other roadside assistance stations. The breakdown emergency service centres operate usually from 7am till 10pm, some closing at 3pm. Membership of the PZM secures assistance to: members of automobile clubs affiliated with the Fédération Internationale de l' Automobile (FIA) and the Alliance Internationale de Tourisme (AIT); holders of insurance polices issued by the Intermutuelle Assistance, Assistance Internationale and SOS; ADAC club members (Warsaw, tel: 290374, 24 hours). Members should contact Autotour Motoring Tourism Bureau 63 Aleje Jerozlimskie, Warsaw 00-697, tel: 6210789, 6286255, fax: 6286254.

CAR RENTAL

The Polish Bureau of Tourism works in cooperation with car rental agencies like Hertz, Avis and Eurocar. This enables you to rent a car at any time at Rent-a-Car in ORBIS Stations. The following conditions must be met: you must be at least 21 years old, in possession of a valid passport, visa and International Driver's Licence. In addition to this, you must be able to pay a deposit of around US$100. Daily rates are based on car type (economy, medium or luxury) and a charge is also made per kilometre.

Warsaw
Americana, 32 Aleja Żwirki i Wigury. Tel: 257275, fax: 255888.
Avis, 65/79 Aleje Jerozolimskie, tel: 6307316 and Okęcie International Airport, tel: 6504871/4872.
Budget, 65/79 Aleje Jerozolimskie (Marriott Hotel), tel: 6307280, fax: 6306946 and Okęcie International Airport, Terminal 1, Arrivals Hall, tel: 467310.
ECU, 65/79 Aleje Jerozolimskie (Marriott Hotel), tel/fax: 6305292.
EuroDollar, 142 Marszałkowska Ulica, tel: 2911249, fax: 258157 and International Airport, tel: 6069202,

tel/fax: 6504733, fax: 460045.
Five, 24 Powązkowska Ulica, tel: 388724.
Hertz, 27 Nowogrodzka Ulica, tel: 6211360, fax: 293875, telex: 812685.
Municipal Cab Company (MPT), 4 Chrzanowskiego Ulica, tel: 107337/102045 ext. 284.
Orbis, International Airport, tel: 469875.
Yossa, 61 Złota Ulica, tel/fax: 249772; International Airport, Terminal 1, Arrivals Hall, tel: 6503121, fax: 6503122.

BY BOAT

In the summer one or two hour excursions are offered by ships sailing between ports on the Baltic coast. There are tours along the Vistula and Odra rivers as well as through the Mazurian Lakes. Tickets can be purchased at ticket desks at landing places.

HITCHHIKING

Hitchhiking is a beloved mode of transport by both Polish and foreign youth, and it is even encouraged by the government! It is necessary to obtain a hitchhiker's identification card, available in any of the 200 PTTK, "It" Tourist Centres and branches of the Polish Society of Youth Hostels (PTSM). There you'll receive a booklet containing kilometre control tickets which enable you to travel 1,250 miles (2,000 km) per person, information pertaining to hitchhiking etiquette and a map. You have to be at least 17 years old to hitchhike legally. The season begins on 1 May and ends on 30 September.

ON DEPARTURE

Customs: Items and objects made prior May 9, 1945 and gifts and souvenirs over the of total value US$100 require a special export licence. Inquires should be directed to the main Customs Office, tel: 268465, 262591 or tel: 6502873 at Warsaw International Airport.

WHERE TO STAY

HOTELS

During the height of the season simple hotels, youth hostels and camp sites are hopelessly overrun. So it's a good idea to reserve accommodation in advance. However, it's usually not a problem to find a bed in the higher price range hotels even during the peak of the season. If you get stuck, don't despair; enquire at the local tourist centre for a list of private homes which take overnight guests. The latter is a good way to come into closer contact with the locals. No matter where you end up staying, don't neglect to register first.

Interhotels are divided into 5 categories: 1, 2, 3, 4 star and luxury-class. The luxury-class hotels correspond in comfort to Western international hotels and are usually run by international hotel chains like the Marriott, Holiday Inn and Intercontinental. They boast sizeable rooms, translating and secretarial services as well as fitness centres, bars and restaurants. Prices are comparable to those in Western hotels.

The local hotel chain, ORBIS, manages some excellent hotels. Among them are the Victoria in Warsaw and the Grand Hotel in Sopot, both of which really earn their stars. The stars granted to some other hotels do not always shine so brightly. Although ORBIS is not inclined to loosen its monopoly on Poland's better hotels, the Polish people are nothing if not enterprising entrepreneurs, so all sorts of possibilities are opening up very quickly in the private sector.

Price categories are based on double room rates for two nights in high season and should be used only as a very rough guide. Expensive: £40–£60; moderate: £30–£40 and budget: £20–£30.

WARSAW

Victoria Hotel (Intercontintal). 11 Królewska Ulica, 00-065 Warsaw. Tel: (22) 279271, fax: 279856, telex: 812516. Expensive.
Europejski Hotel. 13 Krakowskie Przedmie,cie Ulica, 00-710 Warsaw. Tel: (22) 265051, fax: 261111, telex: 813615. Expensive.
Forum Hotel. 24/26 Nowogrodzka Ulica, 00-511 Warsaw. Tel: (22) 6210271, fax: 258157, telex: 814704. Expensive.
Grand Hotel. 28 Krucza Ulica, 00-522 Warsaw. Tel:

(22) 294051, fax: 6219724, telex: 813422. Moderate.
Holiday Inn. 48/54 Złota Ulica, 00-120 Warsaw. Tel: (22) 200341, fax: 300569, telex: 817418. Expensive.
Novotel. 1 Sierpnia Ulica, 65 02-134 Warsaw. Tel: (22) 464051, fax: 463686, telex: 812525. Expensive.
Warsaw Marriott, 65 Aleje Jerozolimskie. Tel: 283444. Expensive.
Zajazd Napoleonski, 83 Plowiecka Ulica. Moderate.

BIELSKO BIALA

Magura Hotel. 93 Żywiecka Ulica, 43-300 Bielsko Biała. Tel: (30) 46545, fax: 45874, telex: 35773. Budget.

BYDGOSZCZ

Pod Orlem Hotel. 14 Aleja Gdańska, 85-006 Bydgoszcz. Tel: (52) 221861, fax: 221607, telex: 221861. Moderate.

CIESZYN

Motel Orbis. 21 Motelowa Ulica, 43-400 Cieszyn. Tel: (386) 20451, fax: 22930, telex: 38234. Budget.

CZESTOCHOWA

Motel Orbis. 281/291 Wojska Polskiego Ulica, 42-200 Częstochowa. Tel: (34) 610233, fax: 655607, telex: 37605. Budget.
Patria Hotel. Ks. J Popiełuszki Ulica, 42-200 Częstochowa. Tel: (34) 247001, fax: 246332, telex: 37269. Moderate.

GDANSK

Henelius Hotel. 22 Heweliusza Ulica, 80-890 Gdańsk. Tel: (58) 315631, fax: 311922, telex: 512458. Moderate.
Marina Hotel. 20 Jelitkowska Ulica, 80-341 Gdańsk. Tel: (58) 532079, fax: 530460, telex: 512184. Budget.
Novotel. 1 Pszenna Ulica, 80-749 Gdańsk. Tel: (58) 315611, fax: 315619, telex: 512724. Moderate.

GDYNIA

Hotel Gdynia. 22 Armii Krajowej Ulica. Tel: (58) 206661, fax: 208651, telex: 54525. Moderate.

JELENIA GÓRA

Hotel Jelenia Góra. 63 Sudecka Ulica, 58-500 Jelenia Góra. Tel: (75) 24080/89, fax: 26269, telex: 75603. Moderate to budget.

KATOWICE

Silesia Hotel. 2 Piotra Skargi Ulica, 40-091 Katowice. Tel: (32) 596011, fax: 596140, telex: 315647. Budget.
Warszawa Hotel. 16 W. Roździeńskiego Ulica, 40-202 Katowice. Tel: (32) 596011, fax: 587066, telex: 315747. Moderate.

CRACOW

Cracovia. 1 Marszałka Focha Ulica, 30-111 Cracow. Tel: (12) 228666, fax: 219586, telex: 322341. Moderate.
Forum Hotel. 28 M. Konopnickej Ulica, 30-302 Cracow. Tel: (12) 669500, fax: 665827, telex: 322737. Moderate.
Holiday Inn. 7 Aleja Armii Krajowej, 30-150 Cracow. Tel: (12) 375044, fax: 375938, telex: 325356. Expensive.
Wanda Hotel. 15 Amii Krajowej Ulica, 30-150 Cracow. Tel: (12) 371677, fax: 378518, telex: 325507. Budget.
Grand Hotel. 5 Slawkowska Ulica. Tel: 217255. Moderate–expensive.

LUBIN

Unia Hotel. 12 Aleje Racławickie, 20-037 Lubin. Tel: (81) 32061, fax: 33021, telex: 642345. Moderate.

LÓDZ

Grand Hotel. 72 Piotrkowska Ulica, 90-102 Łódź. Tel: (42) 339920, fax: 337876, telex: 886293. Moderate.

NOWY SACZ

Beskid Hotel.1 Limanowskiego Ulica, 30-300 Nowy Sącz. Tel: (18) 420770, fax: 422144, telex: 322391. Budget.

OLSZTYN

Novotel. 4a Sielska Ulica, 10-802 Olsztyn. Tel: (89) 274081, fax: 275403, telex: 526426. Moderate.

PLOCK

Petropol Hotel. 49 Jachowicza Ulica, 09-400 Płock. Tel: (24) 624451, fax: 624450, telex: 83302. Budget.

POZNAN

Merkury Hotel. 20 Roosevelta Ulica, 60-829 Poznań. Tel: (61) 558000, fax: 558955, telex: 413434. Moderate–budget.
Novotel. 64/66 Warszawska Ulica, 61-028 Pozań.

Tel: (61) 770011, fax: 773654, telex: 413519. Moderate–budget.
Polonez Hotel. 36 Aleja Niepodległosci, 61-714 Poznań. Tel: (61) 699141, fax: 523762, telex: 413491. Budget.
Hotel Poznań. 1 Plac Gen. H. Dąbrowskiego, 61-898 Poznań. Tel: (61) 332081, fax: 332961, telex: 413751. Moderate.

SOPOT

Grand Hotel. 12/14 Powstańców Warszawy Ulica, 18-718 Sopot. Tel: (58) 510041, fax: 516124, telex: 512851. Budget.

SOSNOWIEC

Novotel. 5 Kresowa Ulica, 41-200 Sosnowiec. Tel: (32) 666046, fax: 695353, telex: 312516. Moderate.

SZCZECIN

Arkona Hotel. 10 Panieńska Ulica, 70-535 Szczecin. Tel: (91) 880261, fax: 880260, telex: 425188. Budget.
Neptune Hotel. 18 Matejki Ulica, 70-530 Szczecin. Tel: (91) 240111, fax: 225701, telex: 422732. Budget.

TORUN

Helios Hotel. 1/3 Kraszewskiego Ulica, 87-100 Toruń. Tel: (56) 25033/8, fax: 23655, telex: 552469. Budget.
Kosmos Hotel. 2 Ks. J. Popiełuski Ulica, 87-100 Toruń. Tel: (56) 28900, fax: 21341, telex: 555147. Budget.

WROCLAW

Monopol Hotel. 2 Modrzejewskiej Ulica, 50-071 Wrocław. Tel: (71) 37041, fax: 448033, telex: 712225. Expensive–moderate.
Motel Orbis. 151 Lotnicza Ulica, 54-132 Wrocław. Tel: (71) 518153, fax: 518577. Moderate.
Novotel. 35 Wyścigowa Ulica, 53-011 Wrocław. Tel: (71) 675051/4, fax: 675275, telex: 715198. Moderate.
Panorama Hotel. 8 Plac Dominikański, 50-159 Wrocław. Tel: (71) 443681, fax: 4411245, telex: 712543. Moderate–budget.
Wrocław Hotel. 7 Powstańców Śląskich Ulica . Tel: (71) 614651, fax: 616617, telex: 715252. Moderate–budget.

ZAKOPANE

Giewont Hotel. 1 Kościuszki Ulica, 34-500 Zakopane. Tel: (165) 12011, fax: 15700, telex: 322270. Moderate–budget.
Kasprowy Hotel. Polana Szymoszkowa, 34-500

Zakopane. Tel: (165) 14011, fax: 15700, telex: 322206. Moderate–budget.

ZIELONA GÓRA

Polan Hotel. 9a Staszica Ulica, 65-175 Zielona Góra. Tel: (68) 70091, fax: 71859, telex: 432290. Budget.

YOUTH HOSTELS

During the summer holidays the Polish Association for Youth Hostels arranges accommodation in converted school buildings. The PTMS is a member of the International Youth Hostel Federation (IYHF).

Travellers bearing a valid IYHF card will receive a discount. You can obtain a listing of Poland's 200 or so hostels and an official IYHF card either at any IYHF office, or directly in Warsaw, from the PTSM at Ulica Chocimska 28. Tel: 022-498128; tel/fax: 498354.

STUDENT HOTELS

Between the months of July and October, Almatur, a travel agency run by the Polish Student Association, offers bargain accommodation in student residences. If you are in possession of an International Student's Card (ISTC), you'll receive a discount. The names of these hotels, further information and bookings are available from ORBIS Offices, or at Almatur-Polish Co. Ltd. Travel and Tourism Office, 15 Kopernika Ulica, 00-359 Warsaw. Tel: 263507, 262356, fax: 2630507.

PTTK OVERNIGHT HOSTELS

The Polish Association for Tourism and Culture (PTTK), 36 Swietokrzyska Ulica, 00-116 Warsaw, tel: 022-208241, arranges holiday accommodation in tourist-class overnight hostels for those interested in activity holidays. They are located in the mountains, along canoeing and sailing routes, as well as in several cities, including Cracow, Poznań, Płock, Sandomierz, Sanok, Sopot, Sczcecin, Szczyrk, Wanlbrzych, Warsaw and Zakopane. The larger of these hostels are complete with restaurants and cafés. Hostels for hikers are usually simply furnished.

SERVICE AREAS

Alongside major thoroughfares you'll find numerous, usually rustically furnished travellers' inns and service areas (*zajazd*), where you can spend the night or merely rest.

CAMPING

The Polish Camping and Caravaning Federation (PFC) operates 240 camp sites divided into three categories. All have access to running water, sanitary facilities and electricity. In addition to these amenities, camp sites in the second category have washrooms, those in the third hot running water in the washrooms and restaurants. Don't expect luxury from these relatively inexpensive alternatives to hotels.

Information pertaining to camp sites is available at all automobile clubs, and a list of camp site addresses and further information is furnished by CAMPTUR, Warsaw, 27a Krolewska Ulica, tel: 022-272408 or Warsaw, 331 Grochowska Ulica, tel: 022-106050.

The camping season runs from 15 June to 30 September. FICC-Carnets card holders receive a 10 percent discount.

It is sometimes possible to pitch your tent on private property. Just make sure you come to an agreement with the owner before doing so.

EATING OUT

WHAT TO EAT

Generally speaking, Polish cuisine is rich, substantial and relatively high in fat. Poles allow themselves a generous amount of time in order to enjoy their repast. A typical midday meal is usually composed of at least three courses: start with soup, e.g. *barszcz* (beet soup) or *zurek* (sour rye meal mash soup), followed perhaps in a restaurant by an appetiser of salmon or herring (prepared in either cream, oil or vinegar). For the main course you may want to try the national dish *bigos* (sauerkraut with pieces of meat and sausage) or *kotlet schabowy* (breaded pork chops). Finish on a sweet note with ice cream, or, more likely if you've been fortunate enough to be dining at someone's home, a piece of homemade poppy seed cake.

Other Polish specialities include *chlodnik* (a chilled beet soup for warm days), *golonka* (pork knuckles cooked with vegetables), *kolduny* (tiny filled dumplings), *zrazy* (slices of beef served with groats), *flaki* (entrails), all kinds of game and *plerogi* (savoury dumplings filled with cream cheese or potatoes).

WHERE TO EAT

In every luxury-class or ORBIS hotel you'll find a well-managed restaurant. In addition to national specialities, hotel kitchens offer a variety of simple,

Middle European dishes. In large cities there are new foreign restaurants. In Warsaw the magazine, *Warszawa, What, Where, When*, has listings of new restaurants.

WARSAW

Bazyliszek, 7-9 Rynek Starego Miasta, Old Town Square. Tel: 311841. The perennial favourite with vistiors and has a good spread of game in season.
Canaletto, Victoria Intercontinental Hotel, 11 Krolewska Ulica. Tel: 278011. Generally recognised as Warsaw's best.
Klub Swietoszek, 6/8 Jezuicka Ulica. Tel: 315634. A restaurant that has soared to become the Canaletto's closest rival.
Kamienne Schodki, 26 Rynek Starego Miasta. Tel: 310822. Widely admired duck dishes.
Wilanow, 27 Wiernicza Ulica. Tel: 421852. Near the Wilanow Palace.
Kuznia Krolewska, 24 Wiernicza Ulica. Tel: 423171. Also near the palace.
Lers, 29 Dluga Ulica. Tel: 6353888. Near the Old Town and moderately priced.

CAFÉS
Krokodyl, 19 Rynek Starego Miasta. Tel: 314427.
Bombonieka and **Fukier**, in the same square.
Telimena, 27 Krakowskie Przedmiescie, literary watering hole.

CRACOW

Wierynek, 16 Rynek Glowny, Town Square. Tel: 229896. Reputed to be the best Polish restaurant in the world. King Casimir III (1310–70) used it, as did his contemporary Emperor Charles IV. To the restaurant's immortal credit the prices are not that steep.
Hawelka, at number 24 in the same square. Tel: 224753. Will not disappoint those who cannot get into Wierzynek.
U Wentzla, at number 18, completes a distinguished triumvirate.
Starpoloska, 4 Sienna Ulica. Tel: 225821. Simple but honest with some respite for vegetarians in a generally non-vegetarian society.

CAFÉS
Jama Michalika, 45 Florianska Ulica, a famous art nouveau rendezvous.
Noworol, Old Cloth Hall, Rynek Glowny.
Ratuszowa, basement, Town Hall Tower, Ryneck Glowny.

GDANSK

Summer brings tables and chairs out onto the pavements all over Gdańsk. Serious restaurants include:
Pod Lososiem, 11 Szeroka Ulica, for superb fish served in the location of the Old Town.

Pod Wieza, 51 Piwna Ulica, also central, excellent stews.
Kaszubska, 76 Kartuska Ulica, fish specialities.

ZAKOPANE

Obrochtowka, Kraszewskiego Ulica, a pleasant little place just out of town.
Siedem Kotow, also on the outskirts.

SZCZECIN

Jubilatka, 41 Wojska Polskiego.
Chief, 16 Swierczewskiego Ulica.

WROCLAW

Polonia, 68 Gen Swierczewskiego. Tel: 31021.

MILKBARS

An alternative to restaurants and good value for money are milk bars (*Bar Mleczny*), which mainly serve vegetarian dishes. They are rarely tributes to decor, so don't expect anything fancy.

SNACK BARS

On practically every street corner you'll find a caravan where you can have a bite to eat, say a hotdog, *bratwurst, zapiekanka* (a kind of baguette with mushrooms and melted cheese),or chips. During the summer season in the tourist resorts along the Baltic Sea coast, small stands sell freshly caught baked or smoked fish.

DRINKING

Poles prefer drinking *piwo* (beer) with their meals. Among the best known brands are Zywiec, Okocim and Warka. Most restaurants offer a selection of German and Czech beers. Vodka is produced in numerous straight versions and 106 flavoured varieties. The basic ingredient is either potatoes or rye. The standard strength is 80 to 90 degrees proof, though there are one or two varieties which top 140 degrees. Various types of vodka (Zubtowka, Jarzebiak, Mysliwska, Wyborowa and Zytnia), or a bottle of good, foreign wine are present on every festive table.

ATTRACTIONS

CULTURAL

MUSEUMS

WARSAW
National Museum. 3 Aleje Jerozolimskie, tel: 6211031. Polish and foreign (Flemish and Italian schools) painting and sculpture from medieval times to the present day; ancient art and Polish handicrafts. Open Tuesday, Sunday and holidays 10am–5pm, Wednesday, Friday and Saturday 10am–4pm, Thursday noon–6pm. Entrance free.
Wilanów Palace Museum. 1 Wiertnicza Ulica, tel: 428101/424809. Contains the Polish Portrait Gallery and Museum of Posters. Tours of the palace 9.30am–2.30pm everyday except Tuesays and holidays. The Royal Park is open from 9.30am till dusk.
Lazienki Museum. 1 Agrykola Ulica, tel: 6216241. Paintings (mostly Dutch school) 18th century furniture and sculpture. Open Tuesday–Sunday 9.30am–3.30pm. Park is open till sunset.
Museum of Archaeology, Arsenał, 52 Długa Ulica, tel: 313221/5. Polish and Slav archaeology from the Stone Age to the early Middle Ages. Open Monday–Friday 9am–6pm, Sunday 10am–4pm. Entrance free.
Frédéric Chopin Museum. Żelazowa Wola (53km/33 miles west from Warsaw), tel: 22300. Eighteenth century manor house and the birthplace of Chopin. Open Monday–Saturday 10am–2pm, Thursday noon–6pm. Piano recitals every Sunday.

CRACOW
Wawel Collection of Art. On Wawel Hill, Wawel 5, tel: 221950, 222529, 225155. Richly furnished castle interiors, valuable art collections contain Dutch tapestries from the late 16th century, regalia and armoury with exhibits from the 16th to 18th centuries.
National Museum. 12 Marszałka Józefa Pilsudskiego Ulica, tel: 222733/763. Ancient art, Polish and foreign painting, art from the Far East, handicrafts and graphic design.
National Museum. Main Building, Aleja 3 Maja 1, tel: 343377/526. Branch houses "Weapons and Colours in Poland" a collection of 20th century art and Polish art from medieval times.
The Sukiennice (Cloth Hall). 1/3 Rynek Główny, tel: 221166. Paintings from the late 18th century to

the early 20th century.
Czartoryski Museum. 19 Šw. Jana Ulica, tel: 225566/226137. Among other exhibits the museum contains European painting and ancient art.

OŚWIĘCIM
The Oświęcim Museum. 20 Więźniōw Oświęcima Ulica (50km/31 miles east from Cracow), tel: 31934. Museum of Martyrdom on the site of the former concentration camp.

WIELICZKA
Museum of Cracow Salt Works. 6 Park Kngi (14km/8½ miles south-east from Cracow), tel: 221947/783266. Historical museum of Wieliczka and a collection of salt celllars on the ground-floor level of the museum.
Wieliczka Salt Mine. Tourist Services Department, 10 Daniłowicza Ulica, tel: 782653. UNESCO-listed site of Cultural and Natural Heritage.

LUBIN
Majdanek Museum. 67 Droga Męczenników Majdanka, tel: 42648/46. Martyrdom museum on the site of the former World War II concentration camp.

ŁÓDŹ
Textile Museum. 282 Piotrkowska Ulica, tel: 846115. Dedicated to the textile industry in Poland with the oldest mechanically operated mill.
Art Museum. 36 Więckowskiego Ulica, tel: 339790. Polish and foreign art from the 19th and 20th centuries.

MALBORK
The Castle Museum. 1 Hibnera Ulica, tel: 33642405. In the former defensive castle of the Teutonic Knights, 13th to 15th century exhibits include weapons, china, ceramics and a magnificent collection of amber.

POZNAŃ
National Museum. 9 Aleja Marcinkowskiego, tel: 528011. Sculpture and art from foreign artists, Polish artwork from the 18th century to the end of World War I.
Museum of Musical Instruments. 45 Stary Rynek, tel: 520857. A collection of musical instruments from all over the world, including Polish and Italian-made violins.
Rogalin. Branch of the National Museum 20 km (12 miles) south of Poznań, tel: 132030. An 18th-century building containing paintings from the late 19th century to the early 20th century, furniture and crafts from the 18th and 19th centuries; the coach house shelters a collection of period coaches.

SZCZECIN
National Museum. 27/28 Staromłyńska Ulica, tel: 335066/3336070. Sculpture and Polish paintings

from the 17th to 20th century, treasures from the ducal dynasty of Western Pomerania.
Museum of the City of Szczecin. 1 Plac Rzepichy, tel: 347249. Interesting exhibits from the 8th and 12th century Slav settlements, objects made from brass and bronze from the 17th century.

WROCŁAW
National Museum. 5 Plac Powstańcōw Warszawy, tel: 38830. Branch of the National Museum containing medieval and modern Silesian art, numismatic collections and crafts.
Post and Telecommunications Museum. 1 Krasińskiego Ulica, tel: 444034/36735. Historical development of post and telecommunications, collection of rare postage stamps.
Archdiocess Museum. 12 Kanonia Ulica, tel: 221755. Collections of religious art.

ART GALLERIES

WARSAW
Zachęta Art Gallery. 3 Plac Małachowskiego, tel: 276909, 275854. Exhibitions of Polish and foreign artwork.
Kordegarda Art Gallery. 15/17 Krakowskie Przedmieście Ulica.
The John Paul II Collection. 1 Plac Bankowy, tel: 2020725/1818. Founded by the Porczyński family. European collections. Open Tuesday–Sunday 9.30am–4.30pm.
The Royal Castle. 4 Plac Zamkowy, tel:6353995. Open from Tuesday–Sunday 10am–4pm. Collections mostly from the 18th century. No tour on Sunday.

CRACOW
Gallery of Polish Painting and Sculpture. Cloth Hall, 1/3 Rynek Główny, tel: 221166. Collections from the end of the 18th century to the beginning of the 20th.

WROCLAW
The Panorama of Racławice. 11 Purkyniego Ulica, tel: 4423344. A monumental painting (120 m x 15 m/400 ft x 50 ft) made in Lvov in 1894, depicting the battle of Racławice in 1794.

THEATRES & CONCERT HALLS

WARSAW
Grand Theatre of Opera and Ballet, 1 Plac Teatralny, tel: 263001/265019.
Ateneum Theatre, 2 Jaracza Ulica, tel: 6267330.
Dramatyczny Theatre, Palace of Culture and Science Bldg, tel: 263872.
Polski Theatre, 2 Karasia Ulica, tel: 267992.
Jewish Theatre, 12/16 Plac Grzybowski, tel: 207025.
National Philharmonic, 5 Jasna Ulica, tel: 267281, 265712.

Warsaw Operetta, 49 Nowogrodzka Ulica, tel: 6280360.

CRACOW
Karol Szymanowski State Philharmonic, 1 Zwierzyniecka Ulica, tel: 220958.
Musical Theatre, operetta stage, 48 Lubicz Ulica, tel: 211630.
Helena Modrzejewska Stary Theatre, 1 Jagiellońska Ulica, tel: 224040, 228566.
Juliusz Słowacki Theatre, 1 Plac Św. Ducha, tel: 224022.

GDAŃSK
Wybrzeże Theatre, Targ Węglowy, tel: 311328.
Baltic State Opera and Philharmonic, 15 Aleja Zwycięstwa, tel: 410563.
Miniature Puppet and Actor Theatre, 16 Grunwaldzka Ulica, Tel: 410123.

POZNAŃ
Stanisław Moniuszko Grand Theatre, 9 Aleksandra Fredry Ulica, tel: 528291.
Music Theatre, 1a Niezłomnch Ulica Tel: 522927.
Poznań State Philharmonic, 81 Sw. Marcin Ulica, tel: 522266, 524708.
Polish Dance Theatre, 4 Kozia Ulica, tel: 524241.

Information about cultural events and opening times of museums can be obtained from: the **Ministry of Culture and Art**, Ulica Krakowskie Prezedmieście 15/17, 00-071 Warszawa, telex: 813762; **Department of Cultural Activities**, tel: 267545 and the **Foreign Department for Cultural Cooperation**, tel: 261896, fax: 261922.

Ticket reservations for theatre performances and cultural events taking place in Warsaw can be bought at the ZASP Office, 25 Aleje Jerozolimskie, tel: 219383/54, or at the theatre box office. In other towns try ZASP offices, or at major hotels.

CINEMAS

In Warsaw consult *Warszawa, What, Where, When* for listings of English-language films.

CALENDAR OF CULTURAL EVENTS

April
All-Polish Student Pop Festival in Cracow.
Springtime Music in Poznań.

May
Contemporary Polish Theatre Festival in Wroclaw.
Chamber Music Days in Lańcut.

June
Polish Pop Festival in Opole.
Jan Kiepura Festival in Krynica, Zegiestow and Nowy Sącz.
International Short Film Festival in Cracow.

July
Organ Music Festival in Gdańsk-Oliwa.

August
International Pop festival in Sopot.
Chopin Festival in Duszniki Zdroj.
Country Picnic in Mragowo.

September
Swietokrzyskie-Fire Race in Słupia Nowa.
International Festival of Contemporary Music "Warszawska Jesien" in Warsaw.

October
International Jazz Jamboree in Warsaw.
Warsaw Theatre Rendezvous.

TOURS

Since the political turnaround in Poland, privately-owned small and medium-sized travel and service agencies offering excursions and local business services have sprung up everywhere. Nevertheless, the former national travel agencies are still worth recommending.

OPERA, THEATRE & CONCERTS

Poland is now the scene of many international music festivals and competitions. Every four years there is the Chopin Competition for young pianists. Annually there is a "Warsaw Autumn" festival of contemporary music and a "Jazz Jamboree" in Poznań. Also every four years there is the Henryk Wieniawski Violin Competition.

Mazowsze is a state ensemble, founded by the composer Tadeusz Sygietyński in 1949 and since his death managed by his widow, Mira Zimińska, a famous ex-actress and cabaret artiste. It consists of a corps de ballet, choir and orchestra recruited from towns and villages around the country, which are constantly scouted for new talent.

The repertoire is based on folk songs and dances, chiefly those of central Poland. Songs like *The Waggoner, The Cuckoo* and *The Girl from Lowicz* have become known all over the world through the company's regular overseas tours which incltdes the Royal Festival Hall in London every four years.

You'll find dates for concerts, opera and theatre performances listed in the calendar of events above. Tickets for concerts, sporting and social events are available at advance booking outlets, hotels and tourist offices, reservations for theatre performances and cultural events taking place in Warsaw can be made at the ZASP Office, 25 Aleje Jerozolimskie, tel: 219383/54. In other towns try ZASP offices or at major hotels. Your best bet is to order tickets several days prior to the date of the performance. Chamber music, jazz and rock concerts frequently take place in arts centres and student clubs.

NIGHTLIFE

Nightlife in Poland is rather modest but there are still plenty of things to do. In most luxury-class hotels there are pubs and night cafés which offer entertainment in the way of variety shows and revues. Two of the most beautiful casinos in Poland are located in the Grand Hotel in Sopot and in the Marriott hotel in Warsaw.

If you prefer a carefree evening of dancing to a hard night of gambling there are several alternatives. In Warsaw you might want to pay a visit to the nightclub Czarny Kot in the Victoria hotel, or, if you're in Cracow, try the Crazy Dragon at the Forum hotel. If discos are more your style, shake a leg in Warsaw at the Park or the Remont, in Gdańsk at the Rudy Kot, or in the resort town of Sopot at any one of the many options. Nightclubs and discos tend to go in and out of fashion with changes in management and it's a good idea to check venues with someone at hotel reception before setting off for an evening's entertainment.

Prostitutes practise at most nightclubs. Keep in mind that cases of AIDS have increased dramatically. Condoms are difficult to come by, so if you think you are going to be needing any it's best to bring a supply with you.

If you're in the mood for cabaret, try the student club Stodola in Warsaw, Zak in Gdańsk, and Pod Baranami in Cracow. Or how about a quiet evening with soft music and good food at a piano bar or candlelit wine cellar? Try the city-famous Café Krokodyl in Warsaw or the Jama Michalikowa in Cracow.

SHOPPING

Visitors can buy imported goods with foreign currency or credit cards in Pewex and Baltona shops. Make sure you save the receipts of all major purchases to avoid difficulties at the border later on. Cepelias, found throughout Poland, are the best place to buy folk art such as fabric, carved, embroidered and ceramic handicrafts, as well as modern jewellery made from metal and semi-precious stones.

In Desa shops antiques, graphic art, paintings, sculpture and decorative objects are sold for foreign currency. It's best to enquire about customs regulations applicable to your purchases before trying to take them out of the country.

Shopping Hours: Food stores are open on weekdays from 6am to 6pm or 7pm and on Saturdays from 7am to 1pm, on Sundays, holidays, and at night, some grocery stores are open in big cities. Other shops and services operate on weekdays from 10 or 11am to 6 or 7pm. In the country some shops may close as early as 5pm. Department stores are open on week days from 9am to 8pm. Souvenir shops are open from 11am to 7pm.

Sailing
Pomeranian Lakeland area and the Great Mazurian Lakes are popular places to sail and there are well-equiped water sports centres at Węgorzewo, Mikołajki, Mrągowo, Ostróda, Iława, Charzykowy, Czaplinek and Szczecinek.

Kayaking
One of the most beautiful places to kayak is the 200-km (125-mile) long Krutynia route, which has tourist facilities, landing stages, bivouac grounds and equipment centres along the way. Other Mazurian routes include the rivers Pisa, Drwęca, Czarna Hańcza and the River Brda route, which runs through the Bory Tucholskie Forest. The 146-km (91-mile) River Gwda route requires kayaks to be transported over dry land. The River Słupia, Drawa and Ina in the Pomeranian Lakeland are popular places for rallies.

Angling
The angling season in Poland lasts all year round. Angling equipment can be easily bought but visitors need a licence to fish. The **Polish Angling Association (PAA)** has branches throughout the country. If you are in Warsaw contact the PAA at 42 Twarda Ulica, Warsaw, tel: 205083.

Skiing
The Tatras in soutern Poland are snow-covered from December to March, in its upper parts the snow stays until May. Zakoppane at the foot of the Tatras, is Poland's winter sports capital, other winter sports centres include Bukowina Tarzańska, Szczyrk, Wisla, Brenna, Ustroń, and Zwardoń. In the Sudety Mountains you should head for Szklarska Poręba, Karpacz, Międzygórze or Duszniki. Zieleniec and Jamrozowa Polana also have comfortable ski slopes and trails. Cross-country skiing is best in the Mazurian and Kaszuby regions in northern Poland.

Gliding
Glider centres are found in Leszno, Jelenia Góra, Żywieckie, Nowy Targ, and Lisie Kąty near Grudzi. Instruction is given on Pirat and Junior gliders, Foka, Kobra and Jantar craft is used for training. You will need: insurance and a health certificate and a glider pilots' or parachutists' licence which been confirmed by the Polish Main Inspectorate of Civil Aviation.

Hunting
All formalities regarding licences for hunting can be taken care of in country of origin through travel agencies in collaboration with Łowex, Animex or Obis.
Animex Co Ltd, 8 Chałubińskigo Ulica, 00-613 Warsaw, tel: 300810; **Hunting Bureau**, tel: 301617, fax: 300537/302634, telex: 814991. **Łowex, Polish**

Hunting Association Co Ltd, 35 Nowy Świat Ulica, 00-029 Warsaw, tel: 262051/2 or 267949, fax: 266242, telex: 817508.

Spas
Detailed information about spars can be obtained from the **Department of Rehabilitation and Health Care**, Ministry of Health and Social Welfare, 15 Miodowa Ulica, 00-246 Warsaw, tel: 6357617.

Horse Riding
Poland had one of the greatest cavalry traditions in the world, and horses still work the land. Arab breeding is an important export industry. There are many riding centres catering for all levels of ability.

LANGUAGE

Polish, along with Czechoslovakian, Slovakian and Serbian, is one of the Western Slavic languages and makes use of the Latin alphabet. As a rule, the accent falls on the next to last syllable. There are the following unusual combinations of letters: **sz** pronounced sch, **cz** pronounced tsch, **rz** pronounced z (as in jalousie), and **ch** is pronounced h.

WORDS & PHRASES

Polish	English	Phonetic
Tak/Nie	Yes/No	*tack/nee-ar*
Dziękuję	Thank you	*gen coo yea*
Proszę	Please	*proshay*
Dzień dobry	Good morning/ afternoon	*jane dobray*
Dobry wieczór	Good evening	*dobray vieer-chew*
Dowidzenia	Goodbye	*dovitzania*
Przepraszam	Sorry/ excuse me	*puh-shay prusham*
Ile to kosztuje	How much is it?	*e-lay toe coshtu yea?*
Chchałbym (he)	I would like	*tuh-chow bim*
Chciałabym (she)	I would like	*tuh-chow wa bim*
Gdzie jest	Where is...?	*juh-jay yest...?*
Jak daleko	How far...?	*yak daleko...?*
Jak długo	How long...?	*yak dwugo...?*
Dobry	Good/O.K.	*dobray*
Zły	Bad/no good	*zuh-wee*
Tanio	Cheap	*tan-yo*
Drogo	Expensive	*drogo*

Gorąco	Hot	*gorronso*
Zimno	Cold	*zhim-no*
Wolne	Free	*volnay*
Zajęte	Occupied	*zigh-vente*
Otwarte	Open	*ot farrtay*
Zamknięte	Closed	*zam kuh ni-ente*
Ja nie rozumiem	I don't understand	*ya nie rozumee-em*
Ja nie wiem	I don't know	*ya nie vee-em*
Ja rozumiem	I understand	*ya rozumee-em*
Ja wiem	I know	*ya viem*
Ja potrzebuję	I need	*ya potsh shay boo yea*
Karta	Menu	*karta*
Klucz	Key	*klootch*
Taksówka	Taxi	*tak soufka*

Here are some hints about the pronunciation of Polish:

$$ó = u$$
$$ń = ny \text{ (as in canyon)}$$
$$w = v$$
$$ł = w$$
$$sz = sh$$
$$cz = ch$$
$$rz \text{ and } ż = zh$$

The ć roughly corresponds to **ch** and the following have rough comparison in sound

$$dź = j$$
$$ś = sh$$
$$ź = zh$$

FURTHER READING

GENERAL

In Cracow, by Adamczewski, Jan (1973).
The Polish August, by Ascherson, Neal (1982)
Cracow: City of Museums, by Banach, Jerzy (ed.) (1976)
Atlas of Warsaw's Architecture, by Chróscicki, J.A. and Rottermund, A (1978)
God's Playground: A History of Poland, by Davies, Norman (1982)
Heart of Europe; A Short History of Poland, by Davies, Norman (1984)
Book of Warsaw Palaces, by Jaroszewski, T.S (1985)
Warsaw: the Royal Way, by Lileyko, Jerzy

Colloquial Polish, by Mazur, B.W (1983)
The Poles, by Stevens, Stewart (1982)
A History of Polish Culture, by Suchodolski's, Bogdan (1986)
Solidarity: Poland 1980–81, by Touraine's, Alain (1983)
A Way of Hope, by Wałęsa, Lech

Polish Literature
Selected Poems, by Herbert, Zbigniew (1977)
A Minor Apocalypse, by Konwicki, Tadeusz
The Painted Bird, by Kosinski, Jerzy
The Issa Valley, by Miłosz, Czesław (1981)
Insatiability, by Stanislaw Ignancy, Witkiewicz (1985)

OTHER INSIGHT GUIDES

The main series of nearly 200 Insight Guides has been joined by more than 100 Insight Pocket Guides and an exciting range of miniature travel encyclopedias, the *Insight Compact Guides*, which present key information in a user-friendly pocket-size guide.

Written and photographed by people who have the first opportunity to introduce their Eastern European homeland to a broader international public, **Insight Guide: Eastern Europe**, is all the adventurous tourist needs to explore this fascinating region.

Insight Guide: Germany captures the various moods and mannerisms of Germany and its people and gives you all you will possibly need for an exciting trip to Deutschland.

ART/PHOTO CREDITS

Photography by

Page 14/15, 16/17, 22, 31, 34/35, 37 38, 41, 44/45, 46, 52, 61, 69, 72/73, 92, 94/95, 100, 101, 104, 107, 110, 118, 124/125, 138/139, 140, 153, 156, 164/165, 189, 191, 192, 193, 194/195, 208/209, 214, 219, 220/221,222, 227, 228, 239, 247, 248/249, 260/261, 262/263, 276, 278, 279, 284/285, 288, 290	Jürgens Ost + Europa Photo, Cologne
9, 18/19, 28/29, 42, 48, 49, 50, 51, 58, 59, 70/71, 78/79, 80/81, 82/83, 87, 93, 98, 120, 121, 128/129, 146/147, 148/149, 152, 159, 163, 168, 174, 180, 183, 187, 206/207, 210/211, 232/233, 250/251, 252/253, 254, 256, 257, 264/265, 273, 283, 286/287	P.A. Interpress, Warsaw
57, 96, 97, 108/109, 142, 145, 204, 216	Agentur für Fotografen
240, 244, 272, 280, 281	Regina Maria Anzensberger, Vienna
20/21, 85, 86, 99, 136/137, 143, 154, 184, 188, 205, 230/231	Christophe Kazor
24/25, 30, 32, 33, 40, 54, 112, 113, 116/117, 119, 201	ATO Picture Archive
3, 76, 130, 172, 173, 175, 238, 268, 270, 277	Alfred Horn
266, 267, 271	Dieter Vogel
43, 74, 161, 259, 269	G. Micula
123, 166/167	M. Socaia
90/91, 102/103, 126, 134/135, 170, 200	Orbis Picture Archive
88, 114/115, 127, 202	C. Parma
62/63	W. Milewski
66	J. Bałanda Rydzewski
178, 182, 203, 212	R. Ziemak
196/197	S. Zbadyński
Maps	Berndtson & Berndtson
Illustrations	Klaus Geisler
Visual Consultant	V. Barl

INDEX

R

S

T

A
B
C
D
E
F
G
H
I
J
a
b
c
d
e
f
g
h
i
j
k
l